MW00640577

LIVING
THE RING
OF FIRE

by

Jacqueline Weet

**Grosvenor House
Publishing Limited**

This book is published by
Grosvenor House Publishing Ltd
Link House
140 The Broadway, Tolworth, Surrey, KT6 7HT.
www.grosvenorhousepublishing.co.uk

A CIP record for this book
is available from the British Library

ISBN 978-1-83975-503-3

DEDICATION

To the grandchildren - Zoe and George in Yorkshire, Japanese granddaughters Ai and Sakura, Philippine grandsons Nicolo, Matteo and Frank and adopted Zimbabwean granddaughter Nicole. I send all my love.

CONTENTS

Acknowledgement   vii
Preface   viii

Part I

Chapter 1   Ancestors And Childhood In Wartime Years   3
Chapter 2   Michael's Ancestors And Childhood Years   17
Chapter 3   New Friends And Experiences In Mallorca   36
Chapter 4   Time For Fun In The Swinging Sixties   50
Chapter 5   Parents Arrive For Their First Holiday
            On The Island   68
Chapter 6   Amazing Revelations From The
            American Major   84
Chapter 7   As Work On The "Bolero" Begins So
            Michael Leaves   99
Chapter 8   On His Return, The Business Is Up
            And Ready To Go   120
Chapter 9   The "Bolero" Soon Runs Into Financial
            Trouble   134
Chapter 10 Diving Lessons In Porto Colom   146
Chapter 11 The Spanish Bullfight   160
Chapter 12 Special Mallorquin Evening
            With The Locals   178
Chapter 13 Troubled Days And Nights   195

Chapter 14 All Back Home In The UK For Christmas   198

Chapter 15 In May 1969 Birthday Celebrations
            With Petronella   214

Chapter 16 With Car Confiscated And Mounting
            Debts, Return To The UK   231

Part II

Chapter 17 Move With The Family From London
            To Yorkshire   239

Chapter 18 Twenty Years Later Divorced, Return
            To London   253

Part III

Chapter 19 First Holiday In South Africa   269

Chapter 20 Adjusting To A Totally Different
            Environment   285

Chapter 21 All The Fauna, Flora And Wildlife
            Of South Africa   297

Chapter 22 White Sharks Galore. Unforgettable
            Trip To Philippines   310

Chapter 23 The Time Arrives To Say Farewell
            To Michael   326

Appendix   329

Acknowledgement

My son Edward, who lent me his eyes,
his relative youth and computer savvy to keep
the words on the page and my wits intact.

PREFACE

The ability to rise above life's challenges.

For more than forty years, the idea of writing an autobiography has haunted me. On four separate occasions, over the course of these turbulent years, I have submitted various versions of this book, all of which were rejected by publishers. Having said that, if at first you do not succeed, to try and try again.

It is sad to say, I believed it was the fate of all children to endure miserable early years. So it followed, married young and then encouraged to go and live on the island of Mallorca in the swinging sixties, was like being born again!

Subsequently, as a person able to adapt, I moved back to the UK where I lived in Yorkshire for twenty years. Eventually returning to my roots, the final years have been spent commuting between the East End of London and South Africa.

PART I

CHAPTER 1

My father named Terence Weet, called Terry for short, was born in Hanwell Ealing and joined the Metropolitan police at the age of twenty-one. In 1936, as a young police officer stationed in Stoke Newington London, he was brought in to assist with the Moseley riots. It was not a good time for my parents. With Terry aged twenty-seven and his wife Ivy only twenty-four, they had endured a tragic accident; the loss of a little girl of seventeen months. In those times unlike today, with little support for a grieving family, this must have placed an enormous strain on their relationship.

With Dutch Afrikaans ancestors on his father's side and a reserved English mother Terry's background was diverse. Billeted in a chateau during the First World War, stealing oil paintings from their frames before bringing the booty back to England, Terry's father was the black sheep of the family. Then again in the 1920's while employed as a clerk for a firm of accountants, charged and convicted of fraud and embezzlement, the father went to prison.

By contrast, the father's two younger brothers served in the Household Cavalry. And at the age of eleven Terry and his older sister Eileen regularly went to watch Trooping of the Colour in Horse Guards parade. Also, at that time the father's elder sister, worked as a top model for Revelles in Knightsbridge. And on many occasions this tall and elegant spinster called Maud, was summoned to Buckingham Palace to model the latest suits and fur coats before Queen Mary.

Caused by the father's drinking and spell in prison, Terry and his sister Eileen had a problematic childhood. While educated in a French finishing school and employed as an assistant working in Peter Jones Sloan Square, their mother enjoyed art and the theatre. As teenagers considerable tension existed between both brother and sister. Greatly favoured by his mother, Terry was only too willing to snitch on his sister Eileen about her encounters with young men.

Leaving school at sixteen with a reasonably good school report, Terry left home to join the Merchant navy. Travelling around the world for six years, he then joined the Metropolitan Police force. And it was while on traffic duty in Stoke Newington High Street, that he spotted Ivy, his future wife to be. Drawn by Ivy's haughty demeanour and striking good looks, his pursuit of her began.

Contrary to Terry's background, with second generation Irish on the father's side and an English mother, Ivy had a happy childhood. While Ivy's mother was a rather over-weight, sedentary woman her father, referred to as Pop, was a lean and wiry outgoing man. Sharing a rented house in Islington, Pop's Irish parents lived nearby. Despite times being hard in the 1920's, employed as a skilled cooper making casks for fermenting beer and spirits, Ivy's father was never out of work. Only occasionally was Pop called away to work at the Guinness factory in Ireland and distillers in the West Country.

Ivy's favourite past time on a Saturday, was to visit her Irish grandmama. Accompanying grandmama the two of them went off to study the expensive hats in Southgate Road market. Rummaging through the piles of velvet cloche hats, adorned with silks and feathers, grandmama would invariably choose and buy one. Then, later the same afternoon, leaving Ivy outside with a glass of lemonade and a packet of pork scratchings, grandmama entered the pub. As a young girl waiting for what seemed forever, grandmama would re-appear with a jug of stout to take home to grandpapa.

Unlike grandmama with her strident and confident personality, grandpapa was a hapless and withdrawn little man. At one point, Ivy remembered grandpapa disappearing from the home for more than two months and it was not revealed the nature of his illness or the treatment he had received. However, upon his return, grandpapa was permanently relegated to a wooden chair placed next to the black grate. Thereafter each Saturday, after receiving his wages, his entire pay packet was given over to grandmama unopened. Handing her husband back one shilling pocket money, grandmama kept the rest.

Perhaps it was the fact that she had one son killed, on the front in the First World War, and another son die later from gassing, that made grandmama so vindictive.

Leaving school at sixteen Ivy gained a scholarship to attend Pitman's college in Russell square. As the only spoilt daughter with two younger brothers, Ivy loved to tell the story about how, during the week, the brothers had their best suits put into the pawnbrokers to buy Ivy silk stockings. Being very musical, each Saturday morning accompanying the film show at the local cinema, Ivy played the piano by ear. Then on Sundays, accompanying her newly acquired circle of friends from Pitman's college, she went by bus to 'The Spaniards' pub on Hampstead Heath. At eighteen, already a confirmed smoker, with her dark hair caught in a headband and wearing a loose-fitting sleeveless dress, plump good-looking Ivy, was off to the Strand to dance the Charleston.

In 1931 the family moved from Islington to a rented house in Tottenham and it was while she was out shopping in nearby Stoke Newington that Ivy met Terry. I do not know how my father eventually managed to win her over. All I do know is that he was far more interested in her than she was of him. Just prior to their marriage in 1933, out of the blue, a little boy of four years was presented to Ivy as a page boy at her wedding. However, for Puritanical-minded Ivy, discovering that this little boy was the offspring of Terry's unmarried eldest sister Eileen, did not go down well.

Being in the police and entitled to accommodation, Terry and Ivy moved into an unfurnished ground floor flat in Grayling Road Stoke Newington. Two weeks after moving into the Victorian house Terry's friends in the Police were invited around for dinner. Walking up the path towards the front door, the two couples were confronted with a large white notice, stuck in the front room window that read. 'ONE WIFE FOR SALE.'

In April 1938, one year before the outbreak of the Second World war, I was born and named Jacqueline. And in 1940, partly due to the proximity of the Orthodox Jewish area of Stamford Hill, Stoke Newington took an absolute hammering from the German Luftwaffe. During the blitz of 1941, with my father out on night duty, the bombing so bad my mother was forced to put me into her bed. When a land mine dropped into the next street, the blast not only tipped us out of the bed but blew the cellar door halfway up the garden. With another bomb dropping directly onto Saint Paul's Church West Hackney, a landmine followed leaving a fifteen-foot crater in the middle of Stoke Newington High Street. With this unexploded device lying in the deep crater, it was left to my father, along with other policemen on duty at the time, to seal off the whole area.

During the constant air raids, like Winston Churchill, my stubborn mother refused to go underground. On one occasion, after the air raid siren had sounded, failing to take cover my mother was admonished by an Air Raid Warden for walking in the street with a child in a pushchair.

It was that same year of 1941, that the Americans entered the Second World war. Again, at that time the bombing in central London was so intense, my father sent both of us down to the family friends in Frome Somerset. As previously mentioned, the reason for the connection with the family in the West Country came via my grandfather Pop. On the odd occasion he was sent to work in the local distillery in Frome, he lodged with this homely country family called the Palmers.

With plenty of good food, fresh eggs and with plentiful meat and vegetables, it was a place my mother loved to visit.

On one occasion, shopping for the family in the centre of Frome, leaving me outside the baker's in a pushchair, my mother went inside to buy bread. Coming back out from the bakers shop she was shocked to find me gone from the pushchair. The reason she felt frantic was because, at that time, the Americans had an army base just outside of the town. And that particular morning, armoured vehicles and tanks were thundering right through the centre of Frome. Rushing up and down the road, looking into shop windows, my mother tried to find me.

"Are you looking for a little girl?" asked two passers-by. "Because we have seen a child in the toy shop around the corner, so sweet." they said, watching my mother racing up the street with the pushchair. Locating the toy shop to find me cradled safely in the arms of a shop assistant while cooing over the enchanting little girl, my mother's reaction was different. Always one to tell the truth, she did not hide her feelings.

On one occasion while coming to visit us, my father was not impressed to discover that, having left me in the care of the Palmer family, my mother had set off on a bicycle to the American army base to attend the Saturday night dance.

In 1943 although old enough to attend primary school, it did not happen simply because I, along with many other children was evacuated out of London. Taken by my father to Paddington station we boarded a packed train bound for the West country. I distinctly remember with the carriages filled with weeping children, while my father managed to find a seat, I sat on the floor in front of his legs. Arriving at a dreadfully rundown farmhouse in the middle of Gloucestershire, with no running water and a septic tank at the bottom of the field, we five evacuees were left in the care of a disgruntled middle-aged couple.

For more than two months, I suffered in that awful place. Each afternoon, when sent back upstairs to rest, I just cried continuously. I remember distinctly one little six-year-old boy, with a patch over one eye, was picked on and bullied more than the rest of us. On one hot August afternoon leaving this boy alone in the coal bunker, the rest of us went down the fields for a picnic.

Meanwhile back in London, taking a break from the unrelenting bombing, my grandparents came to stay with the Palmer family in Frome. Finding out just how close they were to where I was evacuated, my grandmother and Pop came to pay me a visit. Arriving unannounced by taxi, the grandparents were taken into the front room by the farmer's wife. Suddenly, lying with my head on the pillow crying, I recognised my grandmother's voice. Disregarding the house rules about not coming down the stairs until we were told, descending the stairs in bare feet and without knocking, I entered the room.

Totally aghast at my gaunt and unkempt appearance, my grandmother came forward to take me in her arms. Meanwhile shocked at how thin I was tight lipped Pop kept his mouth shut. Following a few curt words from my grandmother to the farmer's wife they left, only to return two days later to collect me. On this occasion, taken by taxi to Bristol station and escorted on the train back to Paddington. I was handed back to my father.

Back in London in September, with sandbags piled high at all the school windows, and issued with a red gas mask, I began preliminary education at Church Street School. One unfortunate little boy of six, picking up a live bullet in the playground, had his little finger blown off. Hardened by the war, it seemed that such incidents were taken for granted.

With rows continuing between my parents, I delayed returning from school. Instead, loitering in the streets looking in shop windows and taking my time, I balanced on the low garden walls in Bouverie road with the favourite place to stop being the Catholic Church. Drawn by the light and warmth of its interior, I relished the quiet and solitude. Tip toeing down the central transept before laying down on the soft green carpet in front of the altar, I gazed up at the gentle lady, draped in a cobalt blue gown, holding a naked baby on her lap. Rarely questioned as to where I had been, often it was gone 5 o'clock before I arrived home.

Throughout the Second World War my mother worked as a part time secretary for a pharmaceutical company in Stamford Hill. With Christmas 1944 approaching money had been put aside in the toy shop, close to where she worked, to buy me a doll. It was about this time that I discovered I had yet another cousin on my father's side called Sybil. Also the offspring of aunty Eileen, this kind cousin had donated a wicker doll's cot to me. On Christmas morning, I woke to find a beautiful doll, dressed in pink and white satin placed in the cot at the bottom of my bed. Also laid next to the wicker cot was a gift from my father. During the previous week missionaries had come to the front door to preach the Gospel. Leaving the Book of Mormon with my father and wrapping it in Christmas paper, the book was left as a present or me.

Despite continual air raids, at every opportunity, I was out in the street meeting up with other children. Playing hopscotch on the pavement, juggling two balls in in the air, or with my skirt tuck into my knickers, performing handstands up against garden wall. At other times I walked through the walls of Jewish homes in Manor Road, laid bare by the German air raids.

Struck down with the usual childhood ailments and sick with measles, I was shipped off to my father's mother in Ealing. As a caring woman, working as an Air Raid Warden and looking after me she cared for both her pets, the garden, and her local allotment. At that time, with Britain desperately short of food and German 'u' boats targeting the merchant ships bringing supplies across the Atlantic from America, Britain was feeding itself. Ill this time with mumps, with my mother at work, it was left to my father to take care of me. Wrapping my painful and swollen cheeks in a scarf while balancing me on the cross bar of his bike, I was taken to the allotment in Clissold park. Sitting on the frosty grass, I watched while my father dug up the winter crops.

In 1944 the first V1 rockets arrived over London. This new form of attack from Germany, involved a flying bomb coming in silently above the ground, before landing to deliver its lethal load. At that time, during the VI air raids, with three different families sharing our Victorian house in Grayling Road, we sheltered together in the cellar. I am not sure what my father's motive was but, on more than one occasion, when the siren had sounded and the doodlebugs came in, I was taken into the garden to watch them approach.

One morning while walking up Bouverie Road on my way to school, the air raid siren sounded. Standing still, halfway between my house and school, I thought about what I should do. Upon hearing the familiar drone of a doodlebug coming in low, followed by the formidable whooshing sound, I knew I was in danger. Running across the pavement to the nearest wall I lay down with my arms around my head. Unaware that I had been seen crouching against the garden wall, the lady in that house came running. Grabbing me by the back of my coat, I was hauled into the broom cupboard beneath the stairs. Listening to the bomb exploding several streets away, we knew we had a lucky escape.

The first time I met Barbara Deeks was while out in the street playing rounders. Having been bombed out of their home in East London, Barbara along with her parents had been given a prefabricated bungalow in Bouverie Road. At the end of the Second World War in 1945, Pop took me to the West End to witness the VE Day celebrations. Then a few days later, following the most joyous street party, a Children's concert was organised and staged in front of the Stoke Newington Town Hall Watching the petite blond, formerly Barbara Deeks and later Barbara Windsor, singing and tap dancing across the wooden stage, I knew then she was something special.

With the cessation of hostilities in Europe so came the years of hardship and austerity. Food was rationed, books had to be stamped to buy clothes and the queues at the butchers and grocer's shops went halfway down the street. Just after the Second World War one of my mother's brothers, having served as a Sergeant Major with the Americans in Anzio and then in North Africa, was demobbed from the army. Arriving back from the Middle East with a box of green bananas, the luxury fruit was distributed amongst the family. It was the very first time I had ever seen a banana and as the fruit was so under ripe, it had to be left in a window for a week before I could eat it.

During those lean years after the war, I was often hungry. In fact, my hunger was only kept down, by meagre school dinners, supplemented by Cod Liver oil and a small pint of milk. With strict rationing in force, each family was entitled to one egg a week. However, in my home that constituted two eggs for my father, one egg for my mother and none for me. On more than one occasion sitting on the floor behind my father's chair I waited, like a dog open mouthed, to receive a mouthful of his food.

During those difficult times, I can honestly say my mother never ever went short of anything. Born under the sign of Taurus, her loves in life were luxury and good living. Aged eight, every week armed with a shopping basket and money wrapped in newspaper, I was sent to the grocer's shop to buy food on the black market. Taken surreptitiously through to the back of the shop, passed a queue of wide-eyed customers, the money was handed over to the grocer. With half a pound of butter and a pound of bacon put back in the basket, I left to return home.

During school holidays I often went to see my grandmother living in Stamford Hill. And because she always took an afternoon rest, Pop and I would have to lie down for an hour in the bed next to her. Once she was up, we shared together tea sweetened with condensed milk and bread with butter and strawberry jam. The thing I loved most was to touch and comb through my grandmother's fine hair. Carefully untying the soft bun of real hair at the nape of her neck, brushing out the tangles the bun was then rolled back with pins.

Visiting the grandparents on Saturdays, the whole family were there to share the special afternoon tea. Always eager to be away from my troubled home, I arrived early. Sent first up the road to the sweet shop, to buy rolling tobacco for Pop and Daisy powders for my grandmother's headaches, I was treated to a bottle of black current cordial. And left to swing, happily, on the front garden gate. I waived to the drivers of the steam engines passing by. Then later going into the front parlour, I played the piano and sang to the tunes made up in my head. Around 5 o'clock sitting at the table with the sons and their wives, savouring the tea of winkles, prawns, cream cheese with celery, followed by luscious cream cakes, it was a joyous occasion.

Quite regularly on a Sunday morning, Pop came to take me to Commercial Street and the market in Petticoat Lane. Because my father was such a stickler about time, if Pop brought me home late for Sunday lunch, my food was left out on the table to get cold. Sitting on the chair close by, he forced fed me until I was sick. However, believing the treatment I received was the norm for all children, I did not protest. On one Saturday lunchtime, hungry and eager to eat the jam suet pudding in front of me, bending low to cool it, I blew into the bowl.

"Jacqueline you have absolutely no manners at all!" My father shouted, hitting me hard on the back of head and forcing my face down into the hot jam. Running into the scullery to grab a cloth and holding it under the cold running tap, I pressed it to my burning face. Fortunately, although the side of my nose and right cheek blistered, I had no permanent scars. While both parents always maintained it was an accident it is true to say, that neither of them moved an inch from their chairs to help me.

That same year of 1947, playing with a friend in her garden and suddenly feeling ill, I was sent home. Later that night, leaning over the makeshift bed, watching me drawing my legs up in pain, my parents thought I might have an appendicitis. However, not willing to accept I was ill enough to call an ambulance, waiting instead until 6am the following morning, an off-duty police car was summoned to take me to the hospital. By the time I arrived at the hospital in Kingsland Road, I had to be taken immediately into the operating theatre to remove the acute appendix. Following the successful operation, the next ten days were spent in the middle of an adult ward.

While my mother's parents came to visit quite regularly, being at work, my mother only came twice. On the other hand, despite the distance and the arthritis, nanny from Ealing came to see me and bearing a gift of fresh eggs. Sadly, with those precious eggs stolen from my locker, I never got the chance to eat them. The highlight for me, during what seemed endless days was when my father, dressed in uniform, came to visit. Watching this six-foot tall well-built policeman come striding down the centre of the ward, filled my heart with joy.

That same year 1947 was the year of the big freeze and from January to April the whole country was encased in ice. While I thoroughly enjoyed sledging down the slopes in Clissold Park, I hated having chapped legs. Sent after school in the dark to a baker's shop in Church Street, knowing full well what would happen when I reached home, did not prevent me from eating a hole down through the middle of the hot bread.

Two years later, passing the 11 plus exam, and kitted out in my bottle green drill slip and cream shirt I started secondary school education at the Central School for girls in Clapton. Settling into the new environment I made a new friend called Ruth, a Jewish girl from Springfield Clapton. The very same stomping ground of the, now, famous Sir Alan Sugar. Because Ruth came from a family of strict, second generation orthodox Jews, although close friends, I was not allowed into her home.

Ruth was a generous sort of girl, who always had money in her pocket. The reason she was always flush with money, was because she was paid half a crown to clean her brother's shoes. After school I was regularly taken by Ruth, to the local shop to pick out whatever sweets I fancied. Invariably my choice would be brightly coloured marzipan fruits and liquorish sticks.

As my father rarely went to see his mother, it was left to nanny to come to visit us. Embarking on the journey, by underground, from Northfields in Ealing to Finsbury Park involved 29 stops. For a lady in her late sixties, with acute arthritis, it was not an easy thing to do. Always, prior to her arrival, a verbal battle would ensue between my parents. Despite now owning his own car, my father refused to collect his mother from the station. Taking another bus from Finsbury Park station, nanny arrived smiling. Then holding on and sliding down the stairs against the wall, she entered the kitchen bearing gifts for us all. As a sensitive young girl, sitting on my hands, I was appalled at my father's cruel attitude towards his mother.

Accustomed to strict discipline in the home, I followed orders at school. Leaning against the front room window looking at homework set for that day, I saw Barbara Deeks go tripping by. There she was, one year older than me, dressed in a tight-fitting short skirt and her now very blond hair stacked on her head and wearing a gorgeous pair of red high-heeled shoes. Still in my, rarely washed, green drill slip, long grey woollen socks and black lace-up school shoes, I jumped down from the window.

"I have just seen Barbara walk by in a lovely pair of red high heeled shoes." I said, standing directly in front of the ironing board in the scullery. "Mum, do you think I could have a pair of red high-heeled shoes like she is wearing?" I said, looking at her.

"You just mark my words my girl" she said, thumping the iron back onto the board. "Her mother Rose is going to regret the day she ever put her daughter on the stage."

It goes without saying that I did not get a pair of red high-heeled shoes and how wrong can mothers be!

As teenagers Barbara and I enjoyed similar interests. At the weekend, the favourite place for girls to be was the Tottenham ice rink where we met up with local boys. The difference between Barbara and myself, was that while I drifted off with any young man who paid me attention, Barbara was more selective in her choice. Always attracted to the bad boys, the young men with a history, Barbara gravitated towards the Hoxton and Diamond gangs of the East End.

Reasonably academic I enjoyed attending Pond House Central school, but my mother had different ideas. Without consulting me she went to see the Headmistress to discuss the possibility of taking me away to attend Pitman's College in Russell Square. Because, according to my school report, I was 'a confident, forthright and pleasing girl' my mother's idea was promptly dismissed by the Headmistress. I was not moved from the school, and the following year became School Captain.

In the 1950's Teddy boys were all the rage. Wearing their draped jackets trimmed with velvet, thick soled black suede shoes and hair greased into a quiff, they were a sight to behold. In this new age of Bill Haley, rock-n-roll and Elvis Presley I saved enough money from a Saturday job to buy a bright orange teddy girl coat with a black velvet collar. I remember my mother shuddered at the sight of the coat and after wearing it a few times I also thought it was hideous. It was the fashion at that time for women to wear headscarves. For my haughty mother, putting aside the fact that the Queen regularly rode a horse wearing a headscarf, she believed it was only factory girls who wore them!

Leaving school at sixteen with 3 "o" levels I began a job in the City of London as a typist working for the Civil Service. It was then that Barbara and I went our separate ways. While she moved up from a local dancing school to appear with Johnny Brandon in a West End show, I developed a teenage crush on a local boy. Following a fumbling session of petting, behind the rhododendron bushes in Clissold Park, I lost my virginity. Later when the young man was called away to do his National Service, sailing away for a year in the Persian Gulf, I wrote him letters.

I never ever had any real form of rapport with my father. Even though my mother was unloving and distant towards me, I was closer to her than I was to him. Although, there were times in my late teens, when I felt sorry for the way my father endured my mother's lashing tongue. Feeling somewhat depressed with her castigating me and criticising my looks, it was Ruth who came to my rescue. Asking me to join her and her latest young man, out on a blind date, four of us met outside a Chinese restaurant in Wardour street. Not only was it the first time I had ever been to Soho but my blind date for the evening, was the younger brother of Ruth's boyfriend. Being introduced to this slimly built, dark-haired and extremely handsome young man called Michael, I did not know that he was home on leave from the Royal Navy, after serving one year in the Persian Gulf.

CHAPTER 2

Where Michael's ancestors were concerned it was a question of the Kelly's and the Cohens. Ancestors on his father's side were first generation immigrant Jews living in Whitechapel East London. Occupying a terraced house on the Mile End Road, Joseph Isaacs and his wife Rose produced a family of ten and consisting of six girls and four boys. At mealtimes, with the tiny kitchen overcrowded, children were forced to sit up the staircase, one behind the other, with a plate of food balanced on their knees. While Joseph was a furrier by trade, the mother Rose spent most of her day next to a black grate in the kitchen, tending pots of soup and cauldrons of hot water for her family. At the age of thirteen, once the boys had been through the traditional ceremony of their Bar Mitzvah, they were out in the London streets earning money by whatever means they could. Meanwhile, the six daughters in the family took different paths. Choosing not to marry, the eldest daughter stayed at home to care for her parents. While the next eldest daughter emigrated to America, another two girls went onto the London stage. Then becoming the mistress to a much older man, the next pretty sister secured herself a lucrative lifestyle in Chelsea. Meanwhile the youngest daughter called Jane, against her parent's wishes and Jewish tradition, married an Irishman with a florist shop in Dalston. Even though from an early age all the daughters drank their father's gin, it was a happy home.

Jane and her husband called John, produced four children. And following Jewish tradition, their first and only son was also named John. With three younger daughters, jealous of the attention given to the older brother, there was tension in the household. As far the girls were concerned, spoilt John was nothing more than a bully who kicked doors down to get his own way.

Graced with curly dark hair, deep brown eyes and chiselled features, John had an eye for the ladies. It was while dancing at the Tottenham Palace, that his roving eye fell on one particularly full breasted woman called Ivy. Totally smitten by John's swarthy good looks, the courtship was short. Seven months after a hasty marriage, a son also named John was born. It just so happened that John's young wife also had the same name as my own mother called Ivy. Two years later yet another son called Michael was born to join the family living in accommodation in St Philips Road Hackney.

With the arrival of the Second World War life was about to change. While John was called up to serve in the Royal Navy, leaving the small boys with the grandparents in the flower shop, Ivy worked in a local factory making uniforms for the troops. Then in 1943, like so many other London children at that time, John and his younger brother Michael were evacuated to the country. Having suffered more than his fair share of childhood illnesses, Michael aged six was a delicate and sickly boy. However, after spending one year on a farm in North Devon with a caring family, and away from the smoke and grime of London, Michael returned a comparatively healthy boy.

For some unknown reason in 1944, the father John was demobbed early from the Navy and soon John found employment working for a bookmaker called Joe Coral. For two young boys, growing up in an environment that lacked discipline and guidance, it was a good place to be. Being his mother's favourite, wily young Michael knew exactly how to dupe her into believing he was too ill to go to school. Sweet and gullible Ivy was easily persuaded to write letters to the school, feigning Michael's illness. Always, when away from school playing truant, Michael was at the flower shop, accompanying his grandfather to Covent Garden market buying flowers. At the end of 1948 yet another son, named Terry, was born to join the growing family.

As promising boys, both passing the eleven plus with flying colours, they both won scholarships to attend good schools. John went to The City of London grammar school for boys and two years later, Michael went to the grammar school in Cowper Street close to Moorfields hospital. On the odd occasion that Michael decided to attend school during exam times, he invariably came top of the class. Unfortunately, inconsistent with his studies and resentful of authority and discipline, most of Michael's time was spent in the flower shop with his grandfather. Upon reaching the age of 15, his parents, John and Ivy were summoned to the school.

"Take him away," said the Headmaster. "Being at school, for Michael is a complete waste of time. He would be far better suited elsewhere".

Having left the school at the age of 15 without any formal qualifications, for the following two years, helped by his father, Michael also went to work for the bookmaker Joe Coral. Starting work at such a young age, he was employed as 'chalker', in the betting shop, marking up the runners, riders, and results of each horse race.

Two years later, at eighteen, Michael was called up to do his National Service. And once again, following in his father's footsteps, he joined the Royal Navy. Setting sail aboard a ship called "The Superb" the British cruiser went first down the west coast of Africa before dropping anchor in Cape Town South Africa. Even though at that time, the strict regime of Apartheid was in force, Michael stated that Cape Town and its surrounds was the best place he ever saw. Upon leaving the Cape before sailing up through the Indian Ocean, and into the Persian Gulf, he returned to England via the Suez Canal. It was while he was stationed at Chatham in Kent, waiting to be de-mobbed from the Navy, that his brother John asked him to come out on a blind date.

Upon that fateful August day I entered a world previously unknown to me. Suddenly launched into a relaxed laissez-faire environment devoid of rules and regulations, emerging from a background of rejection and abuse, meeting Michael was like a breath of fresh air.

I managed to resist for two months before Michael seduced me. On one Sunday afternoon left alone in the front parlour, for the first time going all the way, we made love on the floor. Lying there prostrate and disappointed, I wondered what the fuss was about. Still resting on his elbows Michael looked down to smile at me before rolling off to one side. At that moment, recognising that Michael was a well-rehearsed and seasoned lover, it was several weeks before I began to understand and enjoy the skills of good sex.

Christmas 1957 I was invited to join Michael and his family at a party organised by the bookmaker Joe Coral. Arriving by taxi to a venue in Euston I was ushered into a ballroom with golden chandeliers and the distinct smell of cigars. Standing alongside veneered panels, dressed in double breasted dark wool suits and bow ties, the men stood with partners decked out in beautiful silk gowns to the floor. On this particularly auspicious occasion, wearing a full-length dress of purple satin and decorated in turquoise sequins, Michael's mother looked radiant.

Meanwhile spread out on long tables, draped with damask clothes, was a cornucopia of luxury foods. It was the first time I had ever seen whole cooked salmons with olives and lashings of salt beef laid out on silver platters. While the bar was completely free, the entertainer for the evening was a young man by the name of Bruce Forsythe. And as Michael and I danced together, accompanied by the small band, each time our loins touched I felt his erection.

Early in January Michael's grandfather, owner of the flower shop, died suddenly leaving grandmother to run the business alone. Quickly the family rallied around to help Jane and the wheels were set in motion for John, the son, to take over the florist business from his late father. On Valentine's Day, helped by his grandmother to create a heart of fifteen red roses and presenting me with a three stoned diamond ring, Michael asked me to marry him. To celebrate the engagement Michael took me to Covent Garden to see the opera 'Carmen'. It was at that point that I developed the life-long passion for opera. Hearing the two great tenors Jose Carreras and Pavarotti, in full flight, forever stirred my soul.

My own parents had grave reservations about the sudden engagement. While my father summed up Michael as a "as an East End wide boy" my mother was more subtle and eloquent with her warning.

"The bed that you make, you will have to lie in my girl".

In the following March, handing in his notice with the bookmaker Joe Coal, John began the preparations to move his entire family around into the flower shop in Dalston Lane. However, with errant John spending far too much time in the snooker hall, instead of being home to help his wife, it was a particularly difficult time for Ivy. With her youngest son Terry at school, it was left to Michael and his older brother John to help move the furniture, in phases on wheelbarrows, along the roadside to the flower shop.

Compared to my own strong and robust mother; there was a gentle fragility about my Michael's mother, that I warmed to. At the age of eighteen, welcomed into the family, I already addressed Michael's parents as mum and dad. On one afternoon in April having left my office job in the city, I went to the flower shop to meet Michael. Upon walking into the flower shop, filled with the heady smell of spring flowers, Michael's father John busy mossing a large wreath on a bench.

"Oh Jacqueline, I am so pleased you are here. Do you think you could go and have a look at mummy?" When referring to his wife, "Mummy" was the term he always used.

Where is she? I asked aware that Michael had arrived and was standing behind me.

"I'll take you upstairs to her bedroom." Michael said.

Following close behind Michael, up the stairs and navigating around two wardrobes still left abandoned on the landing. I was taken into the bedroom on the right.

Laying on top of the bed in a wet nightdress and with a soiled sheet beneath her, I looked down at Ivy.

"She looks unconscious. How long has she been like this?" I asked, studying her open mouth and listening to the rasping breath.

"I am not sure, maybe two or three days." He said, looking quite helpless.

"My God that long?" I said, looking back down at her closed eyes. "I think your mother is extremely ill. Do you know the name of her doctor?".

"Yes, Dr Bilinky."

"Well you need to get him here now!" I said, standing up. "I will go and speak with your father."

After an urgent phone call, the doctor arrived. And while Michael and his father went with him back upstairs, I stayed in the back kitchen with grand-mother Jane. The moment the doctor reappeared to use the phone I sensed the urgency in the situation.

"What does the doctor say? I asked Michael."

"He's not sure. Dad and I watched him striking the balls of my mother's feet with a blunt instrument. Dr Bilinky seems to think it could be either meningitis or maybe a tumour on the brain."

Taken immediately by ambulance to the London Hospital Whitechapel, while a team of doctors tried to make a diagnosis, Ivy hovered between life and death. No matter how many different cocktails of drugs she was given, Ivy remained in an unresponsive deep coma.

After more than a month of not coming to a firm diagnosis, following extensive examination by one of the top consultants, the lack of hair on Ivy's pubic area and armpits was noted. Upon learning from the attending medical staff that, during her time in hospital Ivy had not menstruated, a diagnosis was made.

"The problem here is a malfunction of the pituitary gland at the base of the brain, which has led to the malfunction and breakdown of the other glands." Said the consultant, to his junior doctors. "Namely, the thyroid and adrenal glands and the answer is the drug Cortisone."

Over the next week, given more drugs along with Cortisone, Ivy began to regain consciousness. However, given so many different potent drugs, there were side effects. Shouting abuse and screaming at nurses while throwing objects around the ward, Ivy became violent. As a result of this completely uncharacteristic behaviour, Ivy was transferred from Whitechapel and to the Maudsley Mental Hospital in Denmark Hill.

It just so happened that while this trauma in the family was in progress Michael's older brother John, engaged to Ruth and taking Jewish instruction in a synagogue on Stamford Hill, made the decision to carry on with the wedding plans. On the day of the June wedding, attended by me along with Ruth's Jewish family, Michael's father was called away to the Maudsley hospital. Having suffered a sudden relapse, Ivy was back in a coma.

Regularly visiting my future mother-in-law in the hospital, was indeed a traumatic affair. Surrounded by very disturbed patients, Ivy continually begged to be taken home. During the first few weeks in the hospital, escorted by a nurse, Ivy was permitted to wander freely in the grounds and even visit he local shops. However, following three unsuccessful attempts to escape, my future mother-in-law was transferred to a more secure unit in ward 7 called The Villa. For visitors and patients alike, walking passed extremely disturbed women flashing their genitalia as you walked by, was not a pleasant sight. No matter how many times Ivy pleaded, with her arms around

John's neck, telling him she was not mentally ill, he remained unconvinced. Not prepared to go against the medical advice given, he would not sign the papers for her release.

On one extremely hot Sunday afternoon in August, with me in the flower shop along with other members of the family, helping Jane with the Sunday roast, the phone in the hall rang.

"Shit!" John said, walking back up the hallway, "Mummy has escaped from the hospital again!".

"How?" asked his mother Jane sliding the roasting beef and potatoes back into the hot oven.

"It appears she planned it. While they were all outside in the grounds having their Sunday roast and the nurses with their backs turned, stacking three tables one on top of each other, mummy leapt right over the bloody seven feet high wall. The police have been informed and they are out looking for her."

"So what are you going to do now dad?" Michael asked,

"This is the third time she has done this. The hospital knows exactly what she is wearing. She has stolen a red and white dress from the laundry. While the police in Denmark Hill are out looking for her, we just have to wait." John said, running fingers through his thick dark hair.

For the next ten minutes or so while John paced back and forth, Michael and I along with Ruth, John, along with grandmother and youngest son Terry, sat around the oak Victorian dining room table and when the phone eventually rang, we all jumped.

"OK, they have got her." John said, racing back up the side hall. "The Police picked her up in a phone booth. She was trying to make a phone call here to the flower shop. "Hell!" He said, stamping his foot. "I don't believe it. The police have no authority to take her back to the Maudsley hospital. Instead, it is up to me to take her" John said, storming out of the flower shop to collect the white van parked out the front.

"I think it would be a good idea to turn off the Sunday dinner until dad returns."

Another hour and a half went by before, John came back into the flower shop, but this time with Ivy hanging onto the back of his shirt.

"Can you believe it." He said, his eyes blazing and throwing his arms into the air. "Every time I have tried to turn the van around to take her back to the hospital, he said, looking back at his frightened wife, "mummy jumps out of the van in front of the traffic. And I have had no alternative but to bring her home,"

Looking at Ivy's large limpid brown eyes staring, caught like a rabbit in the headlights of a car, she watched her husband's every move.

"Come and sit-down mum." I said, as Terry her young son rushed forward to cuddle her.

"I am not going back to that place am I?." She said, screwing her hands together anxiously.

"Keep her occupied" Said John, avoiding eye contact as the family gathered about her.

Knowing exactly what he intended to do, I followed my future father-in-law out of the parlour and down the hall towards the phone.

"Dad, please do not do that. Do not take her back. You need to give her a chance!"

"I have no alternative but to take her back. We do not have any of the medicine she needs here." He said, starting to dial the hospital number.

"Look, go ahead and speak to the doctors. But tell them your wife is here at home and looking quite well. Get the doctors to send a prescription, by phone, to the chemist here in Dalston Lane, they are open on Sundays. Let us wait and see how she responds to being in her own environment."

With the hospital agreeing to send a prescription for Cortisone by phone, to the chemist in Dalston, the atmosphere in the flower shop took a different turn. From that day forward, supported by Cortisone, Ivy continued to gain strength. With her never ever returning to the hospital and watching her improve day by day, Michael and I set a date to be married in December. Sadly in the November, struck down by a cerebral stroke, my own dear grandmother from Stamford Hill died.

On my wedding day December 28th, true to form operating as queen bee dressed in a silver fox cape, my mother chose not to see my hired wedding dress, until the actual day. And in fact it was left to an aunt to dress me and to curl my hair. With considerable pressure applied to my own father and under duress, he eventually agreed to pay half towards his daughter's wedding. Arriving at St Mary's Church Stoke Newington, accompanied by him in the back of the Rolls Royce, we were waived on to drive around the block. Finally arriving with his brother, looking absolutely drop dead gorgeous in a hand-made navy wool suit, Michael, the groom, arrived late for his wedding. With more than 80 guests present from both sides of the family, including a backdrop in the photographs, of the majestic Jewish women Jane along with the three sisters, Stella, Rita, and Lily all decked out in their mink and chinchilla coats, it was a day to remember. And just nothing could take away the fact that I was a beautiful and radiant bride.

The first home that Michael and I moved into, was a ground floor furnished flat in Tottenham and while my mother-in-law's health continued to improve, concern was shown about her youngest son Terry. Aged ten and being without his mother for several months and left, instead, with his over-bearing grandmother had taken its toll. Reports coming in from the teachers at his school, stated that Terry's attitude and general behaviour was giving concern.

On my twenty first birthday in April 1959 and with my parents not wanting to attend, Michael and I invited as many of our friends as possible. Taking a day off from my job as a secretary in the City, considerable time was spent preparing favourite cakes such as lemon meringue pies and chocolate éclairs. Among the guests invited for my 21st was now famous Barbara Windsor. Wriggling around, provocatively, amongst the guests in a skin-tight black dress slashed open down to her rounded bum, Ruth and I rolled our eyes. What both my sister-in-law and I had not anticipated was that our husbands, along with most of the other men present, would close in around this captivating little blond, like bees near a pot of honey!

I have an idea." Ruth said, watching me handing around a plate of chocolate éclairs to the guests. "What do you think about me aiming one éclair right down the back of Barbara's dress?".

"Would you dare?"

"Just watch." She said, her eyes fixed on the scoop of material at the back of Barbara's dress. One neat throw and the cream laden éclair slipped down to nestle in the fold at the top of her spine.

"Oh!" she gasped, spinning around. "Who did that?"

"Oh, I have no idea" I said, feigning distress. And that was the last time I saw Barbara Windsor.

With the birth the following year in 1960 of our first son named Michael, we moved from Tottenham to a two bedroomed unfurnished flat in Kilburn. The same area of London favoured by the Irish and first-generation immigrants from the West Indies. At weekends, rather than attempting to go to bed, with little Michael in his carry cot, we joined our Jamaican neighbours next door for hot curry and reggae music.

With a second son named Terry born in 1963, the Great Freeze began between the Christmas and the New Year. As temperatures dropped to below freezing, so for the first time in 200 years the river Thames froze over and from January to March London struggled to survive. As icicles hung down from the rooves of houses and pipes in the road froze and split open, so we were forced to collect water from tankers parked in the road.

Our own problem was exacerbated by the fact that with one son aged two and another son less than a year, both boys were still in cotton nappies. Returning from work each bitterly cold evening, Michael was sent straight back up the road to collect water in buckets. With the first three buckets tipped into the sink to rinse the towelling nappies, water for drinking was the second priority. Into February and still with no let-up in the deep freeze our youngest son Terry developed bronchitis. Despite repeated medicine, he was so poorly the doctor was called to the house.

"We will not be able to shift this chest infection while Terry is moved from one hot living room into a cold bedroom. The whole family needs to move into this living room, with the coal fire burning day and night. Go to the shops in shifts and do not move the baby from this warm environment." Said the Irish doctor.

For the next months, taking the two wooden cots into the living room and eating and sleeping close to the coal fire, Terry recovered. With the two young boys sound asleep in their cots, stripping off naked in front of the fire, with a cushion jammed beneath my bottom, we indulged in steamy hot sex. Unlike my own mother, who disliked any form of sexual contact, the chemistry between me and my husband was second to none.

As far as employment was concerned, Michael was certainly going up in the world. Following one promotion after another and an increased salary, somehow, Michael managed to accrue enough money to take out a mortgage on a new home. After three happy years in Kilburn we then moved into a two-bedroomed detached bungalow in Carpenter's Park Watford. With another son born named Edward and another promotion to manager of several extremely lucrative betting shops in Mill Hill and Edgware, life was good.

Flush with spare money we went off on a packaged holiday to the island of Ibiza. Arriving in a turbo propeller plane onto a tiny runway and into a terminal building nothing more than a wooden shed it was quite something. For both the children and me, going abroad for the first time and staying in a top-grade luxury holiday was a wonderful experience. Meanwhile smitten by the bug of endless sun, sea, and cheap booze, Michael was already making plans to return to the Mediterranean the following year.

In 1966, again in a turbo propped plane, we landed at Palma airport on the island of Mallorca. Booking with a travel company called Cosmos, the two-week holiday in a luxury hotel came to forty-nine pounds for each adult and half price for the boys! The name of the resort where we stayed was called Cala Murada. And with hotel, of the same name, situated in an idyllic spot on the eastern side of the island.

"How would you fancy living here?" Michael asked me, setting the second rum and coke back down onto the sun terrace table.

"Are you serious?"

"Yes, of course I am. We are both young and fit. Why don't we return to the UK put the bungalow up for sale and move out here?"

"And do what for God's sake? We have a young family to think of and you have a good job".

"I have been looking around researching this entire area." He said, ignoring the note of caution. "There is so much potential here. It just screams out to be developed. What do you think about opening a bar and restaurant?" He said, getting up to look out at the panoramic view across the aquamarine blue sea.

"How many bloody Bacardi and cokes have you had this morning? It is a crazy idea Michael, you cannot cook."

"I can always learn."

"Really?" I said, taking the youngest child Edward onto my lap while watching the eldest two boys playing crazy golf in the hotel grounds.

"Alright, I understand you need time to think about it, but I am restless. I have had enough of the boring job settling bets all day. I need to try something more challenging. I have already broached the subject with the hotel manager Señor Martinez. His receptionist is going to take us on a guided tour in the hotel car, around the entire area so we can see the layout."

"And where would we live?"

"Señor Martinez has told me there are plenty of villas available to rent here."

"It looks like you have already made up your mind?"

"Come on, let us give it a try. We only live once Jacqueline."

Returning to the UK the following week, sun kissed and feeling euphoric, the bungalow was put up for sale. While Michael's mother and father thought it was a fabulous idea, surprisingly, my own parents raised no objections either. Although by the following January the bungalow had still not been sold, Michael went ahead with his plans. Securing a two-week holiday with his employer Coral's, five tickets on the car ferry from Southampton to Bilbao in Northern Spain were booked. Writing to the manager of the Cala Murada hotel reiterating our plans, a date was given to Señor Martinez confirming our expected arrival in April.

A month later with the date of our imminent departure looming and the property still unsold, the acting Estate Agents were contacted once again. Twice a young woman arrived from the Agents, ensuring us that everything possible was being done to execute a quick sale. Later that same week, hearing letters drop through the letter box, I went into the hall to check the mail.

"Darling, we have got a letter from the Estate Agent." I said noting the logo printed on the envelope. Opening the letter, I began reading its contents.

"Michael, will you please come and read this letter before you go to work. It is from that woman in the Estate Agents and I am a little bemused."

Rushing into the kitchen while looking at his watch, Michael took the opened letter from my hand.

"For fucks sake!" he exclaimed, with narrowed eyes.

"What? Her telling me how pretty I am and that she is attracted to me? And can we meet up somewhere for coffee! It sounds like a love letter. What is this all about?"

"Don't you understand? She fancies you. She is a lesbian."

"What is a lesbian?"

"Look," Michael said, looking extremely exasperated "I am already late for work. You know about homosexuals don't you? And gay men who fancy one another, right?"

"Yes"

"Well you get women like that too. They have sex and make love to one another like heterosexuals do."

"But she does not have a penis.

"No, and I am not prepared to go into any more details this morning."

"So out of the blue this woman tells me she has feelings for me. When exactly do you tell me how you feel about me?" I asked, watching him zip up his navy-blue pin striped trousers.

"At this time in the morning, this cross examination is too much. He said, adjusting the Windsor knot in his silk tie.

"Please answer my question. If ever I raise issues regarding our relationship, you always manage to duck the subject. The only time you ever tell me that you love me, is when your mouth is roaming my body, or you are about to mount me."

"You know I love you I just do not say it all the time."

"But I need to be assured of your love."

"Okay I can see where this is going, back to your shit childhood." He said, slipping, into his pin-striped jacket, and 'Your 'Whatever happened to Baby Jane' mother. It is about time you put that all behind you. Forget about it! We are about to move to a completely different life. See you later." He said kissing me before disappearing into the hall.

"By the way, it sounds like the boys are wrecking the place. You had better go and see what is going on. And bin that letter."

Following a family farewell party and leaving the unsold bungalow in the hands of the Estate Agents, on my birthday the 26th April, we drove down to Southampton. With the inside of the car packed to capacity and the boot filled with bedding and cooking utensils, another two cases were on the roof rack, borrowed from my father.

To say the least, the two-day journey by sea from Southampton to Bilbao was not easy. With the weather in the Bay of Biscay rough, packed in together below sea level, I was seasick. Taking up Michael's maritime knowledge, the only relief I found was to go up onto the top deck in the wind and fresh air and look out at the horizon.

Landing in the port of Bilbao at 6am in the morning, stocked up with a supply of foods and snacks, we set off on the 600 km journey across the top of Spain to Barcelona. Content to just sit quietly in the back of the car, the children were extremely well behaved. Hurtling across the top of Spain, only twice did Michael have to stop the car to allow the boys to pee in a field. In 1967, with little knowledge concerning the rough and unkempt roads, the journey took far longer than anticipated. With approximately 200 Km left to reach our destination, disaster struck. Travelling at speeds above 70 miles an hour and hitting a deep pothole in the road, the roof rack flew off the car crashing into the centre of the road. Discarding the smashed roof rack at the roadside, for another three hours we limped along with the suitcases jammed on our laps. Into Barcelona by eight o'clock that evening we were just in time to see the ferry leave the harbour bound for Mallorca. Asking Michael pull over, Terry and I fell out of the car.

"I am sorry about all this." He said, watching my son and I being sick in the road. "Mind you, missing the ferry did not really matter, because I had not reserved any tickets yet".

Booking into the nearest cheap hotel and not bothering to eat or take off our clothes, dropping down onto the grubby beds, we slept for eleven hours. The next morning booking the ferry tickets and following a hearty breakfast, with 8 hours to kill, we took the children to Barcelona zoo. For all of us, it was the first time we had ever been up close to a 13 feet-high African giraffe. As its mighty head came over the wall and the long purple tongue flicked towards my face, the children rummaged through my large bag.

"Give it something to eat mum." Said Terry.

"Like what? I have only got bananas."

"That will do." Said son Michael.

Feeding an African giraffe a banana proved to be a disaster. Not managing to negotiate the soft fruit, the banana just went around on the outside of its yellow teeth. At that time I had no idea that, years later, I would witness an African giraffe in its natural environment, curl its tongue around the thorns of an acacia tree to nibble at the soft green leaves.

 Like the previous journey through the Bay of Biscay, the overnight journey across the Mediterranean to Mallorca was rough. However, the following morning driving up and over the ramp into the warm spring sunshine was exhilarating. Staying for the first night in a hotel close to Palma, the next morning, armed with a map of the island, we set off on the 60 Km journey through Llucmayor, Campos, Felanitx and onto Cala Murada.

"Hola buenos dias Señor. Como estas?" Good morning and how are you?" said Señor Martinez. "I got your letter." He continued in broken English, "You are now here to find a villa. Good, book into the hotel for a couple of days and I will make the necessary arrangements for my receptionist Bernabe to take you around the area."

Winding down from the tiring journey, for the next two days, we walked from the hotel down the road, between olive trees and passed opulent villas, to sit on Cala Murada beach. On the third morning we were taken in a car driven by Bernabe, to look at three villas available for rent. While the two most well-equipped villas, near to the hotel and shops were good, they were beyond anything we could afford. Left with no alternative, we agreed to rent the much cheaper option some 2Km away from the centre of Cala Murada. A two-bedroomed villa D43, consisting of a lounge and dining room combined. With a bare kitchen containing a fridge, sink and cooker operated by butane gas. While overlooking the front garden path, was one single and one double fitted bedroom.

"It could certainly do with a bit more furniture," I said, looking critically at the dining room come lounge, with its table, four chairs and a wooden cabinet.

"Do you think you can cope? You know I am going to send a couple of large packing cases, with lots of our belongings, when I get back to England".

"Yes I suppose so. I do not have any alternative we are here and that is that." I said, opening one box filled with kitchen appliances.

"Mummy, come and look." Called four-year-old Terry, bounding back through the French doors leading from the garden. "There are rocks and prickly plants everywhere, and sheep in the fields."

After negotiating price and paying the six month's rent, the rest of our time together was spent either on Cala Murada beach or in Felanitx exploring the market and grocery shops. Opening a new joint bank account in Felantix and signing up to receive electricity and butane gas in D43, Michael prepared to leave.

"Take care of yourself" He said, looking at the four us standing on the road. "Until contracts are exchanged on the bungalow, I will continue to work and send money to our account unt in Felanitx." He continued, placing the suitcase and bags in the boot of the car. "I will send packing cases with most of our personal belongings. Are you sure you will be okay? He asked standing close to me.

"It sounds to me that you are starting to get cold feet, are you?"

"No, of course not. It's just such a big thing we are taking on".

"It is a bit late now to say that. And what about our dog Susy?" I asked, placing tree year old Edward in his push chair.

"Once you are settled, I will send the dog out to you by air. Come here and let me kiss you. You know how much I love you darling. I am going to miss you all so much." He said, drawing me close while looking across at his sons. "Take care of the boys and I will be back as soon as I can."

"Bye." I said, blowing a kiss.

CHAPTER 3

Lying on my stomach, with my feet facing the sea and my chin resting on my hands, I was studying a group of bystanders huddled around the bar. Getting up and leaving our swimming togs lying on the hot sand, I walked back up the beach to find out what was going on. Remaining at the back of the group but stretching up onto tiptoe, I looked over the heads of the onlookers. Seated on a chair in the centre of the group, lolling back with a half empty glass in one hand and a cigarette in the other, sat a woman with long dark hair. With one foot resting in the beach attendant's lap, he attacked the ball of the woman's foot. Intently occupied, lifting the tender pink flesh with the tip of a penknife, the attendant was squeezing black sea urchin splinters from between grime ridden fingernails. Meanwhile, the deeply sun-tanned woman, with the large dark eyes, showed little reaction. On the contrary, smiling up into the faces of the captive audience, she remained remarkably cool. Languishing in the chair, dressed in a stylish white swimsuit, it was obvious that she enjoyed taking centre stage.

Deciding to remain unobserved, instead peering around the back of two heads, I looked for my children. Not sure whether it was the intense heat of the late afternoon sun, or the flashing white light bouncing off the tip of the knife, but I was sweating like a pig. It was at this point that I spotted my eldest boys, standing at the front of the group, watching the operation with an unflinching gaze. With the mini operation complete, placing her foot back down on the ground and addressing the barman in Spanish, the striking looking woman ordered a round of drinks. Then turning back to look at the beach attendant, the other foot was placed onto his lap. A few minutes later when the tray of drinks arrived, the barman was thanked again in Spanish.

Meanwhile my sense of curiosity about this striking looking woman was heightened even further when, in a marked French accent, she spoke to my eldest son in English. Taken aback, I watched as Michael stepped forward to collect a glass of orange, followed by Terry also stepping up to take orange juice from the tray. At this point, pushing to the front, I made my presence known.

"Come here Edward" I said, watching my youngest also about to follow the lead taken by his brothers. However, with his loyalty now split between the presence of his mother and the temptation of a cold drink, Edward hesitated. Choosing to ignore me and taking up the drink, Edward then stepped back to place one arm around my thigh.

"Oh, so you must be Eddy's mother?" the woman said, dropping her foot down to the ground. "My name is Anna DeBois" she said, standing up.

"Please to meet you and my name is Jacqueline Weet." I said, stretching out my right hand in greeting.

"I have already made friends with your boys." She said, the large dark eyes focused on my cheap chain store swimsuit and rubber flip flops.

"Well nice to have met you Anna," I said, backing away somewhat embarrassed at the obvious scrutiny of my attire. "We must go," I said noting the catchy tune of "Puppet on a String" coming from the record player. Bumping Edward on my hip to the rhythm, leaving the eldest two behind, I returned to the beach.

Coping alone, in new and beautiful surroundings, I adapted well. With the bonus of being able to choose exactly how and where to spend those early summer days, time passed quickly. Taking breakfast out on the terrace was just one of the many new experiences to be enjoyed in the rented villa. Taking chairs from the lounge and putting them next to deck chairs already out on the terrace, I prepared the breakfast. Anticipating a potential squabble about the amount of precious corn flakes in each bowl, scooping a handful from one bowl, the flakes were distributed more equally. Then standing on the terrace, with my eyes shielded from the morning sun, I called to my brood playing in the field.

"Come on, breakfast is ready."

Bounding across the dark red earth and around wild sage bushes before jumping clear of the rocks, the boys came running. Completely ignoring the wails coming from Edward, who had snagged one knee on a rock. Michael and Terry were the first to arrive.

"Wait for me and where is my tea?" called Edward, always bringing up the rear, while clutching his bleeding knee. Placing the whimpering boy down into a deck chair, I went into the kitchen to fetch the first aid. Intently watching me apply cream and bandage to the graze, Edward dried his eyes on the sleeve of his shirt.

"Come on eat up, we need to hurry today boys. We are expected to be an Anna's for 10 o'clock. She is taking us to Porto Colom today in her car. Isn't that exciting?"

"Oh, I do believe we have come too early." I said, knocking on the front door twice before it was opened. "Would you like us to come back later?" I asked, studying Anna's dishevelled appearance and crumpled nightdress.

"As you can see," she replied, "I have only just got up. But now you are here you had better come in." she said, stepping aside before ushering us down the hall and into the well-equipped large kitchen.

"I already know what the boys like to drink, iced milk chocolate." She said, standing in front of the red tiled breakfast bar. "But you Jacqueline, what would you like?" She asked, opening the fridge door. "Cognac? Pernod? or perhaps a dry Martini with ice? Would you like to know what I am going to take with me into the shower? A cold pick-me-up to start the day." She said, placing three bottles of chocolate drink onto the bar before taking a Spanish beer from the fridge.

"It's a bit early for me Anna. But perhaps just this once I will have a Martini with lemon and ice please." I said, totally mesmerized watching Anna bang the top off the beer on the edge of the sink.

"Please make yourself at home," she said, pouring the chocolate drinks into glasses. "Have a good look around and go out into the garden, the French doors are already open, I have a gardener who takes care of everything. Go up onto the top terrace. The boys will show you where to go. I will catch up with you later after my shower." She said, taking another beer from the fridge before disappearing.

Nursing the drink, I walked through into the lounge. There set close to one wall, was a dining room table in olive wood, with six red leather chairs carved in the traditional Mallorquin style around it. Also placed on the black and white tiled floor, were cane armchairs and patchwork-coloured cushions. Setting down the emptied glass onto a ceramic table and stepping out through the French doors, I studied the garden brimming with early summer flowers.

"Mum," called Terry bounding up behind me. "You must follow me. I will show you where to go up the stairs."

"Did you finish your drinks?" I asked, looking back as Michael and Edward arrived.

"Yes, come on mum." Said Michael, beckoning me towards the steps.

Stopping to look cautiously at the open sided flight of steps, holding Edward in a vice grip we walked together next to the inside wall. Meanwhile spearheading the white steps to the top terrace, Terry and Michael were already standing in front of a wooden door.

"Is it locked?" I asked, going across to try the handle. "I wonder what goes on up here." I said, finding the door unlocked and entering an empty cavernous room with wash basins and toilet facilities at the far end. In fact, the noise created by three small boys clattering around on the concreted floor, disturbing the sleeping lizards, was so loud I retreated out onto the sun terrace.

Compared to the area around the hotel, this side of Cala Murada was quite under-developed and the view across the countryside, one of open farmland, olive trees and pine forest. Although Anna's home was just a short distance from where we stayed, a bend in the road combined with thick undergrowth obscured the view of D43. It was only when Anna came to stand behind me, that I became aware of the smell of a freshly showered woman.

"Well, what do you think?" she asked, her washed dark hair coiled on top of her head and dressed in a diaphanous kaftan in Cobalt blue.

"You look amazing Anna."

"Thank you. I have to tell you that this is just my second home." she said, pointing out at the panoramic view, in the distance, of hazy blue hills. "My husband Edgar and I own a private school in Belgium. Next year we intend to bring students here to spend part of their summer vacation. And this toom at the top, where the children are playing," she added smiling and noting the racket going on. "Is to be a dormitory. It is not yet finished because the villa was only completed three months ago. Anyway, come on boys," she called, through the wooden doorway. "I need to lock up so we can go to Porto Colom." Walking back passed me, to wait at the head of the steps, I could smell the aniseed on Anna's breath.

Throughout the 7kilometer drive to Porto Colom, Anna's driving was so dreadful, I was convinced we were all going to finish up the ditch. Only on one extremely sharp bend, when she was forced to take her foot off the gas, did I let go of the car's dashboard.

"This is pretty." I said, expelling a breath of relief while looking across at quaint cottages, painted in earth colours, leaning against one another like comfortable old men,"

"This is where I buy all my fresh fish." Anna said, swinging the wheel of the Spanish car abruptly to the left before lurching up a small side street filled with potholes.

"Follow me," she said, yanking the hand brake on before the car had stopped. "And leave the boys in the car."

"But we want to come too." Said Michael.

"No, it is better if you stay outside and play." I said, herding them from the car.

Following Anna, we stopped in front of an ochre-coloured dwelling, with a green and white beaded curtain hanging on the front door. Entering the fish shop, away from the glare of the sun, it took time for my eyes to adjust to the interior, with its fridges and freezers standing against the walls. It was only after Anna called twice, that a petite lady appeared through an open door at the far end of the shop. Drying her hands on the striped apron, the woman came forward to greet Anna. Following the customary kisses on both cheeks the two women launched into a conversation, conducted in local Mallorquin, that was totally foreign to me. With even more explicit hand gestures, coupled with pointing to various refrigerators, Anna announced, to me, that we had come on the wrong day for fresh fish.

"You could always buy some of these." She said, pointing to a line of red mullet inside the freezer.

Not wanting to offend, while too embarrassed to admit that I was short of money, I graciously agreed to buy one kilo of the local fish. Following more kisses and farewells and with the mullet in the boot of the car, watching the boys playing in the bowls of dust in the roadway, Anna and I sat in the car smoking.

"Next time we come I'm going to leave you in the car." Anna said, blowing perfect smoke rings out of the side window at the front of the car. "Having a foreigner with me almost doubled the price of the fish."

"That's good coming from you. You are a foreigner too!"

"True, but I speak the language and that makes a vast difference. Besides, I am accepted here as one of them." She said, rolling the cigarette between her painted fingernails. "If you are serious about opening a business here, you had better start learning the language."

"Hang on, I am starting to learn. When buying food in the shops, I am forced to speak Spanish."

"That is good. Do you mind me asking, how old are you?"

"I am twenty-nine. How old are you Anna?"

"I am four years old than you. Anyway, get the boys back into the car, I am going to take you to a bar I know in the harbour close to the water's edge."

With the sun in its zenith, conscious of my fair English complexion, Anna chose an outside table in the shade of tall poplar trees. Once again, instantly recognised, the proprietor of the bar came forward to whisper something inaudible in Anna's ear.

"The first drinks are on the house." She giggled, in a coquettish manner, while pulling away to join us at the table. "It will be Pernod with ice and water for me, and three Lacao chocolate drinks for the boys. And what about you Jacqueline?"

"Cognac with ice please." I said, lounging back with my sunglasses tipped up onto my forehead.

While I paid for the next round of drinks, Anna began talking about her background and how she had been born in the Belgian Congo and educated in an English school in the Congo. However the conversation about how she was then brought back to Belgium was brought to an abrupt end, by the arrival of a lady pushing a wooden cart. Lowering the cart down into the kerb, the lady stopped alongside where we were sitting. Dressed entirely in black, studying her weathered face, I could not help but notice how age and the weight of her gold-hooped earrings had elongated the lobes of her ears. Then taking a large conch shell from the bottom of the cart and drawing a draught of air into her lungs, this woman produced three sonorous notes from the shell.

"Why is she doing that?" asked Terry excitedly, getting down from the table to look inside the cart at the display of fish.

"That is how she attracts her customers." Said Anna, coming around to inspect the array of mussels, prawns and squid laid out on painted earthenware dishes.

"I know these white tube things." Said Michael, joining his brother. "We have seen them in the market in Felanitx haven't we mum?"

"You mean calamari Michael." Said Anna. "That is what they are called in Spanish. I will buy some and when we get back to my villa, I will show you how to cook them."

Later that day keeping her word, Anna prepared us all a meal of calamari with chips and followed by chocolate ice cream.

"I am going to be busy for the next week, so I will not be able to see you." Anna said, leaving us at the front door.

"That is fine Anna that suits me too. As a matter of fact, I am in the process of arranging for boxes from England to be collected at the port. Thank you again for a lovely day and we will catch up again soon."

"That red mullet will have defrosted, so eat it tomorrow."

"We will, thank you for a lovely day." I said, waving goodbye.

The bar standing opposite the hotel Cala Murada is called Pedro's. And today, sheltering beneath the bougainvillea, four men are playing cards. Apart from the fronds of pink blooms rustling in the hot Sirocco wind, nothing moves. (With the following conversations conducted in local Mallorquin) the name of the game the men are playing is poker.

As dealer, Jose the supermarket owner, deals five cards to the other players and is first to call. Studying his hand of two pairs and a queen, a one hundred peseta note is then put down onto the table. Meanwhile Andres the local gardener, seated to the left, studies his 'flush' of spades, thoughtfully, before taking a roll of dirty notes from his trouser pocket.

"I'll raise you one hundred." He says, rolling the black cheroot across his wet lips. before placing two hundred pesetas onto the table. Sitting alongside Andres, Bernabe the twenty-two-year-old receptionist from the hotel Cala Murada is the third man to play. Fanning his five cards between manicured fingers, looking at the 'straight' he holds, he covers the bet made by Andres. At the same time, handsome and dashing Emilio, proprietor of the local car hire firm and fourth man to play, shaking his head, places his cards face down onto the table.

"No way, that's enough for me. Anybody else want to join me for a drink?" Emelio says, looking behind at Pedro the owner of the bar. Engrossed in their hands and the gamble in progress, Jose takes a considerable time deliberating over his cards.

"Come on," growls Andres, grabbing his balls from deep within his trouser pocket. "I do not have all day. I am going to Palma this afternoon. I am collecting packing cases from the port for that English woman."

"Okay, I cover your two hundred and raise another two hundred, to see you." says Jose, looking hard at Andres.

"Thank you," Andres grins, laying down his more powerful hand and displaying his gold eye teeth.

"That reminds me," says Bernabe, standing up and retrieving his jacket from the back of the chair "Jacqueline was in the hotel this morning. She needs a lift to the airport next week to collect the dog. I have already said I would go with her in case she needs someone to deal with customs. It means going again Andres and can you take us in the van?"

"Of course, if she is paying. You know me, always interested in earning money. Especially when it is foreigners paying."

Into June and seated on the garden wall beneath a fig tree, taking refuge from the sun, I waited for Andres to arrive. Admiring the terracotta pots filled with geraniums, all donated by men working nearby, I picked up the letter on my lap. Reading again, the second letter in six weeks from Michael, I studied the details concerning the arrival of the dog in Palma airport. With the letter going on to tell me that the bungalow had been sold and contracts about to be exchanged, Michael went on to assure me that money would be transferred Felanitx. As a final comment, I was asked to conserve money and avoid paying unnecessary bills until his arrival in September.

"Come on boys." I called to the boys in the field and popping the letter back into my pocket. "I can hear the van coming up the hill." I said, jumping down from the wall as the grey van pulled up on the roadside.

"Buenas tardes, Señora. You are looking well today." Said Bernabe climbing down from the front seat next to Andres. "That suntan suits you," He said, walking around to the back of the van to open the doors. "Please climb in. I have put a makeshift chair for you and some sacking on the floor for the boys."

"So you really like living here on the island?" Bernabe said, calling back to me as we set off around the bay towards the hotel.

"How could I not like it? Swimming nearly every day. Keeping fit walking the mile and a half up to the hotel and shops. Not to mention the constant trips to Felanitx for our groceries? And you speaking good English gives me the opportunity to speak English too." I said, smiling.

"Of course, it has to be like that. With so many English tourists arriving, we have to speak the language."

"Do you mind if we stop in Felanitx first? I need to check our bank account."

"Of course tell us which bank, and we will wait outside."

As suspected, discovering there was little money left in the account and with the equivalent of fifteen pounds in pesetas in my purse, climbing back into the van I was somewhat subdued.

"Everything OK?" Bernabe asked waiting to close the door behind me.

"Absolutely fine." I lied.

The plane from Heathrow came was on time. And following an hour of intense negotiation between Bernabe and Customs, including a further payment of six pounds, our dog was released from the wire cage and into our arms. Now left with the equivalent of nine pounds in pesetas to my name, I was relieved the bill with Andres had already been settled. For the entire hour and a half journey back to Cala Murada, Andres only spoke to Bernabe seated next to him. Not that it mattered, with Andres speaking in Mallorquin, I was quite happy to sit alongside the boys with the dog on my lap. Back at D43, while the boys raced around introducing Susy to her surroundings, sipping a cup of English tea I considered the surprise invitation from Bernabe to attend a barbecue.

Protected on both sides by rocky bluffs stretching out to sea, Cala Murada beach itself was a medley of shingle sand and rock. While the central sandy area, sloping down to the water's edge, was designated for swimmers, the shingled area to the right with the deepest water was kept for small craft. The reason the rocky and perilous area on the left-hand side remained out of bounds to all was because, submerged between crevices, lay razor-edged rocks encrusted with urchins.

Sitting beneath a bamboo covered beach umbrella, ignoring the rowdy boys, I was reading an article about the explorer Francis Chichester sailing solo around the world.

"Hi, there." Came an American voice from behind.

Swivelling around but staying seated, I looked up at a late middle-aged American man, with a sandy coloured crew cut.

"May I introduce myself? My name is Ted." He said, leaning forward with an outstretched hand. "And your name is?"

"Jacqueline." I replied, standing up, quite taken by the intrusion.

"Please to meet you. And where is your friend today?" he asked, brushing fine sand from his tanned freckled shoulders." I already know your sons."

"Really?"

"Yes, I was in that group of bystanders at the bar, that afternoon the Belgium woman was having the spines cut out from her feet. Sea urchins are nasty things. If they are not removed, they fester."

"Oh now we are on the same wavelength. You mean Anna? She is back in Belgium."

Meanwhile noticing my conversation with a stranger and bored kicking sand into the sea, Michael came up to stand in front of me.

"Who are you?" he said.

"You are a cheeky kid. My name is Ted and what is your name?" the American asked, studying my eldest with his dark auburn hair and brown eyes.

"Michael." he said, swinging his knees from side to side.

"Well do you know you have more freckles on your face than I have! Okay, so now we have the rest of the troops arriving." said Ted, grinning at Terry and Edward.

"So what is your name young man?" He asked, tussling Terry's mousy coloured hair.

"Terry is a bit reticent. He does not like speaking to strangers." I said looking into my son's hazel eyes.

"Okay, and this little chap?" Ted asked, squatting down onto his haunches to be on the same level as my son. "Do you know young man you have the same large blue eyes as your mother." Ted added, looking up at me.

"He is Edward." I said, noticing the silky long hairs, bleached from the sun, on the American's legs.

"Well what do you know. I am Edward too. But I am called Ted for short. And what are their ages?" he asked, standing up.

"Seven, five and three."

"Wow, you have got your hands full. Now, let me see, can I offer you boys a bribe?" asked Ted.

"What is a bribe?" Terry replied suspiciously.

"Oh so you have got a tongue Terry! Well a bribe is ...." Ted said, hesitating while studying the pedalos parked at the water's edge. "Riding on pedalos, followed by coca cola and ice cream at the bar?"

"Yes please and what about mum?" Asked Michael.

"While we go off for a ride, mum can read her paper. Then later while you boys have ice cream, your mother and I can have a drink at the bar. I am sure you will agree to that plan boys. Let us go and pay for a ride on a pedalo."

An hour later sitting together at the bar, drinking iced brandy and with the boys enjoying cola and ice cream, Ted began telling me how it was that he came to live in Mallorca. Born in California Ted had an American mother and a German father. Formerly a major in the American army, taking early retirement from the military, the pension he received was not only large enough to buy a villa in Cala Murada, but also a yacht and sports car.

"I come to the beach nearly every day." He said, looking out across the bay to the cliffs on the other side. "You cannot actually see my villa from here because it lies back from the road. Can you see that large white villa, standing proud from the rock face, high above the water's edge and festooned with hanging plants?" He said, pointing.

"You mean the villa with the high walls and guarded by Alsatian dogs. Yes, I know that villa because I have walked by it, on my way to Tropicana beach."

"Yes, that's the one. That German owned villa belongs to members of the Krupp's family. Do you know about them Jacqueline? They produced German armaments during the Second World War. Or maybe you are too young." He said, looking over the top of his sunglasses, trying to assess my age. "Anyway, that is enough about me. Let me get us both another brandy and cola for the boys. Then you can tell me how it is that you are here alone with children and without a husband."

Half an hour later after telling Ted all about the plans to build a bar and restaurant in Cala Murada, the American prepared to leave.

"Well it all sounds exciting to me." He said, collecting his wallet. "My villa is situated on the third circle directly behind the Krupp's villa. When your husband arrives, you must both come to my home for a meal."

"Thank you, that would be lovely."

CHAPTER 4

Following the arrival of a hotel maid to look after the three boys, Bernabe drove me back to meet up with holiday makers outside the Cala Murada hotel.

"Okay," said Bernabe climbing up into the coach, dressed casually in a short sleeved white shirt and jeans. "Can I have everybody attention." He asked, clapping his hands together. "This evening we are going to Cala D'Or, to the Ponderosa barbecue. And we have a special guest coming with us tonight. Can you please stand up and show yourself?" he said, beckoning towards me sitting at the rear of the coach. "Jacqueline has recently come to live here in Cala Murada. And on our journey to the barbecue I am sure she will be willing to answer any questions you might have." He said, walking down the central aisle checking that everybody on the list, excluding me, had paid for the outing.

"And this is Benito our driver for tonight." Bernabe went on, placing the clip board on a rack above. He does not speak much English, but I can assure you he is an excellent driver. "Okay, let us go Benito, he said, tapping the driver's back.

The place where the barbecue was held called "The Ponderosa", turned out to be a series of low-slung white buildings in the style of a Mexican hacienda. Strolling beneath one archway festooned in scarlet hibiscus and white oleander, the forty guests in the group were ushered out onto a quadrangle containing cloisters on three sides. Close to one side wall, beneath a roof of slatted bamboo, waiters placed bottles of wine down the middle of trestle tables. On the opposite side of the open quadrangle stood a bar with candlelit tables, while nearby a group of musicians warmed up for the evening's entertainment.

At the upper end of the quadrangle, doubling as a dance floor, was a cascading fountain decorated with stucco cherubs. Drawn by the ambience of an open wood fire, sniffing the burning olive wood and roasting meat, the British visitors mingled freely. Standing together watching sucking pigs impaled through their bottoms, turn on mechanical spits, crispy skinned chickens rotated on poles close to the fire. Meanwhile, attentive waiters circulated amongst the guests, handing out sobrasada sausage and bread soaked in olive oil.

"If everybody is happy? Could you all take a seat at a table please." Asked Bernabe, escorting them to the tables filled with an array of sizzling meats and fresh salad. And as the good food, accompanied by copious amounts of rough red and white wine was consumed, so the evening went from sobriety to something akin to a Bacchanalian feast.

Suddenly standing up onto a chair, Bernabe looked to one waiter to hand him a triangular shaped drinking vessel filled with Madeira wine. Holding the vessel firmly in his right hand and his head tilted back, the handsome Spaniard then allowed the golden viscous fluid to pour into his open mouth. Acknowledging the rowdy behaviour and hand clapping from the audience, Bernabe stepped down from the chair with a bow.

"Now it is your turn. Everybody must have a try." He said, passing the "purron" to one guest. Thereupon, amidst raucous revelry, the "purron" was passed from one holiday maker to the next. However, not surprisingly, more honey sweet alcohol finished up on shirts and dresses, than in the waiting mouths. As the evening progressed, accompanied by the seven-piece band playing renditions of songs by the Beach Boys, the Rolling Stones and The Beatles, so the revellers danced the night away.

Arriving back at the hotel at midnight to escort the holiday makers into the foyer first, Bernabe then took me back to D43 to pick up the maid. Looking across at the lights still on in the villa I was eager to get out and check on the children.

"Wait a moment." He said, holding my head in his hands before kissing me lightly on the mouth. "Thank you for your charming company tonight. We must meet up again."

"Oh, what a lovely surprise Anna," I said, looking up. "I had no idea you were back. We were just about to have a picnic. Would you like to join us?" I asked, lifting the pink and white gingham cloth revealing the sandwiches and fruit cake beneath. "I have just managed to make my first, successful, English style fruit cake using the local flour." I said, lifting the cake out onto my lap. "Move up Terry, and let Anna sit down."

"No not for me thanks. Save it for later. I have had a particularly heavy night and the very last thing I want now is fruit cake. What I need is to go for a swim to clear my head." Anna replied, irritably.

"Suit yourself. "I said, somewhat taken aback by the off-hand attitude and at the same time studying Anna's jittery gait as she walked down to the water's edge.

"Who wants a sandwich?" I asked, turning to the boys next to me.

"No sandwiches mum, just fruit cake for us please." Said Michael.

"Right, but I must save a slice for Anna." I said, cutting three slices and placing another slice in my hand. Biting into fruit cake while gazing out to sea, stunned by a searing pain shooting through my jaw, the cake was spat back into my hand. There, wriggling amongst the chewed piece of cake, was a wasp bitten in half. Conscious that I had been stung on the inside of the lower lip, leaping to my feet, I turned to run up the beach.

"Where are you going mum?" Asked Terry, looking back.

"Please will you give me a glass of water, with vinegar and a slice of lemon?" I asked, relieved that this particular barman spoke reasonably good English.

"What do you want that for?" He asked, filling a glass with water.

"I have been stung in the mouth by a wasp."

That will not do any good Señora. You need sea water. Saltwater is the best thing for stings."

"Oh God" I said, turning away and leaving the glass of water untouched.

"What has happened?" asked intuitive Michael getting to his feet.

"I need to get into the sea now!"

Meanwhile instinctively aware that some maternal crisis was at hand, with arms raised in a primal gesture, Edward screeched with alarm.

"It is alright Eddy, do not worry, Mummy will be okay."

With both cheeks swollen, I waded out into the deeper water. Then diving down close to the seabed, like some whale shark filter feeder. I sieved salty water through my mouth. Returning to the surface, some twenty seconds later, I knew the tip from the barman had not worked. Acutely aware that I now had swollen lips and puffy eyes, I re-emerged from the sea. However any thoughts I might have had about indulging in self-pity were dispelled by the sound of somebody coming up close behind.

"Oh! For fucks sake! What has happened to you?" Asked Anna.

"Do I look that bad?" I lisped, looking at her. "A wasp has stung me."

"Yes you do." She said, stifling a laugh. "You know that East African tribe? The ones where women put plates in their lips to enhance their beauty? Well that is what you look like".

"Thanks that is all I needed." I said, trying not to dribble. "I have got the picture. Come on boys we need to go home".

"No wait! collect your belongings and I will take you to see the doctor in Porto Colom".

Following behind Anna and watching her stride out towards her parked car with an even gait, made me think that a dip in the sea had been more beneficial to her than to me.

Arriving in Porto Colom, Dr Planas was still in his surgery and after examining my mouth and throat, I was given a prescription for Antihistamines.

"You will be much better by tonight Señora." He said, with confidence. "If you had been stung in the throat you could have been in trouble."

Fortunately, having now been resident on the island for nearly three months, I understood most of what the doctor said in Mallorquin.

For the twice weekly visit to Felanitx and the bus departing from the hotel at eight thirty in the morning, meant an early rise for the family. Depending on how many unscheduled stops, the bus took between forty minutes and one hour to arrive at the destination. Haggling with stall owners in the market over prices, forced me to use my limited knowledge of Spanish. And with the bus not returning to Cala Murada before midday, left plenty of time to go elsewhere. Leaving the heavy bags of groceries at the bus station, we set off visiting favourite haunts in Felanitx.

In such intense heat, the first port of call was always a bar situated at the bottom of the town. Around three sides of the square were a petrol station, an abattoir as well as a tobacconist. While in the leafy centre, surrounded by oleander bushes and date palms, were tables with coloured sun umbrellas. The added attraction to the bar, located across the road from the centre, was the fact that it had best toilet facilities in town. For a family, on a hot day, it was the perfect place to be. Never changing the order, it was always double iced coffee and cream for me and triple flavoured ice cream for the boys.

"What about visiting the local church for a change. Then we could stay out of the sun?" I asked the boys, while paying the bill.

"No thanks, mum. We do not like churches, do we." Added Terry, looking to Michael for support.

"No, you go mum".

"Right that means just you and me Edward. You two will have to play somewhere else in the shade." I said, setting off up the hill, with Edward in his pushchair, towards the very old Catholic church at the top.

"Here we are Edward." I said, looking up at the ornately carved, butter coloured, façade and magnificent rose window. "Do not go too far." I called out, as the eldest two boys disappeared down a side alley.

Taking Edward by the hand before climbing the steps together, I pushed open the heavy oak door. However, overwhelmed by the powerful smell of burning incense I stopped at the font.

"Come on Edward, mummy does not want to go any further. Let us go and play with your brothers instead." I said, my mind filled with memories, as a child, visiting the Catholic church in Bouverie road.

Arriving back at 1 o'clock, our kind bus driver carried on down the hill to leave us with the shopping at the beach. However, with loaded bags and tired children, by the time we arrived at the villa, we were exhausted. Having said that, lured on a summer's day, following a quick snack of dry biscuits, sobrasada sausage and all washed down with home-made lemonade we were off once more down to the beach.

Upon arriving at the each with Edward and his bag of toys, the eldest two boys were already swimming in the sea. Sitting upright, wriggling my toes in the sand and with Edward playing, I ignored the eldest two squabbling. Finally giving in, calling them out of the sea, we went up to the bar. Despite attempts to bribe Terry and Michael with iced cola, their behaviour did not improve. Fractious in the heat, Terry managed to tip his chair backwards into the lady's chair behind him.

"Oh! I am so sorry." I said jumping up, grabbing my unruly youngster by the back of his tee shirt.

"Hmm! You must be the English woman I have heard about." Said the American. "My name is Dorothy, and you must be Jacqueline." She said, standing up and pushing the white cotton turban to the back of her head.

"Yes," How do you know my name?"

"Oh it does not take long for news to travel here in Cala Murada. Please come and sit with me. I will ask the barman to bring iced lemon tea for us and orange juice for the children."

Sitting together chatting, telling her about all our plans, I learnt that Dorothy was also a Californian.

"So you intend living here permanently. So what exactly are you doing about schooling for the children?" She asked, eyeing the boys, clattering around the terrace playing tag. "One of my neighbours has children that attend the local school. I could give you all the details."

"That is kind of you Dorothy, but my fried Anna has already taken me to the school at Espinegar to meet the teacher Dona Antonia. They start in September but the thing that bothers me," I said, producing a packet of cigarettes from my bag and offering one to Dorothy. "Is the system of teaching here is so different from England. How does one teacher manage to teach a dozen or more pupils, of differing nationalities and ages?"

"I will tell you, Dorothy said, lighting the cigarette and inhaling deeply. "Within a short time your boys will not only be bi-lingual, but they will pick up a smattering of German, Dutch, French as well as Mallorquin. It is a fact that young children have an inborn ability to speak other languages. "Ugh! she said, taking the cigarette from her mouth to study the label. "Just as I thought, cheap, strong Spanish cigarettes. I only smoke American cigarettes, Of course that is when I can get hold of them. Most of the American brands we buy here are smuggled onto the island." She said, stubbing the cigarette out in the ashtray.

"Anyway I need to leave you now. I have an appointment in Porto Colom. This is the address where I live on the first circle" she said, taking a piece of paper from the elegant leather handbag. "Perhaps you would care to join me for afternoon tea?" She added, writing something down on the paper. "Say in two weeks? I would suggest a date for the Wednesday at 3 o'clock. Now I must go,"

Watching Dorothy scuttle away and at the same time noticing Ted, also from California approaching the beach steps, I wondered if there was some connection between them.

Around tea-time, sitting on the low wall, waiting for the children to come out of the shower, I noticed Bernabe coming down the terrace steps. Spotting me he waived and noticing he was not alone, smiling, I waived back. Now watching Bernabe leaning across the bar, speaking in German to a lovely fair-haired woman, I knew he had moved on. Admiring the blond. wearing nothing more than a crocheted "g" string over her bottom and a bikini top barely covering her ample breasts, knowing that Bernabe was an immature and rushed lover, I suspected that this strapping Fraulein was about to eat him alive.

Following that night at the "Ponderosa" Bernabe came to meet me on the beach and at night, after finishing at the hotel, he also came to visit me in the villa. On two separate occasions, lying on a mattress on the top terrace, above the room where the children slept, we made love. That outrageously reckless and irresponsible behaviour did not last long as, very soon the novelty wore off. I knew it was nothing more than a stupid married woman being flattered by the advances of a Spaniard six years her junior. And for handsome Bernabe, it had been a question of sewing his wild oats.

Because the telephone connection between London and Mallorca was so bad, any descent conversation between

Michael and I was out of the question. Speaking loudly, in between the constant breaks and crackles on the line, I did manage to press home the fact that I needed more money. Eventually, following an argument, Michael agreed to put another 50 pounds into our account in Felanitx.

Meanwhile, only too aware that the conversation, conducted in the hotel foyer next to the reception, had been overheard, I replaced the receiver back on the hook. With bills for electricity and butane gas outstanding, I had no idea how I was going to survive. Conscious that Bernabe and Señor Martinez were watching, taking Susy the dog by her lead, I walked towards them.

"Please," I said, taking the dog up into my arms. "It is about these peculiar lumps I have found fixed to Susy's skin. Look, they are here on her face and in her ears." I said, holding the dog's head fast, while pointing to the grey pea-sized insects half concealed in the long fur.

"They are ticks" Bernabe said without even looking. "Dogs get them all the time in the summer. They pick them up from the sheep grazing in the fields. Ticks feed on the dog's blood. You are going to have to remove them."

"How?"

"Burn them with the lighted end of a cigarette." Said, Señor Martinez "Bring her here I will show you how it is done." He said, lighting a cigarette.

Standing close to the hotel manager, with the dog's head held in a vice grip, the lighted end of the cigarette was brought close Susy's face. Curling her lip and snarling, Susy showed her set of needle teeth.

"Well that is not going to work." Chuckled Señor Martinez. "You are going to have to do it yourself with a pair of tweezers".

"What is more, you must make sure the whole head is removed from the dog's skin. If you do not do that then the tick will just continue to feed on the dog's blood and swell". Concluded Bernabe.

"Charming." I said, placing Susy down on the floor. "Do you know, I am having the most terrible day and I fear it is about to get even worse."

"Look wait a minute Jacqueline. While your boys are playing mini golf in the grounds come into the room at the back. We want to talk to you. We know you are having problems with money and Señor Martinez here, is prepared to advance you fifty pounds in pesetas until Michael arrives in September. Of course as proof of this loan, you will be required to sign this form." Said Bernabe.

"Thank you for your help." I said, signing on the dotted line. "Let us see what happens with the dog." I said going out into the gardens to fetch the children.

Hurrying through our tea of sandwiches and cake, the operation to remove the ticks from the dog began. With Susy, quickly making it apparent that she was not going to allow me anywhere near with a lighted cigarette, the second option was put on the agenda. Prising the insect from the fur with a pair of tweezers, proved to be a time-consuming and bloody affair. Applying pressure while squeezing the bloated bodies, not only splattered blood all over the dog, but also on me. Running my fingers along the Susy's back, even more vampires were discovered buried into her flesh. Shuddering and flushing the tick remains down the toilet, I went into the kitchen to scrub my hands.

"Mum, Anna is here." Yelled Terry, bounding into the kitchen, before turning on his heel to go back out again.

Walking out onto the front step, drying my hands, I watched Anna swinging first Michael and then Terry around in her arms.

"So what do you think of the car," she asked, sauntering up the garden path bending down to cover Edward with kisses.

"Yes, lovely but I am not so sure about your outfit." I said looking at the ruby coloured silk saree, and golden sandals.

"What on earth is that red cast mark, painted on your forehead all about?"

"This is the new Eastern look. It is the summer of love." She said, twirling around.

"I am not quite sure about the Indian look, but I do like the car. Come inside," I said noting the familiar whiff of anis on her breath as she passed by.

"The car belongs to my husband and I have just driven it all the way from Belgium.".

"My God. Really?"

"I am here to ask you to join me at the hotel dance tonight. And can I have a drink please." She asked, flopping back into the deckchair.

"Anna you have already been drinking as well as driving."

"For Christ's sake sometimes you are such a bloody bore. It is about time you let your hair down and started enjoying yourself. I promise, this is only my second drink today."

"I know you are lying Anna." I said, looking down at her before going into the kitchen. Deliberately pushing the door half shut, I poured a small measure of Pernod into a glass before drowning the milky alcohol with water.

"Are you going to come tonight or not?" she asked, scowling at the water-downed drink.

"I don't have a baby-sitter."

"That is not a problem. I can drive to the hotel and get one of the maids to come."

"Alright, see you later."

By the time Anna finally arrived with the maid at 9 o'clock, with the children sound asleep, I had sat dressed in a candy floss coloured pink trouser suit, for more than one hour.

"You have changed your outfit?" I said, looking at her Kaftan of emerald green silk and long dark hair caught in a golden headband.

"Okay! I have got it now. The theme is the hippie summer of love and 'Californian Dreaming.' I said, slipping into silver sandals.

By the time we arrived in the 'snazzy' blue sports car, holiday makers and locals were already seated around tables at the outside bar. While smartly dressed waiters circulated amongst the guests serving jugs of Sangria, the band from Cala D'Or was in full swing. Carrying drinks between us, Anna and I sat at a vacant table. Suddenly, without speaking before standing up cradling the Pernod, Anna disappeared elsewhere. It just so happened, left sitting alone, that as the band struck up with the popular Mexican dance 'La Bamba', that American Ted walked across to ask me to dance.

Invariably on a Saturday night, the local men arrived to sit at the outside bar watching the guests. On this occasion, sitting chatting at the outside bar and talking in Spanish, are Jose and Andres. Kitted out in grey flannel trousers and an open necked shirt, Jose's dark eyes roam the surfeit of sunburnt flesh. Meanwhile, seated next to him, looking decidedly out of place in a double-breasted suit, Andres bites on the cheroot.

"It did not take the American long to pick up the English woman." Andres growls grabbing his crotch and rolling the cheroot with his tongue.

"Hi there" Says raffish Emilio, climbing onto a bar stool in is white flared trousers and black shirt. "What are we drinking tonight? I can see Ted is on form." Emilio adds with a wink.

"He's a notoriously fast worker. The English woman will be yet another notch on his belt." Says Andres.

"Maybe not. 'Ella es muy atractiva y gentile. La quiero.' She is very charming and what is more I want her." Says Jose, caressing the bowl of his brandy glass with calloused hands.

"You are such a randy bastard Jose. She must be at least twenty years younger than you. Better stick to your women in Palma." Emilio says. digging the supermarket owner in the ribs.

"I prefer to leave the 'putas' of Palma to the winter months, when the foreign women have gone home. You never know, my pecker is still in perfect working order. I am not shooting sawdust yet."

"Glad to hear it. It is greetings to the swinging sixties." Says Emilio noticing his own female lover approaching from across the dance floor.

Dancing with other partners for the rest of the evening, and with Anna not seen again, it was left to Bernabe to drive me back to the villa and to collect the maid.

The name of the company responsible for the development of the area was called "Cobassa". And the offices at the entrance of Cala Murada, were quite close to where Dorothy lived. Standing looking bewildered at the address, and still not sure where the house was, I went into the "Cobassa" offices to speak to the receptionist, who presented me with a map. Returning outside to study the map at the roadside, a passer-by stopped to help. And although the gentleman spoke to me in English, I suspected he was German.

"So you found it alright," Dorothy said, greeting us all at the front door.

"Not really. A kind man helped by bringing me to the top of your road. I am not familiar with this area or the layout of the circles." I said, walking into a lounge filled with antique furniture and porcelain.

"It's so hot today I thought we should go into the garden. Please come through" Dorothy said, lifting the cream voile curtains leading out onto the veranda. "I'll tell you all about the villa once we are settled. I have arranged for tea to be served at the bottom of the garden where it is much cooler."

With Edward holding on to the hem of my best dress, we followed the host down a flight of steps and out onto a fan-shaped terrace below. Standing to one side of the terrace, with its sun dial and backdrop of yellow and pink throated honey-suck, was a swinging chair and flounced canopy. And following

Dorothy down a further flight of steps, between pink and red geraniums, we stepped onto a square. On one side of the plaza, tiled in lapis blue. stood an octagonal fountain with ceramic frogs. So totally overwhelmed by this beautiful garden, I had to stop.

"I know, it is lovely" Dorothy said, waiting for me. Then carrying on ducking between palms, mimosa, and lemon trees we arrived at a table laid with a bone china tea service and a cake covered in a muslin cap.

"Please sit down. My maid will serve us here." Dorothy said, ushering us up onto the wooden veranda. At that moment, apparently from nowhere, a maid appeared carrying a tray of sandwiches, glasses of iced orange juice and strawberries in a glass bowl.

"Thank you, Maria. I can manage now." Dorothy said, waiting while the maid set down the tea pot, before disappearing back up the path. "This is my favourite combination. I hope you like it." She said, picking up the copper kettle and pouring the boiling water onto the tea leaves at the bottom of the china pot. "It is Assam mixed with Earl Grey. It is so refreshing on a hot day. Do you not think so Jacqueline?"

Not wanting to show ignorance concerning the pros and cons of the aristocratic teas of the world, I said nothing.

"If the children would like ice cream with the fruit, the maid will fetch it."

"No please do not bother they look quite happy as they are." I said, relieved they were being well behaved. "How lovely this is for them. This is the first time they have had fresh strawberries in Mallorca." I said, admiring my boys, decked out in their best outfits of white shirts and black shorts.

"Did I tell you that I have been married twice?" Dorothy asked, lifting the muslin from the cake. "My first husband was Swedish, and my second husband was an American. It was the alimony I received from two divorces that enabled me to buy this villa. This is lemon drizzle-cake, I hope you like it." she said, cutting the cake into triangular pieces. "I have two children from the marriages. One married daughter living in France, and a son still at University in California."

"So what made you choose Cala Murada to live?" I asked sipping the deliciously aromatic tea.

"Well, I have a half-brother who also lives here called Ted. It was him who introduced me to this place three years ago. Ted is a few years younger than me." She said, pausing to take a packet of cigarettes from her bag. "My half-brother and I do not get on very well now. There has been a disagreement and breakup in the family. These things happen in life you know."

"I think I have already met Ted. He lives on the third circle behind the hotel. And did you say he is your half-brother?"

"Yes, my mother, still alive in California, was also married twice. Her first husband, my American father, died young and she then married a German. So while I have both American parents, Ted has an American mother and a German father. As a result, my half-brother Ted, speaks good German."

"We have eaten all the straw-berries, can we leave the table now please?" Michael asked, looking up at Dorothy.

"Yes, you may. I do like well- mannered children. You can go and play in the top part of the garden. But make sure you behave yourselves and do not go into the house." Dorothy called, watching the three boys run away between the trees.

"I would like to know more about the circles and the layout of the properties in this area." I said, lighting a cigarette.

"Well there are three circles named one, two and three. Where my half-brother lives on the third circle is the most expensive area to buy. While circle two, behind the hotel and where the shops are, is less pricey. Here where I live on the first circle, farthest away from the main part of Cala Murada is the cheapest area to buy."

"Now I understand how the circles are set out like the spokes of a wheel." I said, taking the little map from my pocket. "Each road goes down from the rim to a central point."

"That is correct, and I actually bought this villa from a Swiss family. But they were not the original owners. The original owners were from Berlin. This was one of the first villas to be built in this area at the late 1940's" She said, thoughtfully plucking a eucalyptus leaf from the nearby tree. "You must have heard about the Nuremburg trials?

"Well I was only eight years old, but I have heard about them yes."

"In Germany during the Second World War, a vast amount of money was generated on the Black Market. And at that time Spain, under Franco. was fascist and pro-German. When the war came to an end, some Germans avoided arrest by fleeing the country and taking their ill-gotten gains elsewhere. I am speaking about money sequestrated into bank accounts in Switzerland, South America as well as here in Spain."

"You mean laundered money?"

"Yes of course."

"Mum! come quickly." Yelled Michael bursting through the lemon trees. "You have to come and see what Terry and Edward are doing."

Running like a pair of gazelles back up the path, we found Terry leaping about in the fountain naked, and with Edward lying on his stomach in his pants, his chubby fingers stuffed down the throat of one green frog.

"At least they had the sense to take off their sandals before getting into my fountain!" Dorothy said, laughing. "I will go and fetch some towels while you get them out."

Quickly returning with white towels, Dorothy sat watching me dry the children.

"Really I do not know how you cope with these three on your own."

"I am definitely looking forward to my husband arriving next month that is for sure."

"So you are really determined to go ahead with this idea of building a bar and a restaurant here in Cala Murada?

"Of course. We hope to have the business up and running by next year".

"Let me go and fetch some comics for the boys to read. It will keep them occupied while we talk." She said, leaving me to put the black shorts and shirts, back on the children.

"I hope you do not mind me saying this Jacqueline but really you are being a trifle naïve. Here in Spain things do not get done on time. It is more a question of 'manana' Anyway time is pressing and I have here, from my neighbour Mrs Faulhaber, the name and address of the dressmaker in Felanitx where you can get school uniforms made. Hope to meet up with you again on the beach and I look forward to meeting Michael." she said, politely guiding us towards a gate at the bottom of the garden.

On the one occasion, in August, that Anna came to visit, we visited Felanitx. After buying material for school uniforms and taking the children to the dressmaker to be measured up, there was time to spare before Anna boarded the ferry for Belgium.

"So where would you like to go?" Anna asked. "I doubt I will be back in Mallorca until the late autumn."

"Our favourite bar at the bottom of the town please." I said.

Sitting in the pleasant shady square chatting for more than an hour, first taking us back to Cala Murada, Anna departed for the port at Palma.

During those first four months, living on the island of Mallorca, it was down to my reliable mother typing letters, and keeping me informed as to what was going on.

"Michael came to see us last week, for only the second time." Her letter said, "I understand he is still working and now with the bungalow and furniture sold, he is living with his parents at the flower shop. He is working in a betting shop in Soho and will keep the car until just before he flies out to you the second week in September. And by the way Jacqueline a little surprise. Your father and I have booked a last-minute holiday to come and visit you at the beginning of October."

Following his arrival the next month and refusing to be drawn on the subject of buying a piece of land, Michael behaved like he was on holiday. As far as he was concerned, the most urgent priority to be addressed, was the need to buy a car. Despite my pointing out that during his absence I had managed without transport, Michael insisted that some capital should be invested in a car.

On the day of his departure with the children, on the bus to Palma to buy a Spanish car, I walked to the 'Cobassa' offices. The purpose of this pre-arranged meeting with the Manager Señor Mateo, was to study two plots of land in Cala Murada that were up for sale. With an ordinance survey map spread out across the table, Mateo showed me one plot on the first circle, close to where Dorothy lived, and another plot on the Manzanas, close to where we were staying.

"Of course the plot on the Manzanas is much cheaper than the plot up here on the first circle." Mateo said in good English. "You will need to bring your husband to the offices, so that you can both look at the two plots that are on offer."

"Yes of course." I said.

By the time I arrived back at D43, Michael and three extremely excited boys were standing on the road next to a powder blue Spanish Seat. Noting Michael's state of euphoria, I knew it was a waste of time discussing my visit to the "Cobassa" offices. And instead the subject was postponed until the following morning.

"Okay, I will go with you to have a look at the plots of land for sale. But I am not prepared to make any final decision until your parents arrive in two weeks." he said, getting up from his breakfast table to go out to his new car.

CHAPTER 5

On this my mother's first visit abroad, a two-week holiday with Cosmos, including flight and full board in the Cala Murada hotel, cost fifty pounds per person. On the morning of their arrival, with the children at school, Michael and I drove to the hotel to meet them. Walking through the hotel grounds I could see my parents already seated on the terrace drinking tea. On this first day in October, my mother was dressed in a woollen plaid skirt, long sleeved blouse, and stockings. On the other hand my much-travelled father, looking cool and relaxed, had already changed from a suit into cotton shorts and short-sleeved cotton shirt.

"I just love your inappropriate outfit mum" I said, kissing her cheek.

Well, she said, fanning her flushed cheeks with the English newspaper. "You might have warned me about the heat. And you have lost weight Jacqueline. Have you been ill or something?" Having never ever been what you might call a morning person, and on a plane all night, my mother was cranky.

"No I have not been ill. With this heat you do not eat so much."

"I have brought all the wrong clothes you know." She went on, dabbing her forehead with a handkerchief and scowling down at the 30 denier stockings.

"I am glad someone else has noticed Jacqueline's new image." Piped up Michael. "When I left in April, she was a plump and rosy woman. Now I have come back to a thin and scorched one."

Saying nothing about my husband's unkind remark, turning away, I noticed Bernabe and Señor Martinez standing on the terrace steps. Coming down to greet both parents, followed by a round of drinks paid for by the Manager, we were left to enjoy the company of the family.

"Do you know I am getting quite used to this." My mother said, discarding her navy-blue court shoes and rolling down the thick stockings. "I am off to find my bedroom and unpack. Bye, see you later." She said, padding off across the tiled terrace in her bare feet.

Well what do you know" Ivy called, suddenly appearing over the first-floor balcony. "Terry, you really must come up here and see this view. We have two weeks in which to catch up on all the news. Will you collect us later?" she asked, leaning out to address Michael "We cannot wait to see where you are all living. And the children of course."

"Nice car." Terry said greeting his son-in-law three hours later, dropping the front seat to allow his wife Ivy to get into the back.

"Glad you like it dad." Michael said.

"I am a bit concerned about you buying a car at this stage." Terry said, as Michael began driving down the hill. "Don't you think is it a bit premature? A bit like putting the cart before the horse?"

"No dad. Having a car is an absolute necessity here. Without it we would be virtually cut off. It is seven miles to the nearest town of Felanitx and we need the car to take the boys to school."

When did they start school?" Ivy asked, happily munching her way through a bar of plain chocolate.

"Three weeks ago, and now we are in a rota with other families in Cala Murada taking all the kids to school."

"Hello, this is a lovely spot and what a beautiful beach." Terry said, looking passed Michael out of the window. "So whereabouts are these plots of land you have been offered."

He asked, turning his head to study the barren rocky terrain on the right.

One plot is here on the Manzanas, close to where we live." Michael said turning the wheel of the car to drive up the hill on the right. "The other plot is way back beyond the hotel, near the entrance to Cala Murada. To date, I have not made any decisions about the plots. I have been waiting for you to arrive to tell me what you think dad. And this is where we live." Michael added, pulling up in front of the villa.

"Mm, nice big room." Terry said, stepping through the front door and into the lounge. "But it could do with a bit more furniture, don't you think Ivy?" He said, looking back before placing the two large parcels on the dining room table.

"For me personally, I feel it lacks a few of the creature comforts we are accustomed to Terry." She said, eyeing the room critically.

"I think I will go and prepare some tea." I said, going into the kitchen.

"Good, we have brought plenty of English tea bags with us." said Terry.

"Oh, the children are here." I called, looking out through the kitchen window. "The Spanish teacher knew you were coming. She must have let them out early." I said, returning to stand at the front door.

"Is my nanny and grandad here?" called young Michael, running up the front path.

"Yes we are here. And what have we here?" asked my father, turning the eldest two around for an inspection. "I like your outfits," he said, touching the blue and white striped gingham tunics. "So even little Edward has got a uniform too."

"Well, I am not so sure about the outfits at all." Said Ivy, studying her grandsons. "If you ask me, they look like those wretched Jewish children seen in the concentration camps."

"Oh for goodness sake mum, have a heart!" I exclaimed. "What an absolutely dreadful thing to say."

"You know your mother, never one to pull her punches". Terry said, changing the subject and untying the string on one parcel.

"Is it for us grandad?" asked Terry, helping to rip off the brown paper. "Wow, all our favourite things." He said, retrieving boxes of English cereals. "And look Frosties for you Edward."

"Look there are sweets, chocolates, swimsuits, water pistols and spinning tops." Thank you" said young Michael going into the kitchen to fill the pistol with water. With the children happily occupied, and a tray of tea taken out onto the terrace, the four of us sat down to talk.

"So now Michael, you need to tell us how many families operate in this school rota?" Said Terry.

"Six"

"And they are all different nationalities?"

"Yes they are."

"And do the children speak to one another in Spanish?" asked Ivy.

"Some of the time they do. Other times they speak local Mallorquin and a smattering of German and French."

"Good God! That is amazing." Said Ivy, taking out her packet of cigarettes.

"And how is your Spanish coming along?" Terry asked.

"Don't ask dad." Michael said leaning forward. "At the moment I leave most of the talking to Jacqueline. I have to admit, right now, she speaks better Spanish than me."

"Oh, so you have made a fruit cake?" said my mother watching as I approached the table.

"I heard everything about you getting stung in the mouth." Said my father.

"Yes that is a bit of a sore point, excuse the pun. I have to say mum, now that you have changed into a light cotton dress and sandals, you look so much better." I said, changing the subject.

"Yes after a bath, a sleep, and a light lunch, I am feeling really well."

"Good then I will go into the kitchen to prepare the evening meal."

"So," said my father joining me in the kitchen. "It seems that you have adapted well to this new way of life."

Yes, I have." I said, collecting potatoes from a bucket under the sink. "But Michael's lack of commitment concerns me."

"Well you have been here five months while Michael, has only been here for three weeks! You need to give him time. From what I gather, via letters to your mother, you have been off to barbecues and dances and God knows what else? Where is this friend of yours I have heard so much about?"

"You mean Anna. Well she is in Belgium right now and should be back sometime in the November."

"How old is she?"

"She is four years older than me."

"So how do you feel about Michael's plans?" He asked, watching met cut the chips."

"I just wish he would get off the fence and make a decision for himself. Right now, he is just waiting for you to go with him to look at the plots available." I said, taking lamb chops from the fridge.

For overweight and sedentary Ivy, the idea of clambering over rocks to survey land was out of the question. Instead sitting with me in the front of the car, both of us smoking, we watched our husbands survey the land.

"I am not sure about this plot on the Manzanas." Michael added, shielding his eyes from the sun. "It is a considerable way from the beach. And even further from the hotel and shops. Nobody will ever know we are here."

"How much did you say this plot of land is?" Terry asked.

"Just over 900,500 pesetas."

"How much is that in British pounds?"

"About £1,300 pounds. This plot is half the price of the plot of land we have been offered on the 1st circle close to the "Cobassa" offices."

"And what is the overall cost to build a bar and restaurant?" Terry asked, climbing even higher onto a flat rock overlooking the wooded area below.

"Cobassa" has given me an estimate, of approximately another £1,300 to be paid on completion."

"So that is about £2,600 pounds in total, and you sold the bungalow for just over £5.500 pounds?"

"Yes, I managed to save a few extra hundred pounds and my Company gave me a very nice bonus which has paid for the car."

"So in effect you have less than £3,000 pounds left to live on. That is not a lot of money." Terry said, rubbing his chin thoughtfully. "I have to admit, this is a very picturesque spot to build a bar and restaurant and maybe, with plenty of advertising it might work."

"So what is your opinion dad. Should I go ahead and put in an offer for this plot?"

"You are the one that has to make that decision Michael, not me. If you want my opinion, I feel that you have gone about this whole venture in the wrong way. You should have stayed in the UK working until such time as the actual building was underway. You could have left Jacqueline here supervising the work while you earnt more money. Anyway now you have burnt your boats you have a wife and family to support without an income."

"I have decided, I am going to put in an offer for this plot. We cannot afford to buy the other plot on offer." Michael said, heading down the steep decline towards the car.

"I think I had better leave you to break the news to your wife." Terry said jumping down from the rocks to follow Michael. The next morning with the parents off on a trip, organised by the hotel, to the beauty spots of Soller and Formentor, Michael and I went to the "Cobassa" offices to sign all the relevant documents for the purchase of Plot 28 on the Manzanas.

With a complete change of environment, coupled with endless days of warm sunshine, my parents looked happy and relaxed. While fit and healthy Terry was left to walk, swim, and lie in the sun, Ivy was free to visit local shops, and sit on the terrace conversing with other guests in the hotel.

On the first Sunday of their holiday, and with shops closed on a Holy Day, my mother arrived at the beach looking decidedly out of sorts.

"You know, I hate picnics." She said. "I cannot swim and just loathe getting sand in my clothes. For me personally sitting on a beach for hours is thoroughly boring."

Saying nothing but looking out to sea watching my father and the children enjoying themselves, I needed to think of a way to occupy my disgruntled mother.

"Do you see that lady over there, lying stretched out on the sand?" I said, careful to only nod in the direction of the deeply sun-tanned women, with the ash blond hair.

"The one in the skimpy white bikini, you mean?" Asked my mother, tipping up her sunglasses. "I have to say, she has the deepest sun-tan I have ever seen."

"Yes, she is German and her name Mrs Faulhaber. As a sun worshipper, she is one of the most permanent features on this beach." I said. "I was introduced to her recently on one of the schools runs. Then two weeks ago, while the boys were all playing together here at the beach, I was introduced to her husband. I notice he is not with here today and neither are the children." I added looking around the beach. "Mr Faulhaber has probably returned to sea and the two boys at home with the maid."

"So she has a maid?"

"Yes, they are quite well off. Mr Faulhaber is a captain of a large oil tanker operating in the Far East. "Do you know mum," I said, turning to face her, "At the end of the Second World War, at the age of 21, he was commissioned as a Captain on a "U" boat. He was not shy to tell me that as a rookie, on his very first commission, he was torpedoed by a British destroyer in the Channel. When the crippled submarine surfaced, he along with the other survivors were rescued.

"So what happened then".

"He was taken prisoner and worked on a farm in Kent for over a year. And that is where he learnt to speak good English."

"Now that is an interesting story!" my mother said, lighting a cigarette. "Pity some of our captured men did not always receive that kind of treatment."

Close to the end of their second week, while I stayed in the villa doing housework, Michael took his in-laws to Felanitx. With still plenty of pocket money to spend, while my father went to have his hair cut, Michael accompanied his mother-in-law to a shoe shop. As was her want, Ivy spent a considerable amount of time deliberating over the pairs of shoes set out around her feet. While the attentive shop assistant continued to climb up and then down the ladder bringing even more boxes of shoes to the floor, Michael looked about for something to do. Noticing an opened box with just one new shoe inside, craftily placing one of my mother's own shoes into the box, he closed the lid. Looking on mischievously, he stood back to watch as the shop assistant then placed that particular box back onto the shelf. With Ivy having made a final choice of new shoes to buy the inevitable mayhem ensued. With the concerned assistant climbing up and then down the ladder looking for the missing shoe, it did not take my mother long to work out what had happened.

"You are quite incorrigible Michael." she said, casting her son-in-law a Medusa stare.

"If that had been me doing that," said my father chuckling all the way back to Cala Murada. "I would have been hung, drawn and quartered by now."

Having already said farewell to the grandchildren before leaving for school, standing on the hotel steps looking sun tanned and relaxed, Terry and Ivy waited to board the coach to Palma airport.

"It has been great having you both here." I said, walking up the steps to kiss my mother on the cheek.

"When we come back next year, we expect to see that bar and restaurant of yours up and running." My father added, shaking Michael's hand. "And my order from the menu will be, Spanish Paella for two" he said, waving and boarding the coach. That evening and with them gone, the atmosphere in the villa was decidedly subdued.

"You know despite what has happened in the past, my parents can always be relied upon. As strong and constant characters they will be sadly missed." I said.

"Now that the children are in bed, there is something I need to tell you Jacqueline. In fact it has been bothering me ever since I arrived here."

"Go on."

"While I was in England alone for those four months, just for a short time, I had an affair with one of the cash assistants working in a betting shop",

"You mean Rene."

"What! How on earth........." he stuttered furrowing his brow. "How did you know it was her?"

"On the two occasions you took me to that shop I noticed the way she looked at you. It is what you might call female intuition."

"It is because I feel such guilt and remorse for what I have done, that I am confessing to you now."

"I understand completely A young healthy married couple in their twenties, suddenly parted for several months, these things do happen."

Michael did not speak. But with his dark eyes fixed on me, the look said it all. Because I was such a bad liar, he had chosen not to know. Instead, taking me through to the bedroom we made love.

Wow, my God, you were so fast!" he said, rolling to one side." You even came twice! And there I was thinking that I had come on too rough and too hard." He said, still out of breath.

"Not at all." I whispered. "I just love burning in the ring of fire."

As plot 28 was on a steep gradient, construction on the site had to be carried out on two levels. With the first set of plans, only partially approved, a further set was drawn up and approved by the Manager of "Cobassa." The newly modified plans involved a bar, restaurant, and kitchen on the top level, with a storeroom and modest accommodation below. Sadly, my grandiose scheme of having living accommodation, large enough to house the family, had to be put on hold. During the discussions with Señor Mateo of "Cobassa" it was established that once the existing contract on our villa expired, the following six months would be at a reduced rent.

"With all the plans now agreed, there are a number of formalities that you will need to follow." Said Señor Mateo, taking a fountain pen from his pocket. "These first set of plans have to be submitted to Madrid, for the official seal of approval. Then a second set of plans go to the Police Headquarters in Porto Colom, followed by another set handed over to the Military Headquarters in Palma."

"Do you mind me calling you just Mateo?" Michael asked, signing the first set of plans, and watching them being placed into a brown envelope.

"No of course not Michael. From now on we are going to be working in close contact."

"So Mateo, from what I can make out, I have effectively signed on the dotted line before actually having the permission to build a bar and restaurant. Is that correct?"

"Not quite, this is the formality that has to be followed in Spain. These rules apply, regardless as to whether you are Spanish or a foreigner. Anyway, we will keep in touch," Mateo said, standing up to leave.

Two weeks later, the first set of plans arrived back from Madrid duly approved. However, with the actual construction work on plot D43 delayed, we were left with time to savour the golden days of autumn. Into November and with the midday temperature still in the seventies, lounging around in the sun proved to be Michael's favourite past time. Getting arrangements into place for unpasteurised milk to be delivered by the local milkman, called Pepe leche, we also had a huge supply of logs delivered into the side garden for the oncoming winter months.

"So your idea is that we have outside terraces all along the front and one side?" Michael asked, leaning on the table watching me take seashells from the bucket on the floor.

"Yes, that is why I am collecting shells from the beach. To decorate terracotta pots for the terraces We have to do something to pass the winter months."

"So why don't you come with me to Pedro's for a drink?"

"No thanks, but you go. I am quite happy to be here on my own." I said, studying and grading the colours of the shells.

"By the way, the postman left this letter for you. It looks like a Belgium post mark." He said.

"Thank you, it must be from Anna. I will open it later."

"So you do not want to come with me? Well as I am not on rota to collect the boys from school, I will go to the hotel to pay that outstanding bill of 50 pounds you borrowed in August. After picking up butane gas from Jose's supermarket, I will go across to Pedro's for a game of dominoes and couple of beers. I had no idea you were so artistic." He said, stopping to watch me arrange one glued shell onto a pot. "See you later darling."

Returning sometime later, having left the butane gas in the boot of the car, Michael appeared from the kitchen with a chunk of bread and sobrasada sausage in one hand.

"I have been chatting to Emilio." He said, spreading the spicey sausage with a knife. "And did you know, that before he had his car hire business, he worked as a pilot for the Spanish air force. He was sacked for flying planes while drunk. He told me that at one stage, he had 8% of alcohol in his blood." Michael continued, his cheeks bulging with the salty bread.

"Typical." I said, not looking up and applying glue to another shell. "Boys will be boys."

"And that gardener guy Andres," Michael said, ignoring the sarcasm. "Isn't he the bloke who collected the large boxes and the dog from the airport."

"Yes, that is right he did."

"Well he is a bit of a shrewd character I can tell you. Did you know he has a nickname? He is called s called 'the fox'. Huh! I would not turn my back on him. Half the workman in Cala Murada is employed by him. He earns an absolute fortune tending the gardens of the residents and foreigners here."

"How did you find out all this? I thought you were playing dominoes."

"We were and then Bernabe came across from the hotel to join us. Now in the winter months, he has more time spare. And he was explaining to me, that now you have been on the island for nearly six months Jacqueline, you are eligible to apply for a residence permit."

"Really do I need one?" I asked looking up.

"Yes it will facilitate us getting all our permissions through. He also advised us to go to Palma and see a Notary."

"Hold on! I thought we already had all the permits through" I said, applying the finishing touches to one terracotta pot.

"We will need permission to open up a bar and restaurant, as well as a permit to sell alcohol."

"And what is a Notary?"

"A lawyer for making a Will."

"I see, well I hope you did not spend too much money on beer today. When I was here alone for five months, I managed to survive on fifty pounds a month. And now we are together we are overspent the whole time."

"So what did the letter say?" Michael asked, eager to change the subject, and nodding at the opened letter on the table.

"Because Anna and her husband are busy with the school, she will not be returning to Mallorca until early spring next year."

"Oh, because you are such good friends, I know you must be disappointed. Never mind, leave what you are doing and let us take the dog to the beach. We could stop at the woods for some dry kindling for the fire tonight."

Letting Susy off from the lead and removing our shoes, we trudged hand in hand, across the cool wet sand towards the shingle and rocks on the other side.

"No driftwood today." Michael said, looking along the shoreline.

"Do you know we have not yet thought of a name for our bar and restaurant." I said, stopping.

"I have." Michael said.

"What?"

"I like the name 'Bolero".

"Are you referring to the music "Bolero" by the composer Revel? or the famous dance routine?"

"Both, 'Bolero' is my favourite piece of music. I just love the way the haunting and repetitive melody starts and then slowly builds into a crescendo and climax".

"A bit like good sex you mean." I said, giving him eye to eye contact.

"Yes, like that."" He said, recognising the come-hither look and reaching out to cup my breast. "Let us take the dog back now. We have got more than one hour before the children return from school".

By the first week of December, the laying of the foundations for the bar and restaurant were well under way and the sound of exploding dynamite, clearly heard from the villa. In fact because Plot 28 was so close to D43, by standing on a chair, we were able to see the rocks being flung up into the air.

Using the facilities of the hotel phone, an appointment was made to see a Notary in Palma. Waiting in the appointed offices for one hour, with our limited knowledge of legal jargon, we were grateful the Notary spoke reasonably good English. In a nutshell it was explained that, if either of us were to die, the remaining spouse would be responsible for the property and any outstanding debts. Coming out from the Notary's office, with a large bill to pay, for the entire journey back to Cala Murada neither of us spoke.

Because the local supermarket owned by Jose Casan was expensive, most of our shopping was done in Felanitx. And the following day strolling through the market, between the stalls of fresh vegetables, poultry, and meat we considered what good food to buy.

"Jacqueline, there is some bloke on the far side wall, next to the fish counters, waving at you. Who is it?" Michael asked.

"Oh it's the American Ted," I said waving back. "I told you about him in one of my letters. We met in the summer on the beach".

"Well he has seen us and is making a bee-line in our direction." Michael said, studying the American's outfit of a wool camel coloured trench coat, pale blue jeans, and matching base- ball cap.

"Hi there, how's it going? So this must be the husband I have heard about?" Ted said smiling broadly and extending a hand in greeting. "Please to meet you Michael. So you have decided to live in the sun? Well what a good idea. According to your charming wife here, you are intending to build a bar and restaurant In Cala Murada?"

"Yes, that is the plan." Michael said, stony-faced.

"Look right now, I have some shopping to do but what about you both coming to my home one evening next week? Say for a little light supper and maybe a game of cards, Poker perhaps?"

"That would be just lovely, wouldn't it Michael?" I said, without hesitation.

"Hold on a minute we haven't got a baby-sitter."

"That is not a problem." Said Ted. "The young girl working in the launderette opposite the hotel, she is a good sitter. I am sure she would come for just a small fee. Shall we say next Friday at 7pm? Hold on let me give you my address." Ted said, taking a pad from the back pocket of his jeans. "While we are at it, you need to give me your address at the same time. Has anybody got a pen handy?"

"Yes, I have," I said, eagerly handing him one from my bag.

"Look forward to seeing you both in a week's time," he said, turning around before disappearing into the crowd.

"What were you thinking of?" Michael said, challenging me. "Jumping in with both feet at that invitation. We know nothing about that man." He said, reversing the car out into the road.

"But I do. He is a retired Major from the American Army. And he has a sister named Dorothy, a friend of mine, who also lives in Cala Murada. Why are you so cross with me Michael? If we intend to own a bar and restaurant in Cala Murada it is essential that we mix with the people living here and to make friends."

"Jacqueline, friends do not invite you to play poker. And besides, you cannot even play poker".

"I do play cards." I said, defensively. "I play whist and rummy."

"That is not the same as playing poker".

"I am willing to learn. Let us go and see if we can find the girl working in the launderette. Then once we are home you can give me some lessons in poker."

"I do not think so." Michael smiled.

Arriving at Ted's villa the following week, with my thoughts so preoccupied with the rules regarding poker, I had little recollection of my surroundings. However, what I do remember about that evening was that joining in the gambling game, we managed to lose the grand equivalent of ten pounds.

"Well that was a complete disaster." Said Michael, driving away from Ted's villa. "For us, ten pounds is a lot of money."

"I can only say I am sorry Michael."

"Forget it. I think that is what is called learning the hard way. At times you can be so gullible." He said, shaking his head.

"I know you are right. I promise I will make it up to you."

"Really?" he said with a grin. dropping one hand from the steering wheel onto the inside of my thigh.

While Michael went to deliver the young girl back to the launderette I undressed ready for bed.

"You are just as my father says." I said, greeting him at the bedroom door.

"And what is that?"

"A shrewd wide boy, who I just love to bits." I said, putting my arms around his heck.

"Show me." He said, knocking my legs apart with his knees.

CHAPTER 6

"Well, I don't like that Mr Dewitt one little bit!' Young Michael said, stomping through the lounge door before discarding his school bag onto a chair. "He calls me freckle face and I can tell he does not like us either.

'What makes you say that?' I asked, scooping the deep-fried, golden calamari from the frying pan and onto three warmed plates.

"Every time he brings us home he asks us questions, like what are we doing here and what my dad did when we lived in England" Michael continued, watching as his mother scatter slices of lemon onto the plates. "He is so cross and miserable all the time. He nearly throws us out of the car when we get here." He said, dragging up his three-quarter length grey socks before sitting down at the dining room table.

"Well you can hardly blame him."' Said his father, tipping his head to one side and studying his sharp-eyed son. "He's got my sympathy. It is not exactly a picnic transporting a car full of screaming kids" Michael added, scuffing his son's dark auburn-coloured hair."

"Can't you see that the boy is genuinely upset?' I said, picking Edward up onto my lap and pouring him a glass of coca cola. "And where is your brother Terry? His food will get cold."

"He is playing in the garden with a grasshopper he has found." Answered young Michael.

"Right Michael, listen to me. The next time Dewitt asks you questions about us, you tell him that your father is on the run from the British police. Better still, tell him that your dad was involved in the Great Train Robbery. That will take the wind out of his sails."

"Oh Michael for heaven's sake! You are just outrageous. You cannot tell the boy to say things like that."

"Yes he can."

"I like it dad." Said young Michael, his dark brown eyes alight with amusement.'

"Glad to find you at home," Said Ted, as Michael opened the front door. "As I was in the area, I thought I would look you both up. This is the first time I have been up here on this side of the beach. I have to say you need a car it is a bit cut off up here. May I come in?" he asked, still waiting on the step.

"Yes of course". I said coming through from the kitchen drying my hands on a tea towel. "Please to see you Ted."

"I wondered if you would both like to come again sometime next week, not to play cards this time but to join me for dinner. What do you say?"

"Is that okay with you Michael?" I said, looking to him for support.

"Whatever."

"Good," Ted said, not waiting for a reply. "Look forward to seeing you next week, same day and time."

"Shall we bring a bottle of something?" I asked.

"No, just bring yourselves. I have a really good selection of Spanish wines." Replied Ted walking back down the front path.

"Why on earth did you accept that invitation?" Michael said, shutting the front door. "If you insist on going to Ted's, we are going to have to use young Michael as a baby-sitter. He has just had a birthday and should be capable."

"Good idea, we could always bribe the boys to behave and get themselves into bed."

"How?" asked Michael.

"I can prepare their favourite meal of deep-fried calamari with chips and English Frosties from Jose's supermarket with coca cola that should do it".

"It will save us money and it could work." Michael said thoughtfully. "Ted's villa is only ten minutes away from here. I could always come back, during the evening, to check on the boys."

On our second visit to Ted's villa, I was given the opportunity to look around his lavishly furnished home. For me personally, after sitting in wooden canvas deck chairs, given the opportunity to sink into velvet covered armchairs was a real treat. Following a most splendid meal, cooked, and served by Ted, we sat back to savour good brandy served in cut crystal goblets. Then while Michael drove to the villa, to check on the boys, I helped Ted with the washing up.

"They have eaten all their supper, washed up their plates and are fast asleep" Michael said, on his return.

Sitting together enjoying even more brandy, the conversation went from the phenomenal rise to fame of the Beatles and then onto the inevitable topic of local and European politics.

"Please" He said, standing up to walk across the silk carpet. "Would you folks care to join me? This is an eighteenth-century Bavarian bookcase. And I have an excellent collection of books." He said, running his fingers along the backs of the leather-bound books. "This one here for instance," he said, taking one book down from the shelf, "is an early edition of "Mein Kampf" which in itself is of no great importance, but this portfolio I have here, is." He said, drawing an onyx standard lamp close to a brown envelope before spilling an array of black and white photographs across the oak table.

"This portfolio of photographs, of the Fuhrer, is quite rare.' He said, fingering the shiny image of Hitler dressed in his familiar brown shirt with the red and black swastika on one arm. "And these two here are of the Fuhrer with his mistress

Eva Braun, enjoying a holiday together in their Bavarian mountain retreat. And these close ups of Hitler at Berghof," Ted continued, pushing the holiday snaps to one side, "are probably the most valuable in the entire collection. I can vouch for the fact that very few people have ever seen these photographs of Hitler with his close associates. Like here." Ted said, pointing to the man standing alongside of Hitler. "That's Josef Goebbels and next to him the Nazi Party Member von Ribbentrop. And these are the Fuhrer with Lieutenant Himmler, at a dinner party. Did you know? Ted asked, looking up at his astonished guests. "Berghof" is the place where Hitler prepared his plans to invade both France and Russia. You are both staying quiet. Aren't you going to ask me how I managed to get hold of these treasures from the Second World War? He asked, gathering up the photographs before placing them back into the envelope.

"I have no idea. But I am sure we are about to find out." Said Michael, maintaining a straight face.

"Okay, in 1944, I was in the Normandy landings. After that, I was also involved in the actual Allied push into Berlin. You must know that the Russians beat us to it into Berlin and manged to reach Hitler's bunker before we did. Well anyway we, the American troops, did manage to be the first into the German Army Headquarters. And here," he said, tapping the brown envelope before placing it back into the book-case. "We had what you might call the spoils of war."

"For Christ's sake! What did I tell you about Ted?" Michael said, still stationary outside the villa. "Ted is a bloody Nazi sympathiser. Did you notice how he kept referring to Hitler as the Fuhrer?"

"Oh come on Michael. You cannot say that for certain. Don't you remember, he was a Major in the American army."

"So what! That does not mean a thing. Didn't you tell me yourself that he has a German father and speaks good German?"

"Yes, I did. But you need to be careful what you say Michael. Ted could finish up being a good customer of ours."

"Well you know what they say about never judging a book by its cover? He could have been a double agent for all we know."

By December, with the name of the bar and restaurant agreed upon and the foundations of the "Bolero" in place, we were advised by Mateo to visit the British consulate in Palma. Following that meeting with the Consulate, we were passed on to a lawyer specialising in the opening of businesses on the island. However, on that first visit, not managing to see the lawyer himself, it was left to his British secretary to ask all the relevant details.

"I understand you have already visited the Notary, is that correct?" Asked the secretary.

"Yes," replied Michael.

"Glad to hear it. Coming to Palma sooner rather than later is a good idea. Everything in Spain takes time." She said placing her gold fountain pen onto the desk "I can assure you it will take several months for all the necessary documentation to be drawn up. But first things first,' She said, standing up to straighten her pencil slim black skirt. "For the time being there is nothing more we can do. After Christmas I would advise you to come back again to see me. I might have more news then."

Home for the Christmas holidays, and with the boys at the beach, Michael and I were left to decorate the Christmas tree. With the heat from the log fire enhancing the smell of the freshly cut pine, I climbed onto a chair to place the last baubles and tinsel on top of the tree. At the same time checking that the Christmas parcels from my parents were indeed empty. Michael sat on a deck chair, warming his toes in front of the fire.

"I really do not think much of this turkey we bought in Palma market". I said, prodding the breast with my middle finger. "And the price we paid for it. Scandalous!" I said, turning the bird upside down for a further inspection. "It looks as though it's done a marathon around the farmyard."

"Don't fuss" said Michael, wriggling his toes, "Those extras your mother has sent will help to tart up the old bird a bit."

"Yes, three cheers for her. Only the best is ever good enough for my mother." I said, smiling appreciatively at the extras of chestnut stuffing, cranberry sauce, mince pies and Christmas cake." "The boys are going to turn up their noses at the practical presents." I said, tapping the warm pyjamas and sweaters. "Still she has remembered to put in a couple of toys, chocolate decorations and a fairy for the tree." I said, wrapping the gifts before sitting down to read her letter.

"Oh!" I exclaimed, "Such sad news. My nanny from Ealing has died. And apparently she has left me money in her Will".

"How much?" Michael asked looking up.

"Two hundred pounds." I said, putting the letter down "She was always so kind to me. I remember her giving me a bike to ride so that I could go with her down to the allotment. And on one warm spring day she made me stop the bike to listen to the sound of a cuckoo. She was a lady who not only loved life, but all nature too. And I will miss her."

"You will have to find out how exactly you can receive the money."

"Yes that is a good point." I replied.

On Christmas Eve, with so much Christmas fare for the table, Ted was invited for dinner. Unexpectedly, on his arrival, he came with a present for the boys. And while they played under the tree with the gift of a fort, constructed in wood with Confederate soldiers and Indians, Michael and I sat with Ted near to the fire drinking Spanish beer.

With the arrival of an extremely warm and sunny Christmas morning, leaving the scrawny turkey to cook, with the boys wearing only short sleeved shirts and shorts, we set off for the beach with Susy. However, with the arrival of the New Year, the weather changed dramatically. Into January and following three days and nights of incessant rain, all work on plot 28 was brought to a halt. With the arrival of yet another Saint's Day and the children home, pacing up and down like restless lion cubs, it was decided to take them out.

"I tell you what,' Michael said. "Let us take a trip up into the mountains on the west side of the island. We have never been up there."

"Brilliant idea." I said, grabbing all our winter coats.

Eagerly piling into the blue Seat to drive across the island, what we did not know was, that the weather for the day was wind and driving snow. No matter how many times Michael tried to switch on the heating system in the little car, he could not manage it. And as we climbed even higher into the mountains and around icy treacherous bends, so we began to shiver and freeze.

"We need to get into the first café we see." Michael said, stopping the car on a thick blanket of snow "I think this little village is called 'Valldemossa.' Come on boys get out".

Slipping and sliding across the car park towards the lit bar, we took shelter inside a warm bar filled with local men. Situated in the centre of this cavernous room, on a raised plinth, was a fiercely burning log fire. While looking skywards, thick acrid smoke, curled up through a copper funnel in the roof. However, on this particularly stormy winter's day and with an East wind blasting down from the mountains, plumes of acrid smoke blew back down into the room. And while the local men drinking their favourite tipple of Palo appeared impervious to the problem, coughing, and dabbing our eyes we sipped mugs of steaming chocolate. Totally smitten by the rural setting, I was up and away across the flagged stone floor to study the bench seats made of local stone.

"What are you looking at?" Michael asked, following close behind, rubbing his eyes and blowing his nose.

"These seats and the gorgeous tapestry cushions. I just love them. I'm going to ask the proprietor where he bought this furniture from." I said, placing the mug of chocolate down onto a sturdy, three-legged, coffee table made of olive wood.

"And look Michael, these little stools? They would be perfect for our bar. Wait here while I go and speak to the owner."

"Here we go." Michael Said. glancing at his sons. "Your mother is off with some big idea."

Some minutes later returning to the family I had, written down, the name and address of the manufacturer in Manacor who supplied the furniture.

"And guess what? The proprietor has also given me the address of another company in Manacor where we can purchase all the fixtures and fittings for our bar. We must make a date Michael to go to Manacor."

By the end of January, with a slight improvement in the weather, building work resumed on Plot 28 and Mateo came to pay us a visit.

"I think it would be in both your interests, if Jacqueline learnt to drive the car."

"Really?" Michael said, surprised.

"With a bar and restaurant, both of you driving will be essential. And can I ask you Jacqueline? have you made sure that all your papers and documents are in order?"

"I think so What exactly do you mean?"

"At the end of your six months here in Mallorca, did you go to the Police Headquarters in Porto Colom to get your passport stamped?"

"Yes, Bernabe has already told us about that and Michael took me at the beginning of November."

"Good, you must make sure that you stay on the right side of the Guardia of Civil. I know times have recently changed for the better in Spain. However still entrenched in the past, when General Franco ruled Spain with an iron fist, the Guardia remain comparatively loyal to him."

As advised by Mateo, and while the boys were at school, armed with the name and address of the person we needed to see, we drove to Felanitx. What Mateo failed to tell us was that the driving instructor spoke little English. And with my limited knowledge of Castellano Spanish, I was hard pressed to understand what the instructor told me concerning taking a driving test in Mallorca. Listening attentively the patient instructor managed to explain that just prior to my arrival procedures for taking a test had changed.

"Oh really? So what do I have to do?"

"First," the instructor said, ducking beneath his desk to reappear with a booklet not unlike the British Highway Code. "You will have to sit a written examination in Palma. And only if you pass the written examination will you be allowed to take a practical test at the driving centre on the outskirts of the city."

"I notice that this copy is written in Spanish. Can I take this written test in English?" I asked, turning the pages.

"No, I am afraid not. You will be expected to know the Spanish Highway Code from cover to cover.' He said, tapping his pen on the desk.

"You'll never be able to do that!"' Michael said, shaking his head.

"Who said so? Thank you darling for your show of confidence."

"Would you like to give it some thought first Señora?" Asked the instructor, noting my frisson of irritation.

"No, give me all the forms I will need please. And put my name down for lessons. Let me think. Shall we say a date sometime at the end of April, to take the test? That would give me a couple of months of driving lessons and time to get my head around this Highway Code. Thank you for your time Señor, you have been most helpful."

"I'll be in touch in the next week or so and let you know when I can fit you in for the driving lessons. In the meantime, take these "L" plates with you." The instructor said, ducking down for a second time beneath his desk. "It might be a good idea if your husband takes you out a few times around Cala Murada so that you get used to driving and handling the car."

"Right here we go." I said, sitting behind the wheel before circling around the car part on Cala Murada beach.

Okay, you were quite good with the gears. This afternoon we will take a few trips around the quiet streets. In the meantime, while we are here, we can go and collect driftwood from the beach.

"Hello there." Called Ted following close behind. "How is it going with you two? I haven't seen you for a while." He said, walking faster to catch up.

"We are well. I have just been trying my hand driving the car." I said, stopping on the cold wet sand.

"Well done, during these winter days you need to find things to do. I am wondering if you would both like to come next Saturday evening? For a little light supper and a film show?"

"What kind of film show? Michael asked warily.

"I have travelled widely and have some really lovely shots from around the world. Including Europe, Africa and of course here in Mallorca. What do you say? Will you come?"

"We would love to come, wouldn't we Michael. I said, jumping in to answer for him "What time on Saturday?"

"Shall we say seven o'clock? See you both on Saturday. Happy hunting looking for driftwood." Ted said, turning back along the beach.

In the 1960's Manacor was not only famous for the manufacture of cultured pearls but also it was the centre for the manufacture of fine quality Mallorquin furniture. Nowadays, Manacor is famous for producing one of the best tennis players in the world, namely Raphael Nadal.

You know? "Michael said, standing watching me gloat over furniture in the shop window. "It won't be too long before we are completely out of money. And totting up the price of this furniture you are studying, it just does not add up. We are not going to be able to buy all the things you want for the "Bolero".

"It's a bit late to think of that now,' I said, keeping my eyes fixed on one particular picture hanging in a side window of the shop."

"But I think I've come up with the solution." he said.

"What?" I asked, stepping even closer to the window to study the delightful scene, rendered in beaten copper.

"Not including the furniture but for all the other things we are going to need for the kitchen and that are so expensive here, it would be worthwhile me taking a trip back to England to buy them there.'

"You must be joking." I said, looking up at him. "What about the travelling expenses involved like the car ferry and the petrol?"

"I have already considered all of that, and we would still be in pocket. Besides my Company still owes me money which I could collect while I was there. Of course it means I will have to go on my own. It would not make sense to take you and the boys with me. I will need all the extra space in the car to bring back the essentials."

"I notice you are saying 'will', which implies you have already made up your mind. You have only been here for four months and now you are going to leave us yet again." I said, looking back through the shop window.

"Just think Jacqueline, you could compile a list of all the things you need for your kitchen and if you agree, I could use the money left to you, by your grandmother, to buy a combined record player and radio system for the bar. You know how much you love your music, and particularly opera and the classics."

"Italian opera would not be suitable for the bar." I replied flatly, knowing full well Michael was attempting to win me over.

"Okay well then I will make sure I record all the latest music around. Including Elvis Presley who you adore. So what do you think?"

"That picture in the side window is just so beautiful. I can see it now as the focal point on the wall behind the bar. I am going into the shop to take a closer look." I said, pushing open the door and walking inside.

"You realise it is going to be extremely expensive." Michael whispered.

"Of course, but where you are concerned everything is expensive Michael. So I will ask my mother to buy it for me next birthday in April".

Looking closer at the copper picture and discovering that behind the miniature town, were tiny light bulbs illuminating the scene, convinced me to place a deposit there and then.

"Okay I will agree to your latest plans, on the proviso that you bring back my sewing machine so I can make tapestry cushions for the bench seating in the bar."

On this third visit, following a light supper of home-made soup and fresh Mallorquin bread, while Michael went to check on the children, Ted began erecting a screen and projector for the forthcoming film show. Then following Michael's return, settled into the comfortable armchairs and prior to switching out the lights, we were given a resume of what we were about to see.

In the early fifties, having served as the American Attaché in the Congo, the first few slides were of Ted circulating amongst local tribes, in the more rural areas of central Africa. Then switching from Africa to Germany, accompanied by a commentary, the following scenes were of the Brandenburg Gate, the Berlin wall and Ted's own apartment in Berlin.

"Now," he said, switching on the onyx lamp and lifting one slide up to the light, "the slides you are about to see…? hmm, yes these are photographs taken of Magaluf in the early fifties. I am sure you will be interested because as you will see," he said, switching off the light, before flicking the slide onto the white screen. "apart from two hotels at one end of the beach and a few villas dotted here and there, Magaluf beach was nothing more than a vast expanse of virgin sand. Nowadays, of course, it is quite different. Ah yes," he continued as shots appeared of girls in bikinis lying around a swimming pool, "these are three Parisian girls that I took with me on holiday to Magaluf that year. In fact, the holiday started with me sharing the villa with the three girls. However, following a week of not being able to get into the bathroom for hours on end, the holiday finished up me and one girl and the others in a flat nearby."

As more shots appeared, so the girls were seen playing netball, topless, on the beach. Then progressing from topless to completely naked; the Parisian beauties were photographed frolicking in and out of the sea.

"Wow!" Michael said, spinning around to look at Ted. "That must have been a bit risqué on a Spanish beach in the fifties?"

"You can say that again Mike. Those scenes were taken early in the morning when the beach was deserted and with no police around. Of course, at that time, Spanish women were not permitted onto a beach unless they were adequately covered. And I mean totally covered in black. "Oh sorry folks" Ted said, as another blank slide appeared on the screen. "This is just a little warning device I have to remind me that when showing film shows to an elderly aunt of mine, I need to stop there. What do you say, shall I go on?"

"It is all fine with me," Replied wide-eyed Michael, looking across at me.

"It is okay. "I said, shrugging my shoulders.

The next dozen or so shots that followed, were of women wearing nothing more than laced suspender belts and stockings. While further images were of naked girls posing across a bed. The last shots of one woman, with her legs straddled across the back of a chair, reminded me of the images taken of Christine Keeler.

"Now be honest Michael", I said, as we sat looking at each other outside Ted's villa. "You really enjoyed that didn't you."

"Yes and so did you. I could see by the expression on your face you were affected by what you saw. Anyway I do not see anything wrong with a bit of soft pornography between consenting adults."

"Even though I have never seen pornography before, I have to say, it did not offend me. Undoubtedly Ted is an interesting character."

"Stops life becoming a bore." Michael said, turning the ignition in the car.

"Yes, something like that." I said.

The next morning, after the sexy film show, a letter arrived from the Solicitor in Palma setting out the latest position regarding the applications for the bar and restaurant. Having had the initial plans approved by the authorities in Madrid and until the building was complete, nothing more could be done. Sitting by the fire in the low deck chair, with the letter on my lap, I watched Michael come out of the bathroom freshly bathed. There is nothing more appealing for a young fit woman to see, than a sweet-smelling man wearing white fitted boxer shorts, emphasising the heavy rounded shape of his genitalia.

"Come here," I said, "and take off your pants."

After going to Palma to buy the ferry ticket, as it was Terry's birthday, on his way back from the port he stopped at Jose's supermarket to buy a cake.

"Hi, there Mike. What have you got there in those two large boxes?" Asked Ted meeting him on the steps.

"It is young Terry's birthday today. We are having a bit of a party and these boxes contain his favourite cakes, ensaïmadas with custard cream."

"Well will you wish him a happy birthday from me".

"Yes, and I have to say you will not see me for a while Ted. I am leaving for the UK in two days."

"That is a bit of a surprise. For how long and why?"

"About three weeks. There are a few things I need to attend to. And because so many things we need for the business and the kitchen are more than double the price here, it will be worthwhile me going back to buy them in the UK."

"I understand, that makes sense. And I do hope the film show the other night did not offend either you or Jacqueline."

"On the contrary Ted." Michael said, smiling while waving the American goodbye.

CHAPTER 7

Watching rivulets of condensation running down the misted windows, I felt depressed. Without heating in the bedrooms, and with shoes and clothing in the wardrobes going green, damp was beginning to creep through the inside walls. Even the cupboards in the kitchen, close to the oven, smelt musty. With lonely days and even lonelier nights, my time was spent attempting to learn the Spanish version of the Highway Code. In Michael's absence the only contact I had with the outside world was one letter from my mother. Followed a few days later, with a letter from the driving instructor setting out dates for lessons, and a date in April to sit the written exam.

Then as the spring sunshine suddenly appeared lightening my spirits, the moment the children returned from school, we went to the beach. Walking back with the boys running on ahead, I stopped to study the work in progress on plot 28. Initially delighted to see that the roof was in place, I was dismayed to find that the eight inch in diameter drainage pipes, leading from the roof, had been fixed onto the inside walls. The very next morning, with the boys taken to school by the Belgian father, I was off walking up the hill, beyond the hotel, to the "Cobassa" offices.

"Good morning Mateo, I said, walking into his office. "I have a complaint to make. I have noticed that on plot 28, the eight-inch drainage pipes, running from the roof to the ground level, have been placed on the inside walls. That is just not acceptable."

"Unless stated otherwise, placing drainage pipes on the inside walls, rather than the outside is normal practice here.

Once the premises are complete you won't see those pipes because they'll be concealed behind wood panelling."

"But I do not want wood panelling Mateo. My plan is for bench seating hewn from local stone flush against the walls in the bar. So I cannot have drainage pipes there."

'I must warn you now, that if you want to change the existing plans and put the pipes on the outside, it is going to cost a lot more money".

"How much more?"

"At this stage," Mateo said, stroking his soft black Viva Zapata moustache. "As a rough estimate I would say," he continued, taking a white folder from the drawer below his desk, "Yes, here we are. It will be approximately an extra two hundred thousand pesetas." pesetas".

"That is about five hundred pounds in sterling? Am I right?" I said, converting the amount in my head.

Yes, according to the present exchange rate, the total cost of the work carried out would then be approximately three thousand pounds in sterling. Can I ask, have you discussed this with Michael?"

"No, he is still in the UK."

"Do you know when he is due back?"

"I don't, I have not heard from him. All I do know from the letter I have received from my mother is that he arrived there safely."

"Would you like to wait until he returns to make before making a decision?"

"No. I will decide myself." Noting Mateo's handsome Latin features.

"So changes to the pipes onto the outside walls. The extra cost will involve you signing another document now. Do you agree with that?"

"Yes, I said, looking straight into Mateo's green eyes.

"Okay, so I'll speak with the foreman working on the site and get the necessary changes made" He said, rummaging through a drawer to produce another form.

"I will need to complete a copy of these new details for you to give to Michael on his return."

"Good" I said, not looking up while signing on the dotted line. "I have noticed Mateo, that both you and Bernabe speak very good English."

"That is because we both attended schools in Palma, where English was the compulsory second language." He said, smiling.

"When it comes to speaking another language, we British are sadly lacking."

"That is not entirely true Jacqueline. I have heard you speak Spanish in the hotel, and it is quite good. Speaking of languages, how is the Highway Code coming along? Have you got a date for the written test yet?"

"Yes, I'm down to sit the exam in April. But I am not coping very well learning the Spanish Highway Code itself."

"Alright, so when Michael returns, I will come each week to help you."

"That is most kind." I said, standing up to leave. "In the meantime I wait to see the alterations made to the drainage pipes at the site."

Still working as a secretary and assistant Registrar at Stoke Newington Town hall, Ivy had seen little of her son-in-law. Staying with his family in the flower shop, the only information she could convey, in the last paragraph of her letter, was that after collating all the items put on my list, he would then return to Mallorca. So it was, out in the spring sunshine tending the new plants in the stone troughs, the sound of a car approaching up the road, made us look up.

"It's my dad. He is back" Yelled young Michael, jumping clean over the garden wall.

"What have you got for us?" Yelled Terry, charging down the path towards his father, jammed in alongside huge boxes.

Climbing out to stretch his legs, Michael stood back watching as the family dived into the car, fingering the parcels. Helping him carry boxes into the villa, before ripping off the brown paper, I discovered an electric mixer, a blender, a mincing machine, as well as many other needed gadgets for the kitchen. Meanwhile going back and forth, piled high with smaller parcels, Michael carried in the booty from the car. Pulling open the packets and tipping the contents onto the dining room table, I found custard powder, cake decorations, cake flour, as well as glace cherries and dried fruit.

"You are an absolute darling." I said, running across to cuddle him.

"You can thank me later." He said with a wink. "First you need to open that parcel from your mother. While you do that I will go and fetch your sewing machine and new tape recorder from the boot of the car."

"Look at this? Boys we are having a bonanza." I said, opening the first parcel filled with summer blouses, shorts, and a new swim-suit."

"What is inside the other parcels for us? Asked young Edward.

"Well first I can see cotton shorts and shirts."

"That is boring!" Said Terry, stamping one foot.

"No wait! Look what is underneath the clothes? Chocolates, biscuits, baked beans and your favourite Frosted cornflakes."

"Quick, get the milk and the bowls" Yelled Terry, fleeing to the kitchen.

Leaving the children to scoff Frosties, walking back outside, I joined Michael at the back of the car. Standing back Michael watched, as leaning down into the opened boot, I rummaged around looking for the tapes.

"Catching sight of your black lace knickers has turned me on." He said, hauling me to my feet. "Can you feel it? It is about time I had some reward for the things I have brought back for you."

"Hold on a minute tiger." I said, pulling free of his grip. "You did not think to write to us once. It was only through my mother that I knew you were still alive!"

"You should know me by now. I do not write letters" He whispered, holding me hard against his groin. "Look I have got money for the boys from my parents. Let me give it to them now. They can go to the supermarket and Jose will change it into pesetas Then they can buy whatever they want. Once they have gone, join me in the bedroom." He added, breathing heavily.

As the roof was now in place, the walls complete and the drainage pipes put on the outside of the "Bolero", we celebrated with a bottle of champagne. With the workmen busy inside the building plastering the walls, it was time to pay another visit to Palma. And on this occasion we were introduced to the Lawyer himself.

"Sorry no further developments right now" He said. "Come back and see me again at the end of April." Feeling reasonably satisfied with the latest news from the Lawyer, we returned to Cala Murada.

"Look I have got a letter addressed to me" I said, picking it up from the mat.

"Who's it from?' Michael asked, checking his watch to see if it was time yet to collect the children from school.

"It is from Anna." I said opening it. "She is coming with her husband and some of the students from the private school in Belgium.'

"When is she coming?'

"'She's does not say that. With Anna you just have to wait until she turns up." I said, placing the letter into the pocket of my skirt.

'So, aren't you going to let me read it?' Michael asked, watching me thread the bobbin on the sewing machine.

"I've told you what it says.' I said biting the cotton in the bobbin with an eye tooth. "She's a bit like you, she does not like committing herself." I said, turning the heavy tapestry material around to run a line of stitches up the side seam.

"Why is it, nowadays, I seem to be the subject of your razor-edged tongue?'

"Not now Michael. I said, ignoring his petulance, while keeping my eyes fixed on the line of stitching appearing from behind the flying needle.

On Mateo's arrival that night, there existed an ulterior motive behind Michael making the Mallorquin feel welcome. With tuition on the Highway Code at an end, Mateo was invited to share a glass of Spanish brandy.

"I have studied these latest figures given to Jacqueline and I need to confirm the total amount we will still owe. After paying the deposit, we now owe about £3,000 pounds is that correct?"

"Yes approximately."

"How long have I got to pay that back in instalments?"

"The maximum time for credit here is three years. Of course there will be ten per cent interest on top of that"

Wow that is a lot of money" Michael said, stroking his chin. "So can you also tell me Mateo, what are the chances of me being able to obtain more credit to buy the furniture and most of the more expensive commodities needed for the "Bolero"?'

"Let me explain something to you. There are two types of credit that operate here in Spain. To buy the expensive items like, refrigerators, gas stoves and a coffee machine, you would need to use the first type of credit. That involves a binding contract of Credit letters, settled on a specified date. The second type of less binding credit, involves Credit letters that are not signed." Mateo said, stopping to sip his cognac. "That means no set date for the amount to be paid. It is just up to you how they are paid. But, of course, the drawback with that type of loose unbinding credit is the longer it remains outstanding, the higher the interest becomes."

"So let me get this straight. With signed Credit Letters they have to be paid on time."

"Definitely."

"Right, I understand. So could you arrange for me to meet with some Credit companies in the "Cobassa" offices."

"For what exactly?"

"To buy all the extras we are going to need."

As requested, seated around a table in the 'Cobassa' offices, with various credit companies present, Michael signed all the documents necessary to obtain the two-and-a-half thousand pounds of credit needed to purchase all the things required for the "Bolero." As soon as the team of smartly dressed businessmen had left, so Mateo and Michael sat sharing a bottle of Rioja red wine.

"So Mateo, you were telling me. You are thirty-one and not married and your permanent home is in Palma with your parents?"

"Yes."

"And what do you do in your spare time?"

"I am a black belt in Judo. And I run a Judo club in Porto Colom teaching youngsters the sport. My other leisure activity is sea diving. Not diving in the conventional way, with bottles, but I dive in the traditional Mallorquin way, holding my breath."

"Holding your breath? For how long?"

"Up to about two minutes."

"Really, that makes me feel quite inadequate. Incidentally, while we are here talking could you give me the name of a good carpenter to make the kitchen units for the "Bolero?"

"The man you need to see is named Rodriguez. He has a factory in Felanitx." Mateo said, producing a local directory from a drawer in his desk. "He is a very fine craftsman and here is where you can find him." He said, writing down the address on a piece of paper.

"Something else. Jacqueline wants to know if the interior walls of the "Bolero" can be in a particular colour? She wants the interior of the bar painted in oyster pink and sage green in the restaurant."

"The quotation we have given is for white walls. If you want coloured walls, it will involve more money. I can discuss that matter with Jacqueline, when I come next to give her tuition on the Highway Code."

On Mateo's next visit, following the lesson, he stayed for dinner. And while I went to the kitchen to wash dishes, the two men sat discussing the suitability of various types of wood needed for the bar.

"Mahogany is going to be very expensive, because it's imported from Africa." Said Mateo.

"I heard that remark." I said, poking my head round the kitchen door. "Having anything else, will only be false economy."

"I need to emphasise the point that the initial quotation is now increasing." Mateo said, running his pen down a line of figures on the page before him. "With the drainage pipes now on the outside walls, together with coloured paint, high quality tiles on the floors and now a request for mahogany on the bar, we are now looking at?" he continued, writing down the new set of figures and compiling a total. 'Something in the region in sterling of about a further thousand pounds. Of course, all these increased costs need be authorised by you in writing Michael."

"So over three years, four thousand pounds mounts to one thousand two hundred and fifty pounds a year?"

"Yes and also there will be ten percent interest to add."

"That is going to be a tall order." Michael said, looking back as I came into the room.

"Not if we make a profit from the beginning." I said.

"That is not very likely Jacqueline." Michael said, with raised eyebrows.

"As well as tourists, we need to attract the custom of the residents here in Cala Murada. Anyway, it is a bit late now to start getting cold feet. We are already committed up to our necks." I said.

"So when do you anticipate that the construction of the premises will be finished?" Michael asked.

"Things are going according to plan. The "Bolero" should be completed by the end of April. And incidentally, how are the legal aspects coming along?" Mateo asked, placing his pen back in his pocket "That's the most important thing, because you cannot open the premises until you have all the necessary permits."

"We have been to see the lawyer again, and according to him everything is under control. We have another appointment at the end of April."

"That is good. And your comment Jacqueline, about the residents being important customers, reminds me there is another topic that needs to be discussed. Are you aware that a Residents Association operates here in Cala Murada?" Mateo asked, addressing Michael.

"No, this is the first time I have heard about it."

"Well, it was set up, some years ago, for the benefit of foreigners making permanent homes here. This Residents Association, which meets monthly, gives the villa owners the opportunity to voice their opinion regarding matters concerning the area as well as to discuss problems."

"Go on," I said, joining them at the table.

"I happened to be present at the last meeting when Mr Dewitt, Chairman of the Committee, raised an objection to a bar and restaurant being built in the Manzanas."

"What!"

"No need to be alarmed Michael." Mateo said, raising one hand. "His objection was overruled by "Cobassa.""

"Isn't that the guy, on the school rota, who harasses the boys when they are in his car?' Michael asked looking sideways at me.

"'Yes and probably that outrageous story you told Michael to tell the Dutchman, about you being involved in the Great Train Robbery is the reason he raised an objection."

"'Sorry? I'm afraid you have lost me." Mateo said, furrowing is dark brows.

"It is just a private joke, please go on. So how many members serve on this Committee?' asked Michael.

"Nine in total. Mr Dewitt the Dutch Chairman, four Germans, three Belgians and the American Ted."

"Oh, that follows. Trust a previous American army major to be there on the front line." Said Michael.

"Excuse me Mateo, but I do not quite follow. You are telling us this, now the construction of the "Bolero" is almost complete." I added.

"What the Committee decides is not that important. Ultimately the decisions are made by my company. And it is "Cobassa" that makes the final decision as to how the land is developed. In theory, it is in the interests of the company to take on board complaints raised by the Residents Committee. While in practice, The Residents Committee is nothing more than a paper tiger."

"So why did your company quash the objections raised about a bar and restaurant being built on the Manzanas?" Michael asked.

"Simply because as the very first British to arrive here to start a business, it was in our interest to allow you to build on this side of the beach. Also with The Residents Committee made up predominantly of German, Dutch, and Belgians, we needed to attract more British. And for that reason all objections raised regarding the construction of the "Bolero" were thrown out."

Living in such a comparatively quiet area, my ears were attuned to the sound of cars coming up the hill. Alerted to the sound of a throaty car stopping outside, I looked out of the kitchen window. Spotting Anna climb out of a low-slung gun-metal grey Mercedes sports, I raced down the path to greet her.

"Why didn't You tell me you were coming? And my God Anna, you look so bloody tired." I said kissing her on both cheeks.

"I have driven for two days without stopping. That is why I look tired. Can I come in for a drink?" She said, walking passed and heading for the front door.

"Of course, but I do not have any Pernod. It will have to be Anis mixed with water." I said, leaving her to sit in a deck chair.

Returning from the kitchen with the Anis to watch her sniff the cheap alcohol mixed with water, wrinkling her nose and shuddering, the entire contents of the glass disappeared down the throat.

"So where's this husband of yours?" she said, "I've come here first, especially to see him. And where are my darling boys?' She asked, clonking the glass down on the floor before standing up and rocking sideways.

"They are still at school." I said, catching hold of her. "So how much have you had to drink before you arrived here?"

"Not much." She answered, yanking her arm free. "Stop questioning me. I am just very tired that is all. I need to go now. I've left the students in the villa".

"You have students with you?"

"Yes, while I drove my husband's car, they followed behind in the minibus".

"And your husband Edgar?"

"He's coming next week, with the teachers."

"Go and get some sleep Anna. It is Saturday tomorrow, and the boys will be home from school. We will all come and see you then."

On the most beautiful spring day, with Michael still in Felanitx, I stopped on the road to admire the view. Set against the backdrop of a cerulean blue sky and sweeping down from the hazy mountains, looking like white and pink powder puffs, almond trees were in full bloom. And while the boys ran on, in ever decreasing circles, I stopped once more to smell the fresh, viridian green grass. As I arrived at Anna's front door, so Michael pulled up into the driveway behind me. Whereupon, coming to open the door herself, Anna fell upon the children with open arms. Meanwhile standing back, Michael watched the exuberant stranger kissing his sons.

"Well here you are at last. Please come in Michael" Anna said, leaning forward in an embrace, as he ducked quickly beneath her open arms.

"Please" he said, noting the rancid smell on her breath, "We Brits do not kiss strangers."

"Oh you are just so stuffy. Then you must hold my hand." She said, guiding him down the hallway and into the lounge. Duly assembled in the lounge, the process of introducing us to the guests began. Upon discovering that many of the Belgian teenagers spoke good English, settling into a chair, Michael socialised with the students. And as a self-professed competent chess player, finding out that most of the teenagers played the game, made for an entertaining morning. And while some female students, entertained the boys, Michael was left to play chess.

"I hope you do not mind Anna, but I have to leave shortly. I have an appointment with some carpenters at noon. Will it be alright if I leave Michael to come back with the children later?

"Of course," she said, reaching out for the Pernod with ice and water.

"You know Anna," I said, watching her sip the milky substance "It is only early in the day, and already you are drinking."

"Off you go, good-bye. Please I do not want any lectures." she added with a wave.

At precisely noon, the carpenters arrived from Felanitx to discuss the fitments needed for the kitchen. Standing leaning up against one breeze-block wall, the two men listened as I spelt out my requirements. With heads bent low over note pads, the carpenters began jotting down all the details concerning the fixtures and fittings needed. And while I continued rattling on in Spanish, the two men suddenly stopped writing. First looking at each other in amazement and then holding their sides, the two Mallorquin men began to laugh out loud. Completely taken aback, by this sudden outburst of uncontrolled merriment, all I could do was to look on bemused.

The moment men left, absolutely determined to unravel the mystery of my obvious 'faux pas', I went back to the villa to confer with the Spanish dictionary. Going carefully through the Spanish alphabet to locate the two words that the carpenters had repeated back to me several times, I discovered that 'Cajones" with an 'a' was the correct 'word for a wooden drawer. While 'Cojones' with an 'o' was the slang expression for testicles or balls. What I had been asking the carpenters to make was 'two wooden balls to be fitted underneath the kitchen table'.

For the next three days I avoided visiting Anna. And when I did go, it was a Belgian student who came to the door.

"Madam DuBois is not well today." He said, keeping me in the hall.

"Well can I see her?"

"She is still in bed." He replied looking behind him at the bedroom door. "You had better knock first."

Knocking and getting no response, upon entering I was confronted by Anna hanging over the side of the bed, being sick into a bowl. Gasping for air and wiping the green bile from her mouth with the back of her hand, her head flopped back onto the soiled pillow. Then aware that somebody was standing close to the bed, opening her eyes to speak, she dived once more over the edge of the bed.

What are you doing to yourself?" I asked, coming close to push back the tangled knots of damp hair from her clammy brow. Pulling me even closer to grip my arm, the smell of stale vomit and unwashed flesh made my stomach churn.

"Help me." She said, her dilated dark eyes filled with some inexplicable terror. "You need to know what is going on. The students are neglecting and ill-treating me all the time. I have had nothing to eat today and I have wet the bed. Can you help me Jacqueline?"

Not quite sure about what my position was in Anna's home, after washing her down and changing the bed linen I went back to o D43.

"So where have you been all morning?" Michael asked.

"Did you get to see the lawyer?" I asked, not wanting to be drawn on the subject.

"Yes, and today he was cagey about everything. In fact he seemed surprised that the "Bolero" was going to be finished on time. You cannot imagine how much paperwork there is still outstanding. We need to have a Sanitary Inspection of the premises, as well as an inspection by the Guardia of Civil. And God knows what else! It also appears that we will need special permits to work. The only good point to come out of that visit to Palma was the fact that the lawyer seems to think the price we paid for the land and the property is cheap."

"So how was your day?" He asked. "Don't tell me. You have been to see that potty friend of yours?" Michael said, watching me wipe dirty brown marks from my white sandals.

"At times Michael, you can be such a bloody insensitive brute! Yes, I did go and see Anna. And she is not very well at all."

"Come on Jacqueline, you are just so gullible. Anna is a first-class manipulator who exploits you all the time. More fool you if you are taken in by it, that's all I say."

"You could be right. There are things going on in that place that do not add up. Those students for example, they are so damned lazy. They just sit on their back sides, doing nothing. And the girls are even worse than the boys! When I asked them to help me with toiletries and to find clean linen for Anna's bed, they simply shrugged their shoulders. With their legs dangling over the sides of the chairs, they carried on painted their nails!"

"It sounds to me as though the students know Anna far better than you do. If you decide to take on the responsibility of something that has absolutely nothing to do with you, what do you expect. Besides, is not her husband due to arrive very soon? Wouldn't it be better to let him sort his wife's problems?'

"It's just that she is my good friend and I know she has a drink problem."

"Okay, you have been warned. I'm off to Pedro's for a game of cards and a beer with the men."

On the next visit to the villa, it was the black African teacher who answered the door. Guiding me straight through into the lounge I was surprised to see Anna standing next to a stranger, looking bright-eyed and bushy-tailed and wearing a smart trouser suit of green silk.

"Jacqueline, how absolutely lovely to see you.' She said, placing one arm around the shoulders of this heavily built little man. "Please let me introduce you to my husband Edgar. He arrived from Belgium yesterday,"

Shaking hands with Edgar, while studying the, previously, wayward, and indolent students, it was obvious that he was captain of his ship. Oblivious of the trauma caused on the previous visit, with Edgar now in control, Anna swept around the room fawning before him like a lapping dog.

"In two days," said the African teacher translating for Edgar. "Monsieur Dubois will be celebrating his birthday. And he would like you and your family to come to celebrate the event with cake and champagne."

"Will you come?" Anna asked.

"Of course, thank you." I said, addressing Edgar.

Arriving two days later for the birthday celebration, Anna looked dreadful. Drunk and with reddened eyes, it was obvious that she had been crying. Meanwhile, electing to ignore his wife completely and standing at the top of the table, Edgar cut the cake before making a brief speech French. Leaving the children to plough their way through mammoth slices of iced cake, the rest of us were left to toast the birthday boy in French champagne.

"I am now speaking on behalf of Edgar." Said the African teacher in impeccable English. "We were wondering if you would like to vacate your present villa and take up residence here in this villa, at a greatly reduced rent."

"That is a bit of a surprise. I will give it some thought." Said Michael.

"We understand. The only restriction to renting this property would be that, during the summer months, the top dormitory would remain empty for the use of Monsieur and Madame DuBois and the students. And something else, we wondered if you and your family would all like to join us for a game, to be played on Cala Murada beach next Saturday?"

"At what time?"

"8 o'clock by the beach bar. Can you manage that?"

"We will let you know." Michael said, cautiously.

As it turned out, the game to be played on the beach was not unlike the game played by the British boy scouts. With students in one team and teachers in the other team, the purpose of the game was for a winning student. to get down onto the beach and retrieve a prize without being caught.

"So where exactly do we fit in?" Michael asked, as we stood waiting by the bar.

"As we are the catchers, you will be with us teachers" said the African touching his chest. "As soon as we have dropped the students off at various points in and around Cala Murada, it will be down to us to capture them before they get onto the beach. And by the way, to avoid detection, the students will be dressed in dark colours. At the same time to avoid being spotted, we teachers will also wear dark clothes but with white bands on our arms so that we can be distinguished from the students."

"It sounds like good fun." I said, clapping my hands.

"One more thing I need to add. So that the students can avoid being spotted, they are permitted to blacken their faces." The teacher said.

"Really? Then shouldn't you be with them?" Michael said, laughing. Appreciating the British man's sense of humour, the black African teacher laughed too.

"And where do the children fit in?" I asked.

"They will have to go with your husband in the back of his car."

With the game of confederacy in full swing and with students left at various points in and around Cala Murada, we the team of catchers were left lying in wait. However, in one of her usual cantankerous moods and not prepared to join the game until she had had a drink, Anna and I were left sitting at the bar on the next beach, overlooking Tropicana. Studying Anna's bizarre appearance, enveloped in a black silk jacket and an oversized hood shading her face, I was annoyed.

"I think, in order to avoid detection," she said, throwing back the hood and giggling. "What we need to do is to approach Cala Murada beach on this footpath up here, along the top of the cliffs. What do you think Jacqueline?"

"But walking along the cliff edge, in the dark? That could be dangerous."

"No, because I have got a torch." "

Minutes later creeping along, armed with one torch between us to show the way, the pair of us set out walking along the dark and precipitous pathway towards Cala Murada beach. Of course, as I had not been drinking, I was truly scared. Dropping some twenty minutes later, on our backsides over the rocks, we slid down tentatively into the shadows of Cala Murada beach.

"So what now?" I whispered.

"Well some teachers should already be close." Anna said, "So, stay here, while I move further along the beach. If we are going to stop the students getting onto the beach, we need to spread out." Pulling the black hood over her head and dropping to her knees Anna began to crawl away.

Lighting a cigarette, while staying alert, while hearing scuffles coming from the beach I suspected that teachers had already arrived. Then noting the sound of motorbikes coming down the hill, stubbing out the cigarette, I peered over the rock. There silhouetted against the yellow streetlights, I recognised the outline of the Guardia of Civil police. Parking their bikes, dressed in their distinctive dark green cloaks and black pill box hats, the two policemen came walking through the flower beds to stop at the beach wall.

Anxious to stay hidden, I was still close enough to hear the conversation between the policemen speaking in Castiliano Spanish. With both men lighting up cigarettes the casual conversation, suddenly came to an end. Alert as meerkats, looking first sideways and then back to walk along the promenade, they stopped nearer the beach.

"*Quien es en la playa?*" Who is it on the beach?" Called the first Guardia.

With only silence coming from the beach, but now acutely aware that something untoward was happening, calling again, the policeman demanded to know whoever it was on the beach to show themselves. The very fact that I could hear the movement and whispering coming from the centre of the beach, meant that the policemen could hear it. Upon hearing the sound of a gun holster popping open, holding my breath, I peeped out from my hideaway as there, flushed out like rabbits from a burrow, four shadowy figures walked sheepishly back up the beach. Instantly picked up in the powerful torchlight, Anna and teachers stopped still below the beach wall.

"And just who are you?" Demanded one policeman, in Spanish, while brandishing the gun in their faces.

"And what exactly are you doing on the beach at night?" Asked the second policeman, aiming the torch directly into their eyes.

"Contrabandos!" He said, waving his revolver menacingly, before jumping from the promenade down onto the sand. "And you," he said putting his torch directly beneath the African teacher's chin. "un mono, mono." he repeated. (Monkey in English)

Now with the atmosphere turned into an electric storm, slightly drunk Anna, looked back to where I was hiding.

"Jacqueline, will you please come out from where you are and help us?"

"Oh dear God!" The very first thing entering my head was the warning from Mateo, to stay on the right side of the Guardia of Civil. There I was, waiting to obtain the permits and permissions to open a bar and restaurant here on the island, and now being exposed by my so-called friend. Stepping out from behind the rocks, to reveal my presence, I too walked up the beach to join the group.

"'Ah it is you Señora" Said the first policeman, picking me up in the me torchlight. "We know you. You came the second time to Porto Colom to get your papers checked and your passport stamped." He said, smiling at his companion. "You live here in Cala Murada with your family" He said, placing the gun back in its holster. "'You are going to open a bar and restaurant here. Isn't that right?"

"Yes."

"So, would you mind telling us what you are doing here on the beach? And who are these other people?" He asked, with obvious disdain, while keeping a wary eye on the African teacher.

Struggling in stinted Spanish, I endeavoured to explain the game we were playing on the beach.

"Playing Boy Scout games on the beach at night, is breaking the law. We Guardia patrol the beaches, looking for smugglers and contraband goods arriving from North Africa all the time. And for that reason games are never allowed to be played on beaches after dark. Do you realise Señora, just how close you came to being shot?" The policeman asked, caressing his black leather holster."

"I do," I added with contrition.

"And who is this?" Asked the second policeman, watching Michael approach.

"My husband, don't you remember he was with me when I came to Porto Colom?"

"Yes, now I do." He said flatly, his eyes diverted.

Of course, with all this distraction and furore taking place, two Belgian students managed to stroll, unchallenged, down to the centre of the beach to retrieve the chocolate hidden by the flagpole. And by the time other teachers and Edgar arrived on the scene, the excitement was all over. With Anna falling about Edgar's neck, telling him all about how she had nearly been gunned down, keeping a cool head, Edgar invited the Guardia to join him in the hotel. Leaving the boys with students, drinking coca cola in the gardens, the evening continued on a light-hearted note in the bar.

"Do you know, that was a bit odd the police not remembering me." Michael said, drinking his morning coffee "Because, that second time, I was with you to get my passport and papers checked as well."

"Maybe it was your blatant lack of diplomacy and respect for the Guardia that did not go down very well."

"I know exactly what you are implying by that sarcastic remark. It would be a damned sight easier if the police spoke bloody English."

"I think you have just proved my point Michael."

Arriving in a trouser suit, made of gun meal grey leather and her braided hair piled on top of her head, Anna came to say goodbye.

"We are all leaving now for. You have our address Michael, and we await to hear your decision about renting the villa." She said, sliding behind the wheel of the Mercedes Anna was gone.

CHAPTER 8

Passing the written test on the Highway Code, on the first attempt, the recently modified Spanish driving test proved far more difficult. With no driving on the road involved, instead, the test stated that the car had to be driven through the gears before bringing the car to a stop. That first part posed no problem, it was the second part, involving reversing the car into a small parking space between bollards in a time limit, that caused grief. Then moving to drive the car at speed, through a series of chicanes before reversing around white poles, I knocked into them. Following yet another failed attempt, apologising to the instructor, I abandoned Michael's car.

"This driving test is an absolute joke. Michael said, walking across the road to join me "It's more like taking a lesson in how to be a rally driver. I do not think you have a hope in hell of passing the test."

"The problem is Michael, that this car is comparatively new which means that the steering wheel is stiff. Turning the wheel round from one lock onto the other lock, in a strict time limit, is not easy."

Two lessons later and with only marginal improvement, shaking me by the hand the instructor wished me luck. It so happened that the day scheduled to take both the written and practical test was my thirtieth birthday. My initial joy at passing the written examination for the first time was soon short lived. Driving to the examination centre to take the practical, proved to be disastrous. Reversing the car into a parking space through tight chicanes, in a time limit, I careered into every single one of the white poles.

"Come on cheer up better luck next time. It is your birthday." Michael said, placing his arm around my waist. "Why don't we drive up to Manacor. We could chase up the order on all the furniture for the "Bolero" and at the same time collect that picture you have put a deposit on."

"Yes, let us do that. I know that picture is going to cost more than my mother has sent but I still want to buy it."

As promised, by the end of April, the construction work on the "Bolero" was complete. However, with the property still without power and with the electrical appliances due to arrive at any time, a visit to the "Cobassa" offices was required.

"I have to say, you cannot have the necessary cabling, to install electricity, for another month." Said Mateo, reaching for his notepad. "So what I would suggest is that I give you the name and address of a local electrician who will be able to arrange for power on a temporary basis. He will be able to lay a cable linking the "Bolero" to the overhead pylons on the opposite side of road."

"Is that legal?" asked Michael.

"We are turning a blind eye." Replied Mateo.

With that problem solved Michael stopped at the hotel to finalise the details regarding the move from D43, to Edgar and Anna's villa, at the end of May. Standing in for Edgar the Belgian accountant, employed by the hotel, took the 30,000 pesetas deposit from Michael. Watching Michael complete the relevant documents regarding the move, the reticent late middle-aged Belgian, smoked his pipe.

"By the way," said Bernabe following Michael back out into the reception of the hotel. "I have been contacted by your lawyer in Palma about sponsoring you and Jacqueline. I have signed the documents and sent them back. So you should soon get all the permissions you need to open the business. And I was thinking Michael, as you are going to need staff, I thought I would let you know about a young married couple, staying in Felanitx, who have recently come from the mainland. They need work, what do you think could you employ them?"

"Ugh, a married couple? I am not sure about that. I'll see what my other half have to say about that."

Finding the address in Felanitx, written down by Bernabe, was not easy. Neither Michael nor I had ever ventured down the back streets of the local town. After a long walk and eventually coming across a run-down house with unpainted shutters and crumbling brickwork took us both by surprise.

"That's it, goodbye."' Michael said. Scrutinising a dirty and ragged piece of curtain hanging over a broken pane of glass at the front door. "I am not going in there. I will stay outside."

"Right." I said, resolutely, stepping over the broken paving stones and into a dimly lit room, stinking of raw sewerage. Moving in from bright sunlight and into a treacle dark atmosphere, it was a few moments before my eyes focused on the group of four men and four women, all in black, huddled around a wooden table. Stepping forward smiling while stuttering a few words of greeting, the faces on the entire group remained expressionless. Following what seemed like an eternity, one young plump woman wearing an old-fashioned black dress down to her ankles, stood up to speak.

Straining to understand a single word of what was being said to me, totally bewildered, I shook my head. It was only when the young woman resorted to physical demonstrations and pointing, did I slowly begin to comprehend this new dialect of Spanish I had never heard before. The young woman together with her husband from Murcia in Southern Spain both needed a job. Dismayed at the poverty and feeling cornered, I retreated outside to get help.

"Forget it and do not even think about it" Michael said, looking up at the ragged curtains and broken glass.

"I am sorry, I do not think you are right for the job." I said, standing at the door looking back into the gloom.

"Do you think they understood what you were saying?"

"I have not the faintest idea Michael, they are from southern Spain."

"I tell you what," he said, as we drove back to Cala Murada, "That Belgian guy, the accountant working in the hotel, he is a bit of an odd-ball."

"Yes, he is. Bernabe told me all about him once. He worked for the Belgian resistance during the Second World War. He was captured by the Gestapo and tortured. When you went to pay the deposit, did you notice he had a thumb missing on his left hand?" I asked looking at Michael.

"No, I can't say I did."

"Under interrogation he was strung up by his thumbs and one was pulled off."

"Charming, that could account for his miserable demeanour. You know we have an appointment tomorrow to go to the school to see the children's teacher. What is her name?" he asked, pulling up outside the villa.

"Dona Antonia."

In the most charming rural setting, three miles out of Cala Murada and on the road to Porto Cristo, was the school our children attended. This pristine white oblong building with its bell tower and stone well, was attached to the local farm. And for the dozen or so children attending the school, outside recreation were the fields and visiting the nearby farm. The meeting with the teach Dona Antonia went very well. According to her, all three boys were happy children, who had adjusted well into the new environment. Not only were they starting to read and write in Spanish and understand basic counting but also related well to children from different nationalities.

Ten days later, resulting from an unfortunate incident, I failed my driving test for the second time. Heading towards Palma on the road from Felanitx to Campos, we witnessed a bad road accident. A white car, coming up two cars behind us, suddenly braked forcing the lorry close behind him, to collide with the white car.

"For fucks sake! I could see that was going to happen." Michael said, his eyes peeled on the rear-view mirror. "Vehicles driving too close to one another. Did you see that? The lorry has clipped the side of the car and flipped it over onto its side. You stay here in the car while I go and see if I can help".

Several men, including Michael, were required to lift and then rock the damaged white car back onto four wheels. With Michael helping, the lorry driver and other bystanders managed to extricate the three very shaken passengers from out of the car and onto the roadside. At the same time, still pinned down at the chest by the steering wheel, the stricken driver had to be left jammed behind the wheel. Observing the crash, the owner of a nearby garage phoned for help.

Unfortunately, with the three shocked passengers standing on the roadside wailing, it was another twenty minutes before one policeman arrived on a motorbike.

"Okay let us go, that policeman has called for an ambulance. What are you doing? Get back in the car you are already late for your driving test" Michael said, walking up to me with splatters of blood all over the front of his white shirt.

It goes without saying that on this occasion, knocking down every obstacle in sight, I failed the driving test in a most spectacular fashion.

"You were late Señora, and if you fail again for the third time," the examiner said, tapping his fingers on the book," you will be obliged to go through the whole procedure again and including the written test."

"Do you know," Michael said, as we headed back into Palma to see the Lawyer. "I think we should have told the examiner that we had witnessed an accident. Maybe he would have been more sympathetic."

"Perhaps."

Waiting in the foyer of the Lawyer's office, it was another half an hour before we managed to get seated in front of him.

"Work permits cannot be issued for the "Bolero" until a compulsory sanitary inspection has been carried out." He said, peering over his thick rimmed glasses.

"So how long after the Sanitary Inspection and necessary permission from the police, will we have to wait before all the paperwork is complete?" Michael asked,

"At this stage I cannot really say. Maybe another two weeks. Sorry, I know it is very frustrating. These things take time in Spain" He said, shrugging his shoulders dismissively. And for the entire fifty-kilometre journey from Palma to Cala

Murada, Michael remonstrated about the incompetence of Spanish lawyers.

"Do you know, until we saw him in February and gave him the completion date for the "Bolero", I don't think a bloody thing had been done. He's been sitting on his back side for three months doing fuck all!"

"Michael, lawyers are much the same the world over. I am beginning to think that if we want to get around this red tape and open our bar and restaurant, we are going to have to do most of the work ourselves. What an absolutely dreadful day we have had." I said, wearily. "When we get home, we should go to the beach for a swim.""

Later sitting together on the sand in our swimsuits, I heard somebody call out my name. Standing up and pushing my sunglasses back up onto my forehead, I looked back to see who it was.

"Oh Michael, it's that young couple from Felanitx who need a job."

"Well you know exactly what to say don't you" he said, not moving an inch." I'll leave it entirely up to you to go and tell them our decision."

Walking up the beach, following a brief conversation, I returned to join Michael still gazing out to sea.

"Well?"

They have told me that they are nearly out of money and they are now desperate for work. Please, can't we give them and chance?"

"'No."

"Sometimes you can be such an unfeeling bastard I actually hate you." I said bursting into tears. Rarely seeing me cry, looking shocked, Michael got to his feet.

"Now come on darling, it has been a bad day, and that is why you are emotional. I am not the hard-nosed bugger you make me out to be. That young couple will get a job somewhere else. What I want to know is how the devil they knew where to find us."

"They went into Jose's supermarket.' I said, wiping my eyes. "They were actually on their way to find our villa when they recognised us on the beach."

"Come and let me give you a cuddle."

'No, do not try and get around me." I said pushing him away.

"Okay, have it your way." He said, banging his hands on the hips. "But do not say I did not warn you. Go and catch them up and tell them they have got a job.' He called out, as I raced back up the beach, onto the promenade and up the road towards the hotel.

"I just managed to reach them as they were boarding the bus back to Felanitx. Thank you Michael."

Passing the driving test on the third attempt and returning from Palma to the "Bolero" we found a note pinned to the rustic arch built at the entrance. With an estimated delay of four months, before a telephone could be installed, 'Cobassa' had been taking calls for us. And this latest message, from Mateo, was to confirm that manufacturers in Palma were on their way to deliver the refrigerators to the "Bolero" that afternoon. Not stopping for lunch, Michael was off to locate the electrician, agreed upon, to install the electrical appliances. On his return, snatching up the car keys from the kitchen table, I was away running down the path towards the car to drive on my own to the "Cobassa" offices.

"I was just on my way to deliver another message to you from Palma." Mateo said, coming down the steps smiling.

"Get in the car Mateo. I have just passed my test." I said, eager to show off my driving skill. "I will drive you back here later."

"When I came with the message earlier, I could not help noticing the progress made in the gardens. I did not know

Michael was such a good gardener." Said, Mateo, getting out of the car and waiting beneath the rustic arch at the entrance.

"He's not. It is all Vicente's work. You know the young husband and wife team we took on at the beginning of last week? Well Vicente is fantastic in the garden." I said, as we walked together up the path and onto the top terrace.

"And did he construct that new rockery filled with plants?" Mateo asked, stopping to look at the well-watered holes dug around the tender plants. Well he certainly is a man of the soil."

"He's wonderful. He has spent the entire week, from dawn until dusk, digging out all the small rocks and stones from around the plot. With nothing more than a rubber bucket and a spade, he has transported all the rocks and builder's rubble and use it as the foundations for the rockery. What is more," I said, walking along the terrace, 'Vicente's wife Narcissus? She is so good with the boys and the household chores and what is more she is willing to learn."

'So where did the geraniums and other flowering shrubs come from?' Mateo asked, leaning out over the rustic balustrade at the, flourishing, terracotta pots below.

'Aren't they gorgeous?' I said following Mateo down the terrace steps fingering the dark fleshy leaves of the red oleander in full bloom. "All delivered to us courtesy of Andres. Something about good luck charms for the "Bolero".

"Really, then you must consider yourself honoured. It's not very often Andres gives anything away."

"I can honestly say, I said, walking back up onto the top terrace." I have always found the Mallorquins to be both helpful and courteous. You know Mateo? I just love living here."

Moving away from the outside terrace, to step inside onto the black and cream tiled floor, the smell of cut timber and varnish filled the air.

"I like the warm colour chosen for the walls, it goes well with the dark wood and the tapestry cushions. It adds ambience to the place." Mateo said, strolling around and noticing a four-door refrigerator, standing on the chequered floor directly in front of the bar.

"Well hello you two," Said Michael, his head popping out from the first open door at the end of the refrigerator. "Would you like to hear the latest? We have a fridge without a motor."

"Honestly? So what about the refrigerator for ice-cream?' I asked, looking across at a white fridge standing nearby.

"That's okay because the motor is built in." Michael replied, clambering out through the fridge door."

Meanwhile, through the open door at the other end of the red four door refrigerator, the electrician appeared to confirm that the appliance had indeed been delivered without a motor.

"This is just what we needed." Michael said, standing up straight.

"Come on now Michael, it's not all bad. Your wife has passed her driving test and now I have a message from the Sanitary Inspector in Manacor. He is coming tomorrow to carry out the inspection on the property. Once you have that under your belt you will be almost home and dry."

"'I would not bank on that Mateo. I would like to take a bet that he does not arrive until after his afternoon siesta."

"Oh for goodness sake Michael!" I said, lifting the flap to go behind the bar.

"I think a celebration drink is called for here." I said, taking the unopened bottle of Carlos I brandy down from the mahogany shelf.

"Hang on a moment, that is the best vintage cognac you have there."

"I know Michael and quite frankly I don't care." I added, breaking the seal with the edge of a small knife before pouring out four very generous measures into goblets. "'Here's to passing the driving test and the success of the "Bolero". I said, raising my glass to the electrician.

By the middle of May, with the young married couple Vicente and Narcissus settled into the modest living accommodation underneath the property, we had moved from D43 into the more salubrious surroundings of Edgar and Anna's villa. And proving to be compliant hard workers, it was not long before a sound relationship was established between me and the couple from Southern Spain.

Although initially, the boys showed a certain amount of caution towards the strangers, they too began to accept having them around. On the other hand, the fact that this couple from Murcia, spoke a dialect of Spanish Michael had never heard before, meant that the relationship between him and the staff was somewhat strained. Constantly criticising them for the way they appeared to cut off the ends of words, in his presence there existed an atmosphere of tension.

Following an invitation for the couple to join us for an evening meal in the new surroundings, relations between Michael and the staff worsened. During the somewhat laboured conversation, it was Narcisus who struck the final blow. Wanting to talk about her background she went on to say that, prior to arriving on the island, both she and Vicente had only ever worked in the maize fields of Southern Spain. Hoping to stem the character destruction in progress, I went to the kitchen to serve pudding to our guests. However, quite innocently, Narcisus then went on to explain how, in her teenage years, she had carried water in a jug on top of her head to the men working in the fields. Not even daring to look at the expression on my husband's face, I went back into the kitchen to prepare the coffee.

At four o'clock the following afternoon, the Sanitary Inspector arrived from Manacor. Following a detailed inspection of the bar and restaurant, we were given the assurance that a Clearance Certificate would be issued and sent to us within a week. Ten days later and we were still waiting for the penultimate permission needed to open the business. One month after completion and with little money left in the bank, the "Bolero" remained closed to the public. Very aware and distressed by the displays of open warfare between Michael and me, our three boys looked on in silence.

On two consecutive Saint Days, leaving the children in the care of Narcisus, Michael and I set off to locate the Sanitary Inspector in Manacor. Eventually finding the address it was the housekeeper, answering the door, who told us that the Sanitary Inspector was not at home. Leaving a note and with a promise, from her, that she would pass the message on we left.

Returning to Manacor the following morning the housekeeper had better news. Written down by the Sanitary Inspector, she had the name and address where our signed, Certificate of Sanitation could be found. Wandering up and down the narrow streets, hiding from the punishing midday sun we attempted to find the location. While hiding in the shadows, mewling like some a schoolboy with his satchel, Michael continued to complain.

"What a ghastly mistake we made deciding to come and live on this bloody island." He went on mopping his brow. "I have had enough. Let us just forget it today and go home."

"No, look Michael." I said, coming out of the side street before entering a small square. "That is the name of the place we are looking for, let's go." Half walking and half running and crossing the square, we staggered into the stiflingly hot interior of the bar.

"I have had this document sitting behind my bar, waiting for collection, for nearly a week." Said the owner of the bar taking the Sanitary Report down from behind a bottle of whiskey at the back of the bar.

Returning to Cala Murada, armed with the penultimate permission, our sense of elation was taken even higher. Having been delivered that morning, the wrought iron tables and matching chairs with cream and green striped parasols were out on the terraces. With Edward seated with Narcisus playing snap Vicente, stripped to the waist, was applying the finishing touches to the garden. The only thing marring this otherwise tranquil scene, was the fact that a washing line had been rigged up on the front of the terrace. With Narcisus having abandoned the space located at the back for washing there was now a line, running from the balustrade across to a nearby olive tree, filled with a row of spanking white knickers. Relieved from our success in Manacor, while Michael and I fell about laughing, the couple from Southern Spain looked on bemused.

Into the month of June and Michael's parents, along with friends, arrived to stay in the hotel Cala Murada. On this her first visit abroad, Ivy's beautiful magnolia coloured skin had turned a light golden brown.

"You look so relaxed and happy mum, lying there in the sun."

"It is an absolute joy to be here away from the stress at home."

"What stress are you talking about?"

"It's young Terry, he's given us more than a few problems."

"For sure that stems from your illness ten years ago."

"You are so right. Me being admitted into hospital for four months and leaving nine-year-old Terry with my overly domineering mother-in-law greatly affected him. Shall I tell you Jacqueline, I remember absolutely nothing about my illness. I remember going to the hairdressers and then nothing else, nothing about going to hospital. All I do remember is waking up in an alien environment and surrounded by disturbed patients."

I never ever did tell Ivy that it was me who discovered her so gravely ill.

While praising the ability of the grandchildren to speak Spanish and filled with optimism about her son's future, her husband John had misgivings. Querying the position of the "Bolero", in relation to the beach and hotel, John was not convinced that enough business could be generated to support a family for a whole year.

As their holiday entered the second week, still without the permission from the Police to open the premises, we decided to test the skills of our staff. Behind closed doors, and with the family and friends seated around tables in the restaurant, the dummy run began.

While the food prepared was considered a success, what with Michael corking the bottle of wine, coupled with Vicente's gaffs serving the men before the women and dropping cutlery on the floor, the evening was described by the big-hearted Londoners as thoroughly entertaining. Just prior to their imminent departure back to England, John decided to impart a few words of advice to his son.

"You need to put up signs close to the beach and around the hotel." Said, his father pushing a fistful of pesetas notes into Michael's hand. "It is most important that the British tourists know exactly where you are."

"What's this money for?" asked Michael, looking down at the large bundle of notes.

"Take it. We have all had a wonderful holiday. It is just a little whip round. All our spare pesetas, we thought you could do with it."

It just so happened that this generous amount of money, donated by the family, was enough to cover the first Credit Letter due on the electrical appliances.

CHAPTER 9

Sharing a late breakfast of sobrasada sausage with bread, spiral shaped yeast buns called *ensaïmadas,* and black coffee laced with cognac, four men are seated at a table in Pedro's. Present for their eleven o'clock break, but separate from their boss Andres, the workmen stand against the bar. Meanwhile, leaning forward on the table reading the headlines of the newspaper, Bernabe orders a white coffee.

"Look who is coming. The local Gigolo is back," says Andres, flashing his gold eye teeth and digging Jose in the ribs. "Buenos Dias, Emilio. Come estas? Good morning Emilio, how are you? Back from your sojourn on the mainland?" Asked Andres, studying his friend's cream linen suit.

"Yes I'm back, dried out and rested."

"So how is your mother?" Jose asks. To witness Jose, early in the day, wearing a formal dark suit, silk shirt and tie, is unusual. However, with new contracts to be signed and even more foreign produce flooding into his supermarket, Jose is going to Palma.

"I can see you have benefited from the stay with your parents. Abstinence over the winter months seems to have done you good."

"Not total abstinence Jose. I only forgo sex while I am there."

"And now you are back one hundred percent fit to woo the ladies" Andres says, winking.

"It's funny you should say that. I am off to the airport now to meet her from the plane."

"How do you manage to maintain this amicable arrangement with her seventy-year-old husband? Surely he must know what is going on." Andres says.

"Of course he does. But while she remains happy, the old man continues to turn a blind eye."

"It looks like General Franco is on his way out." Bernabe interrupts, quoting from the paper. "He is about to hand over power to thirty-year-old Juan Carlos."

"'Huh! That is not before time. Once he goes, not only will I be able to own a passport, but I will be set to make my first million. Jose says, standing up about to leave.

"The redeeming feature about old man Franco, was the fact he recognised the potential of the Spanish sun. Realising that it was a commodity that could be sold, he instigated the massive tourist industry we have today." Says Bernabe.

"Well said young man. And so are you off whoring in Palma as usual Jose?" Asked Andres, looking across as his waiting workmen.

"'Not quite, business first and a woman later."

"I don't know Jose." Says Bernabe, collecting his working jacket from the back of his chair. "Does your wife have any idea what you get up to in Palma?"

"At the moment Bernabe you are a young pup in love with a beautiful Spanish girl. But with time, attitudes change. I work hard for my money and, just occasionally, as a reward for my labours I like to enjoy time with women in Palma."

Waiting until Jose and Emilio have gone, Bernabe then speaks to Andres.

"By the way," Michael has asked me to approach about a loan. They are still waiting for clearance to open the premises and in the meantime they have little money."

"How much do they want?' Andres asks lighting his black cheroot.

"They are talking about thirty thousand pesetas. What would be the interest on that amount?"

"Three thousand pesetas."

"That is steep Andres."

"'It is up to them. They can take it or leave it. Three open Credit letters to be paid back by the end of November."

"Look Michael, the Guardia of Civil are here. Two policemen have pulled up on motorbikes in the car park." I said, peering around one of the shutters on the window.

"Where," Michael asked, coming into the bar from the kitchen.

"No, stay back. Do not let them see you. They have just come under the arch and are walking up the path between the flower beds."

"Right I am going to find out what they want."

"No stop and wait. They are now circulating around the whole front of the property. You know what? They are looking to see if we have opened the premises without permission. Okay they have now turned around "I said, noting the back of their flat-backed patent hats caught in the afternoon sun. "They are returning to their bikes. Now for sure we will get clearance to open the "Bolero".

The very next day Mateo came to relay the news, received from the Police in Porto Colon, that we had permission to open the "Bolero". Visiting Felanitx market to fill up the fridges, and while Narcissus and I prepared recipes in the kitchen, Michael and Vicente stocked up the bar. However, on the opening day, the only customers to arrive for their mid-morning tipple, were Bernabe and Emelio.

"Well," said Emilio, hoping to break the obvious tension. "I like they design of this bar constructed in local stone. And the bar top made of Mahogany, sets it all off nicely." He said, climbing onto a bar stool.

"Yes, there is certainly a nice feel about the place." says Bernabe looking around, "What we need to do now is to spread the word around Cala Murada that you are open."

"That is exactly what we need." Said Michael.

At 4 o'clock that day Californian Dorothy arrived for afternoon cocktails and after studying the menu in detail left, promising to return the next evening with a friend.

"This is my friend Petronella, and she lives on the third circle close to where my brother Ted lives." Dorothy said, guiding the elderly Dutch lady towards a table close to the French doors in the dining room. At the same time, while they were left to read the menu, two unknown Germans also arrived for an evening meal. With all four customers choosing prawn cocktails as a first course, followed by entrecote steak with chips and salad and then ice cream with chocolate sauce. the evening went very well.

After two weeks in Edgar and Anna's villa, a young Belgian woman arrived to occupy the dormitory above. And on the third day of her stay, this young woman came rushing into the bar of the "Bolero" to report having seen suspicious activity taking place in the living accommodation below.

Apparently in the late afternoon, while lying out of sight sunbathing on the terrace roof, she was alerted by the sound of a car stopping on the road below. Initially not unduly perturbed, it was only after hearing thumping noises coming from directly below, that she decided to investigate. Peeping over the edge of the sun-terrace wall, she was just in time to see three people, two men and a woman, scramble back into a car before speeding off down the road.

'So what did you do then? Michael asked.

"I ran down the outside steps and noticed that the French doors leading into the lounge were open, "The young Belgian continued, in somewhat broken English.

"Thank you for coming to tell us. Would you like a glass of wine?"

"Yes please, I am quite shaken. I must say that at no time did I enter the villa."

"Right." Michael said, I am on my way."

After extensive investigations throughout every room downstairs, the only thing found missing, was my three-stoned diamond engagement ring taken from the jewellery box on the dressing table.

Thereafter with clockwork regularity and always in the late afternoon, over the next ten days, four more robberies took place in Cala Murada. For the most part, the targets chosen for the robberies were villas owned by German and Belgian families. With the robberies taking place while occupants were away, it became apparent that these opportunist thieves had knowledge concerning the movements of villa owners.

With policemen hiding in bushes and crawling about on their hands and knees looking for the thieves, the robberies were halted by one particularly astute maid. Working in the villa belonging Señor Martinez and spotting three persons climbing over the wall of the villa opposite before running back to the hotel, she raised the alarm with the manger. Just as the robbers were about to board the afternoon bus back to Felanitx, they were apprehended by The Guardia of Civil. While rumours abounded around the two men and one woman from mainland Spain, the suspicion remained that the thieves had worked with an accomplice from inside the area.

Financially, June turned out to be a disaster. No matter how hard Narcissus and I worked in the kitchen preparing an array of culinary delights, just a handful of customers visited the "Bolero".

"We cannot go on like this Jacqueline." Said Michael shaking his head. "We are paying two staff, who are literally eating us out of house and home and still we are not attracting enough customers to pay the bills."

"Yes, I agree with what you are saying. The reason we are struggling is because Pedro's bar and restaurant still takes the lion's share of the custom in Cala Murada. Look Ted is a regular, who brings friends, and I have noticed what they order. Their favourite starter is nearly always the speciality of prawn cocktail with fresh cream sauce. Well known and influential in the area, Ted also eats regularly in Pedro's. Let us see if we can attract more of the wealthy villa owners, by reducing the price of the favourite starter."

Whether it was down to the idea of reducing the price of the house speciality, or the fact that July was the start of the holiday season, but many more customers began to arrive. And by far the greatest proportion of the customers seated in the restaurant were German, Belgian and Spanish.

Anna's tip, the previous year, about integrating into the Spanish way, and speaking the local dialect, had put me in good stead. Now able to pass the time of day in Mallorquin with the fish lady of Porto, I was given the best fish and the largest prawns at a low price. However, characteristically careful with money, it did not take the Germans long to forego the main course. Choosing instead the house speciality of Double prawn cocktail with salad, followed by ice cream with *double* chocolate sauce.

"Trust them, to work out how to get their money's worth," said Michael with a wry smile.

As it turned out, fortunately for us, this well-known German trait was not perpetuated in other nationalities. Coming to eat at least twice a week, Ted was turning out to be one of the "Bolero's" best customers. On one of his regular visits Ted arrived with a lovely woman on his arm. Noticing his sister Dorothy coming up the terrace steps close behind, knowing the interest that would generate backstage, Michael came into the kitchen to spread the news.

"I thought that would happen." I said, looking out through the porthole in the kitchen door and watching Dorothy enter the dining room "I can see that Dorothy has gone to a table on the opposite side of the room, with her back towards her brother."

Whether it was down to some sort of game that Dorothy wanted to play out in front of her brother and his latest girlfriend, or perhaps she was just having a bad day, but nothing on the menu that day was to her liking. First complaining about the cutlery being placed in the wrong order in front of her, followed by the entrecôte steak being tough and the wine not kept cold enough but Dorothy was a dissatisfied and feisty customer.

"Take some advice from someone who knows about these things." She said, looking over her spectacles while settling the bill. "Vicente will never make a waiter in a million years. As far as the "Bolero" is concerned, he is a liability. You would be better off to employ someone else."

"What is more," Michael repeated, extending the case for the prosecution while leaning against the kitchen sink. "I personally do not like the way Narcisus cooks the food. She uses far too much olive oil and garlic which upsets my stomach. And because I have personally heard customers complaining about that too, I have decided to give them both a month's notice.

"Really. And just how are we going to cope alone with three boys and the business?'

"I have already thought of that. We can get a maid to help with the cleaning and us get more organised as a team.'

"Michael you are absolutely useless in the kitchen."

"Then, I will have to get better."

With the young couple gone by the end of July, and with the children home on school holidays, so the pressure mounted. Totally occupied with running the business there was little time left to tend the needs of our young sons. Always it seemed, the moment we sat down as a family to share a meal together, so customers would arrive to be served. Subsequently banished to the kitchen to sit on the back step, the boys ate their food balanced on their knees. Up until then it had always been Terry who was the most difficult boy to control. But now even the eldest son Michael was becoming resentful and disobedient. Meanwhile, as far as young Edward was concerned, this sudden neglect by his parents was manifested in a different way. Quietly retreating into his shell, the only

LIVING THE RING OF FIRE

time Edward allowed food to pass his lips was if, seated on either his mother or father's lap, he was fed with a spoon.

"And another thing,' Michael said, bursting into the kitchen. "Those German customers. They never sit at the table I want them to sit at. Instead of sitting at a table that has been cleaned, they always choose to sit at a table that has been used and is still dirty. They are an absolute pain to deal with" he said, peering at the customers through the port-hole in the dining room door.

"Michael," I said, pushing the tray of food into his hands. "'If you continue with this attitude, we won't have any customers left at all."

As if adding insult to injury, Mateo arrived to tell us that the application to have signs advertising the "Bolero" put up at the beach and the hotel had been turned down by the Residents Committee.

"The problem is 'Cobassa' and the residents want to prevent the sometimes, unregulated development that has happened in Callas de Mallorca, from happening here." Concluded Mateo.

'Well thanks for that Mateo. You might have told us that *before* we bought the land."

The two ways chosen to get around the devastating news was to type and then distribute notices through villa doors. Meanwhile with the children home from school for eight weeks, they happily distributed leaflets amongst the holidaymakers on the beach. Now at the height of the tourist season, by incorporating European dishes, such as Sunday Roast, Paella, Steak Tartar, and English Steak pies, August was a good month.

Extremely early one morning, leaving me sleeping and the maid busy mopping all the floors in the bar and restaurant there was a knock on the bar door. Irritated that somebody had arrived when the "Bolero" was still shut, Michael went to open the bar door.

'Well hello. You must be Michael." Said one of the three very sunburnt young men. "We met your little smashing kids on the beach yesterday afternoon. And they gave us these notices about you. So we decided to come and find where you were." Said the second young man with a distinct Yorkshire accent.

"Are you, by any chance serving English breakfasts?" Asked the third man.

"Well we weren't, but we are now. Come in boys and have a drink on me. Come tomorrow morning and I can guarantee a full English breakfast will be on the menu."

All in full swing the following morning, serving English breakfasts to the three Yorkshire lads, completely unannounced, Anna also came into the bar.

"This is my son Julian, 'She said. "And this is my friend Claude" She said turning to smile at the Adonis-like creature standing, silhouetted in the doorway against the sun.

"I did not know you had a son." I said.

"Yes, he is my son. Did I not tell you that Edgar is my second husband? We will be staying for about two weeks in the dormitory upstairs in the house. I have already left other friends in the villa.

"And who is that young man?" I asked, studying the young man wearing a sarong and carrying a bass guitar."

"He is a very good friend of mine".

"Really" I said, eyeing the much younger man than her. After stopping to consume Pernod, a Vodka and Coca Colas, Anna and the entourage left without paying the bill.

Extending the menu to accommodate the sudden influx of wealthy Spaniards, taking vacations in their holiday homes, a very tight schedule was put in place. At night once meals had been served, leaving Michael to manage the late-night drinkers, I returned to the villa with the boys. Each morning reversing the routine and leaving Michael to sleep, taking the children, I returned to cook English breakfasts and prepare food for the day. Then again in the afternoons, leaving Michael on the terraces serving customers tea and home-made cream cakes, I went to the beach with the boys. Circulating amongst the English and Spanish tourists, listening to the compliments made, I noted the firm favourite was English roast beef with Yorkshire pudding, followed by traditional English strawberry trifle.

Unfortunately, as things improved in the "Bolero" so the circumstances in the villa took a turn for the worse. Having Anna present upstairs in the dormitory with her friends, was like having some unseen canker in the place. In the early hours, with her pacing up and down on the concrete floor in high heeled shoes, it was impossible to sleep. After on particularly horrendous night, leaving the children and Michael to sleep, bleary-eyed I struggled up the road to serve the early English breakfasts. And one hour later, Michael arrived to take over from me.

"Why don't you go back and catch up on some sleep. You look absolutely dreadful."

"Yes I will. I need to go back, to bath the boys and do some washing".

Walking back towards the villa, from a distance, I could hear sounds of my sons screeching from the dormitory above. Standing at the foot of the concrete steps, leading to the top terrace, I called out their names. Calling for a second time, yelling at the top of my voice, all attempts were drowned out from the noise coming from the room above.

'Right!' I said, stamping hard up each step, making my presence known. "You wait till I get up there." I said, striding purposefully across the sun terrace. Just in time to jam one foot in the door before being shut in my face. Annoyed and with adrenaline rushing through my veins I burst into the room.

"What the hell is going on?" I uttered, aghast.

There stretched out on camp beds and mattresses, strewn about the room, the occupants languished in various stages of undress. While posing, wantonly, on top of one grubby mattress, wearing a swimsuit and strumming his guitar; was the young man with the flaxen curls. On one other camp bed wearing a transparent nightdress screwed into a ball around her naked thighs, and with the son Julian sitting cross-legged next to her, Anna sang at the top of her voice. Squinting across the room in the shafts of morning sunlight I could see, like something from one of Picasso's Blue period paintings, two naked waif-like creatures holding a towel in front of their groin.

Standing watching the boys racing about the room like wild savages, I knew I had a mutiny on my hands. Catching hold of Edward, as he flew passed, I whipped him up into my arms. However, completely ignoring my command, Michael stood defiantly next to half-naked Anna. Furious at this display of blatant disobedience, bearing down on my eldest, I slapped him hard. Now, acutely aware that retribution was about to be metered out and determined not to be caught, Terry fled out through the open door. Stopping to look back with disgust at Anna, the young family was herded from the sordid scene. And the next day, after making the regular visit to buy fresh fish and prawns from Porto Colom, I sat in the kitchen with Edward on my lap.

"Anna has been here this morning. She sends her apologies about what happened yesterday. She has had to return to Belgium, in a hurry. She knows that the dormitory is a bit of a mess. She expects to return in two weeks when she will clean it all up then. You are not saying a thing. Have you heard what I am saying Jacqueline?" Michael asked.

"yes, leave it to me."

With the lunch-time trade at an end, leaving the children with Michael, I returned to the villa. Taking the spare key from the garage, climbing the outside steps I went over to unlock the dormitory door where, the smell of unwashed flesh and sex pervaded room. Studying the crumpled sheets, soiled with body fluids, I began collecting the beer cans, spirit bottles, and remnants of half consumed food into a bag. It was while picking up butts of hand-rolled cigarettes that I found pieces of foil, milk bottle tops and bent spoons tucked into the side of one bed. Lifting the mattresses, along with boxes containing coloured tablets, I found needles syringes and blooded pieces of cotton wool. For the rest of the afternoon, armed with a bucket of hot water a broom and a mop, I eradicated all the paraphernalia associated with drug addiction. Just weeks after moving into the comfortable surroundings of Edgar and Anna's villa, we were once again back in D43. What is more, returning to basics, with lower walls open fields, we again had problems with ticks. Not only did Susy come in from the fields covered with ticks on her back, but they were found embedded in Terry's backside.

CHAPTER 10

Back in our first villa, with nights of unbroken sleep, I felt like a new woman. Parking the car and striding out along the quayside, I stopped to admire the ever-changing green and purple shafts of sunlight dancing on the sea.

"So what are you doing In Porto Colom so early in the morning?" Came a voice from behind. Immediately recognising Mateo's dulcet tones, I looked around.

"Good morning nice to see you. What am I doing here? The usual things, buying fresh fish and prawns from the fish lady. But today I am also here buying lobsters."

"Lobsters that must be a new addition to the menu."

"Yes it is. We have this Belgian couple named Monsieur and Madam Brichot. They are new customers who have requested lobster Thermidor for their Ruby Wedding Anniversary."

"I know them well. They are a charming husband and wife who came to live here in Mallorca directly from the Independence of the Congo. It would appear they could not face going back to the damp and cold of Belgium. Monsieur Brichot was Commissioner of Police in the Congo. He certainly has some stories to tell. Anyway, have you had any breakfast?"'

No, not yet."

"Then come and join me." He said, guiding me towards the nearby café, before holding the chair for me to sit. "I have to say that you are looking very well today. In fact, decidedly better than the last time I saw you.' He said beckoning the waiter to our table.

"That is all thanks to you Mateo giving us the opportunity to go back into D43. Staying in Anna and Edgar's villa turned out to be a nightmare." I said watching the waiter collect the fresh rolls and ensaïmadas from beneath a glass hood on the bar.

"Anna being a nightmare is nothing new. Said Mateo, pausing to break the *ensaïmadas* in two before dipping one half in the cup of espresso coffee "I will tell you something in strict confidence. "Cobassa" is not happy at all with the way things are going with the DuBois family. The truth of the matter is that apart from the initial deposit, paid by Edgar, the rest of the money owing on that villa is outstanding."

"So it's Edgar's villa? I thought the villa was jointly owned."

"No, the villa belongs to Edgar. Anna is his second wife."

"Yes so I head. And what about the son Julian that I met for the first time?'

"'He's Edgar's son from his first marriage."

"That figures," I said, recalling the sordid scenes in the dormitory.

"Anyway, let us not dwell on Anna. How are things going with the business?" Mateo asked, pouring me a cup of expresso coffee.

"Things are improving. With customers now requesting what they would like to eat, I am expanding the menu all the time. I am now producing French dishes like Steak tartar, Spanish gambas alla plancha, American grill steaks, and well as all the English favourites."

"In the very first year, with many mouths to feed, you could not possibly expect to make a profit. But, in time, I have no doubt that you will turn the "Bolero" into a success."

"I hope so, but right now, most of the signed Credit Letters remain outstanding. We are not earning enough to pay them. In fact," I said, pausing to light a cigarette. "Michael is considering selling the new car to raise the cash to pay off some of the mounting debts."

"What! But how could you possibly manage without a car?" Mateo added, incredulously.

"If we buy a small two-stroke motor bike instead, Michael thinks it could be done. I admit that the idea of riding a motor bike leaves me cold. Anyway, that is enough of our problems, you still have not told me why you are here this morning."

"I'm diving here in Porto Colom. I have a boat moored down on the jetty. Why don't you join me sometime? I know for a fact that you are a good swimmer."

"I do not know about that. I have never dived in my life Mateo."

"All the more reason for you to try. If Michael gives his permission will you join me?"

With my husband only too pleased to be left serving English breakfasts to his new friends from Yorkshire, I waited on the roadside for Mateo to arrive. Some twenty minutes later, arriving in Porto Colom, Mateo parked his yellow German car on a long ramp. Then collecting the diving equipment from the boot of the car, I was escorted down the jetty to a craft moored up against the sea wall. Looking on with apprehension, I watched as masks, and flippers, along with a harpoon gun were loaded into the stern of the boat. Hanging back I waited for Mateo to come back for me. Then lifting me from the quayside, into his arms I was hoisted over and into the pitching craft. Following one strong pull on the steel cable the outboard motor spluttered into life. As the small craft chugged out along the sea wall so a group of men, standing beneath the lighthouse, called out.

"What are they saying Mateo?" I asked, attempting to decipher the Mallorquin language.

"It is just the usual macho jibes from local men teasing me about taking a foreign woman out to sea.' Mateo said, smiling. "Actually, they are all good friends of mine.' He said waiving back to them. "They are literally the true connoisseurs of the sea. The men that have taught me everything there is to know about free diving."

"You mean diving down without bottles and just holding your breath?"

"Yes."

"How long do you hold your breath for?"

"I am not sure, maybe two minutes. Sometimes more, it depends on what I find at the bottom."

"How deep do you dive?"

"Fifteen meters or so."

"Good God, and all on one breath?" I asked, looking down at the darkness below.

Moving out beyond the harbour wall, so the wind picked up and the sea became choppy. Watching spume being flung up into the air before crashing back down onto the rocks, Mateo looked concerned.

"Is something wrong?' I asked, struggling to push the fair hair back from my face.

"It's the wind coming up from Africa churning up the sea." He went on studying the white horses curling on the crests of the waves. "We will be not be able to go out too far this morning. We'll have to stay close and shelter near the coast."

"Good." I said, relieved.

Turning the rudder hard to port, before skilfully manoeuvring the boat around a group of fearsome looking rocks into calmer water, Mateo hurled the anchor out from the stern.

"It's quite shallow and sandy here." He said, looking over the side. "This will be an ideal spot for you to attempt your first dive. I presume you did bring your swimsuit with you?" He said, beginning to strip off the white track suit and revealing a conservatively cut black swimsuit beneath.

"I already have my swimsuit on underneath." I said, standing up, wobbling about as I pulled off the cotton track suit.

"Aren't you going to join me?' Mateo asked, putting on the pair of flippers.

"Actually, I'm happy to just watch you." I said, admiring his powerfully built torso.

With the flippers in place, and facing backwards on the edge of the craft, with the mask pulled down over his eyes and under his nose, Mateo flipped back into the sea.

"Come on get in, its lovely." He said, playfully blowing a stream of salt water into the air.

"I do not think my equipment is good enough." I said softly, studying the flippers borrowed from Michael and snorkel on loan from the boys. "Here we go." I said, making the most ungainly belly flop forward into the sea.

"Where on earth did you get that mask and snorkel attachment from?" Mateo asked, paddling back and forth to stay afloat. "It looks like something you purchased from a street vendor on Palma Nova beach."

"You are not far wrong. I think with such poor equipment, I should give up now and call it a day." I said, eagerly turning back towards the boat.

"No, come here and let me tighten up that strap a little." Mateo said, swimming close to inspect the mouthpiece and pipe attached to the side of my head.

"It's okay, I will be able to manage." I added, acutely aware of the proximity of this handsome Mallorquin man. "I just hope there is not anything dangerous down there." I said, frantically treading water and looking down into the dark green depths between my legs. "I would hate to go back minus something." I said, clinging onto the boat with one elbow while spitting into the face mask to clear the mist on the lenses.

"Like what?' Mateo asked.

"'Well sharks maybe?" I said, relieved that my period had finished the previous week.

"The only sharks we have here, stay in the far south of the Mediterranean. We do have Moray eels of course. But as you are not likely to be putting your fingers in any crevices, you'll be okay."

"Oh yes, now I remember. That German lady who was bitten on the thigh by a Moray eel when she was snorkelling from Cala Murada beach."

"That is right. She was using a harpoon gun and the fish she had caught, was tied to a belt around her waist. Coming out from the rocks, the Moray eel took quite a lump out of her thigh. Anyway, are you ready? First, I will dive alone."

Still hanging on to the boat I watched as, taking an enormous draught into his lungs, and rolling forward into a right-angle dive, with the grace of a killer whale, Mateo disappeared below. With the snorkel mouthpiece in my mouth and my head down in the water, I watched Mateo descend to the bottom, where the sand puffed and shifted in the undertow. Moving from one rocky crevice to the next, between lacy fronds of seaweed, the Mallorquin swam through shoals of blue and golden harlequin coloured fish.

"Are you ready? It is not too deep." He said arriving back onto the surface. "Only about six meters. Stick with me and you'll be fine." He said, taking my arm.

"Six meters, that is nearly twenty feet! I don't think I am going to be able to go down that far."

"Yes you will. Just remember stay calm.' Mateo said towing me away from the boat. "Every action you take, in a dive, needs to be done slowly. Inhale deeply several times to fill your lungs." Mateo said, coming close. "Then take several large, big breaths deep down into your abdomen before taking the breath you intend to dive with. Get used to expanding your chest." He said, supporting the back of my head with one hand" "Breath as a baby does. Take one deep breath through your mouth and fill your diaphragm."

Attempting to remember the instructions holding on tightly, diving together, we went down to about ten feet. However, stricken by an excruciating pain in both ears, struggling free of my instructor, I bolted for the surface.

"Okay I know what your problem is"' Mateo said, coming back to the surface. "Lift the mask away from your face, and with your mouth shut, pinch your nose hard. You need to release the build-up of pressure in your ears."

Following another two attempts, I did manage to dive much deeper. Accordingly given the circle sign of approval by Mateo's hand followed by a thumbs up, filled with exhilaration at my achievement, I returned to the surface.

So did it all go according to plan?" Michael asked, leaning out over the balustrade watching us approaching up the path.

"Yes, very much so." I replied.

"Good glad to hear it. You deserved a break. Emilio is in the bar right now, and I am about to speak to him about buying our car." Michael said, going back inside.

"I must leave you both now, lots of things to do in the office." Mateo said, walking back down the steps towards the parked car.

"So what kind price would you be prepared to give me for the car?" Michael asked Emilio.

"Sorry Michael will you repeat that? Do you know, you are the first foreigner I have ever met that the longer you are here the poorer your Spanish has become." Says Emilio, offering Jose 'tapas' from the dish placed on the bar.

"Will you buy my car." Repeats Michael, this time in English.

"It sounds a bit like you in trouble financially Michael."

"Yes I am, we need to raise cash."

"How old is the car?"

"We have had it ten months."

"I will think about it and let you know."

Meanwhile spearing a mussel onto a tooth-pick Jose, supermarket owner and agent responsible for collecting debt on Signed Credit Letters, listened to the conversation.

"Do you know?" Emilio says, leaving the bar to walk down the steps with his friend. "Michael has already hinted to me that he is thinking of returning to England for the winter to earn more money.

"And leave the Señora on her own?" Answers Jose. "I am still waiting for them to pay the first signed credit letter."

"It is difficult for them. But I tell you what, when I have been there late at night, I have noticed the Guardia drinking on the outside terrace. The police like the seclusion away from prying eyes. And there is always a good atmosphere in the "Bolero."

By expanding the menu, along with even more unfamiliar faces, August turned out to be a good month. However, into September, as takings began to decline, so an unfortunate incident occurred. Two days prior to the expected transfer of ownership of the car to Emilio, deciding it would be prudent to stock up with butane gas, Michael drove to the supermarket. However, having discarded one seat on the driver's side, in bushes, to make room for extra gas, on his return the seat had gone. Extremely Irritated by such foolishness, without one front seat, Emilio greatly reduced the price he was prepared to pay for a car.

You know Jacqueline, we are now in so much debt, the money we are taking is just a drop in the ocean. And because we are getting nowhere, I have decided to return to England for the winter."

"Without us?"

"Look we have the dog Susy to think of. And besides where would we all stay in the UK? I have given it a lot of thought. For the winter months if you and the boys move into the bedroom underneath the restaurant it would cut down on the expenses."

"Once again you have made a decision without consulting me. You are set to leave us again. No, Michael," I said pushing him away, please do not touch me."

Arriving at the end of September for their second holiday, to discover we were without a car, my parents were shocked.

"So is that now your mode of transport" Asked my mother, peering over the balustrade at the little two-stroke motorised bike parked against the wall.

"Yes and not only that. Because we no longer have a car we have been excluded from the school rota." I said, sadly.

"So how exactly are you going to get the boys to school?" asked my father.

"We have bought two small cycles for the eldest to ride to school.

"And what about Edward?" Asked my mother.

"We will have to take him on the back of the two-stroke." Said Michael.

"It all sounds disastrous to me." Said my mother, lighting a cigarette.

However returning Cala Murada and to be involved in the promotion of a new bar and restaurant, Ivy was in her element. Not only was it the ideal opportunity for her to display her talents as an orator, but it was also an outlet to exercise her considerable charm. Dressed in her finery, mingling with the guests from the hotel, telling them all about the business started up by her daughter and son-in-law, it was a good way to promote business in the "Bolero."

"I have to say, that was money really well spent." She said, gazing up at the picture in copper, with lights illuminating the streets of Manacor. With the temperature still in the eighties, along with local residents, the bar was filled with British holiday makers. And while my mother relished the role of being a hostess the Belgian couple, Madame and Monsieur Brichot, danced to the music coming from the music player behind the bar. At the same time with my father helping behind the bar the chosen drink for the ladies' present was, either Sangria, or Daiquiri cocktail made from white rum, lime and grenadine syrup dipped in sugar.

"So how is it going with you and Michael?" My father asked, coming through into the kitchen to join me. "Michael has been telling me how difficult you have become lately." He said, taking up a tea towel to dry the plates. "He says that you are bad tempered all the time and uncooperative. Is that right?' He went on, placing the dried plates into a rack on the draining board. "I notice you are not answering me. May I remind you, that this whole venture was just as much your idea as it was your husband's. And you have only yourself to blame for the difficulties that you are now both in."

Without saying a word, I continued to plunge the dirty dishes even deeper into the hot soapy water.

"Right, I need an assortment of sandwiches for the bar." Called Michael, thumping his way through the swing doors by his backside. "And two prawn cocktails followed by rare steaks with salad and chips in the dining room." He said, in a raucous cockney voice, before disappearing back into the bar.

"So what did you think of that display of boorish behaviour?' I asked, my father.

"My God! I have completely forgotten what I was saying".

"It was something about me being a difficult person to live with. Could you help me please dad?" I asked, opening a packet of bread. "Start buttering the slices while I fetch the salad, ham and cold chicken from the fridge. While you do that, I will attend to the cooked meals for the restaurant."

"I am sorry to have to go back to a prickly subject," he said, starting to butter the bread, "But what is this crazy idea I have heard? You and the boys staying here while Michael returns to England?'

"We are really struggling and need more money. There does not appear to be an alternative." I said, opening the fridge to collect chicken and ham. "Besides, there is nowhere for the boys and I stay in England.

"That is a point. I just think it would make more sense for you to shut this place altogether during the winter months."

"Dad we have only just started to make an impression around here. The other bars in Cala Murada stay open during the winter and so we need to do the same. There are plenty of residents living here all the year round and they need to be encouraged to come to the "Bolero" during the winter months too." Rubbing the raw entrecôte steaks with crushed garlic black pepper and salt, I placed them under the hot grill. "We have made up our mind. The boys and I, will stay here for the winter."

"So tell me again." He went on, daintily putting lettuce, cucumber, tomatoes, and various meats, onto the slices of bread. "If the weather turns wet and cold, how are you going to get the boys to school?"

"I have already thought of that. They will have to be transported in relays on the back of the two-stroke bike."

"So how are the orders coming on?" Called Michael through the doors.

"All coming up now." Answered my father.

Taking the opportunity to ride the two-stroke bike, Terry sped off down the road from the hotel ahead of the family. Meanwhile, also heading for the beach, meandering down the hot road carrying the picnic basket, Ivy, along with Michael, myself and two boys stopped at the bar.

"Wait for me, and where is my tea?" Called out Edward, forever bringing up the rear.

"You know I just hate picnics and absolutely loath sitting on the beach" said my mother, flopping down into a sun lounger and glaring at Terry.

"What about a swim to the next beach?" Suggested Michael, hoping to avoid a possible confrontation between his in-laws.

"It looks like the boys are having a good time anyway." Said Terry, studying his grandchildren frolicking, like seal pups, in the sea.

"I don't mean them. I mean a competition between us."

"You can leave me out. I am happy to stay here sitting on the beach." Terry replied.

"No alright, what about us?" He said, looking at me.

"How exactly are we going to do that?" I asked.

"You swim the first leg from here out of the bay and along the coast to Tropicana beach and then I will swim back. We could hire a pedalo and then I could paddle close to you while you swim. It cannot be more than two or three kilometres from here to Tropicana beach."

"So you are not going to join us dad?" I said, knowing how good a swimmer he was.

"No thanks We are quite happy to be left with the kids. Leave us to open the picnic basket." He said, rolling a cigarette.

Waiting for Michael to collect a pedalo from the beach attendant, I was left studying the calm sea. In the early afternoon, with Michael paddling along nearby, the swim from one bay to the next went off without incident. However with the arrival of the Sirocco wind some three quarters of an hour later, when Michael entered the water, there was a marked swell on the sea. Less than three hundred yards out from Tropicana beach, Michael appeared to be in trouble. Battling against the strong wind and oncoming waves, waving his arms above his head, Michael called out for help. Slowly bringing the pedals of the craft to a stop and turning the rudder to port, I waited. As I thought, the moment I began to move slowly towards him, so the apparent drowning came to an end. Striking out with a lusty stroke, Michael began to swim towards me. Turning the rudder sharply to starboard, I began to paddle away.

"Jacqueline, come back, I am drowning." He said, spluttering and spitting out water.

"No you are not." I said, standing up from the seat. "You can bloody well swim back you double crosser. Squealing to my parents about what trouble I give to you. Stabbing your wife in the back like that. Showing absolutely no loyalty to me,. goodbye." I said, sitting back down on the seat to peddle away.

Arriving back somewhat ahead of him, I discarded the pedalo at the water's edge. Minutes later, stopping to pull the pedalo up out onto the sand, Michael joined me.

"You absolute bitch! Have you gone mad or something?" Do you realise I could have drowned?" He whispered, avoiding being heard by the family seated on the sand.

"No you would not. And I did like the drowning act."

Without a car, my father hired a car from Emilio for a few days. Taking it in turns to organise the days, I went with my parents to visit the old part of Palma and the magnificent Catholic cathedral. On another occasion, leaving me to serve the afternoon teas with cakes, Michael went with my parents to visit the enchanting resort, with its famous fruit and vegetable market, called Alcudia. Not being able to spare more than two days away from the bar and restaurant they were left to explore, with the aid of a map, the magnificent Sanctuary of Sant Salvador near to Felanitx.

Prior to my parent's departure back to England, a special evening was organised. Utilising the children and Michael, notices were distributed at the beach and to villa owners advertising the event. Guests arriving in the "Bolero" that night, included Monsieur and Madame Brichot, Ted alone, his sister Dorothy with her Dutch friend Petronella, Emilio with Bernabe, and two German couples. Including my parents, the tally in the dining room that evening, was thirteen.

While I waited in the kitchen, to receive the orders, Michael circulated amongst the guests studying the menu. On this occasion, as guests of honour, Michael went to my parent's table first.

"And what wine would you like?" He asked my father.

"A good dry red wine please. I will leave it up to you Michael to choose."

"What would you and mum like as a starter?" Michael asked, pointing to the selection on the menu.

"What are you having Ivy? I fancy the prawn cocktail. Would you like that too?"

"'Yes, lovely, thank you."

"And for your main course?" Michael asked, jotting down their order on his notepad.

"Ivy has already said she would like the Sole baked in white wine with sautéed potatoes and vegetables. And I will have the entrecôte steak, chips and salad with Chateaubriand sauce".

Turning around slowly to face the kitchen door, Michael delivered the order as follows.

"ONE STEAK AND ONE FISH!" He bellowed between cupped hands, like a Regimental Sergeant Major.

Refusing to react but with narrowed eyes, my mother sat tight-lipped. Meanwhile as stony-faced customers looked on in utter amazement, my father broke the silence.

"Do you know that has made all the hairs on the back of my neck stand up on end." He whispered to Ivy.

CHAPTER 11

The day of Michael's departure, on the 2nd of October, was truly a sad day. Not only was is it son Michael's birthday, but with so many commitments and creditors to appease, there was little to celebrate the event. Instead, standing on the terrace we watched as, taken to the airport by Emilio, Michael disappeared down the road. And on the very same night that he left, Jose arrived in the bar.

"During the winter months you need to change your menu to accommodate a different clientele." He said, taking a sip of his favourite tipple 'sol y sombra', dry Anis stirred into rough cognac. "At lunch times, you will be expected to cater for the palate of the local workmen which means adding roasted red peppers soaked in olive oil. And something else, mussels with garlic and parsley or maybe black olives served with cured 'Serrano' ham. In the evenings, you can change to cater for the palette of the residents."

"So tell me Jose, how comes you know so much about these things when you own a supermarket?"

"Because when it comes to making money, I am an expert. Trust me, I know exactly what will go down well here in the "Bolero". It could be good, leave it to me." He said, getting down from the stool and leaving.

So that more time could be spent with the somewhat neglected children, I decided to close the "Bolero" each Monday and Thursday. At the same time with a real upsurge in trade, I had to ask the maid cleaning the premises, to come four nights a week to help in the kitchen. Also, with the sudden early arrival of autumn rains, the routine for getting the boys to school had to abandoned and a new system put in force. Taking the eldest, on the pillion at the back of the little motor bike, Michael was transported the two miles to school. Leaving him at the gate, belting back to Cala Murada together Terry and Edward, hanging on like limpid mines behind me, were transported to school.

With this new coterie of customers arriving to eat and drink in the "Bolero" I was able to settle a bill, that stood outstanding for more than three months, with the local milkman. As this sense of camaraderie began to develop, so new faces began to appear. At lunchtimes, with Jose present, every stool in the bar was taken. Farmers, workmen and businessmen from Felanitx socialising and enjoying the tasty 'tapas, of sobrasada sausage accompanied with pea sauce on toast. On one such evening, sitting in the dining room with his regular German mistress, handsome Emilio was eating his favourite meal of 'Moules Marinieres'.

"I know of the Catholic school in Felanitx who needs a teacher" he said, savouring the dish of fresh mussels in wine, garnished with parsley and double cream. "The local priest in the school is looking for somebody, out of school hours, to teach his pupils the rudiments of English. I thought you might be interested." He said, slurping the liquor from the plate with his spoon.

"No too much for me to go at night in the winter. It is bad enough ferrying the boys to and from school on the bike each day. Thanks anyway Emilio.

On the Wednesday evening two ladies, accompanied by a young man, came into the bar. I recognised the ladies from having seen them, lying on the beach, during the summer months. But the young man with them, was a total stranger. Very quickly it became apparent that these elderly ladies, with French accents, had quite different personalities. While one lady was outgoing and bubbly, her companion was timid and withdrawn. Accordingly it was the lady, with the exuberant personality, who was receiving the lion's share of attention from the shifty-eyed young man. For over half an hour, amidst frivolous laughter both ladies flirted with the young man. Standing back while the gullible pair paid for their cocktails as well as his beer, the young man with the sickly grin, nipped and patted their wasted flesh. Wriggling skittishly on the bar stools, enjoying the attention heaped upon them, the two women giggled. Watching them fool about like vain teenage girls made me think of the famous painting by the Spanish master Goya, with his cruel interpretation of advancing age.

Three more rounds of cocktails and the pair were really drunk. It came as no surprise that the outgoing lady, with the peroxide blond hair, was having difficulty maintaining her balance on the stool. And while she wobbled about, gently patting the young man's cheek her friend, with lipstick smeared into a cupid shape above her top lip, lay in a crumpled heap across the bar. Humming a tune and obviously bored out of his head, the young man looked about for something to do. The moment he slipped down from the bar to stroll unobtrusively out onto the terrace, leaving the bar door ajar, my curiosity was aroused Standing at the back of the bar, drying coffee cups with a tea towel, I watched as the young man moved about the terrace, stopping twice, to retrieve something from the ground before placing it into his jacket pocket. Re-entering the bar, the young man, then slipped back onto the bar stool alongside the vivacious and still conscious lady. Not taking my eyes away for an instant I watched as, taking an object from his jacket pocket, the young man placed his closed fist on the bar in front of him. With the speed of a striking serpent, a plump black cicada beetle was dropped down between the folds of the woman's Georgette blouse. Because the lady was so drunk, moments elapsed before, pulling open the blouse, she spotted the shiny insect buzzing up against her sagging breasts. Screaming at the sight of the cicada trying to escape, leaping from the bar stool, the woman fled to the lady's toilet. Re-appearing visibly shaken and buttoning up the Georgette blouse, she climbed back on the stool.

"I flushed it down the toilet you very naughty boy" She said, smacking the young man's hand. Meanwhile yet again, the young man was putting one hand back into his pocket.

"Excuse me ladies," I said. "I think you should know that your boyfriend here has another beetle in his pocket. I know because I saw him collecting it on the terrace."

"So what have we here? The owner of a bar who does not know how to mind her own business and wants to spoil other people's fun eh? Well I think.." he said, getting down from the stool and walking, purposefully towards the hinged flap at the end of the bar, "..we should have a game with her."

Aware that the Susy the dog was asleep at my feet, banging her into life,. before heading towards the end of the bar to apply my full weight to the flap, I looked back at the l open pen penknife lying next to the sink.

"Good evening." said Mateo walking across to stand at the bar. "You okay? You look like you have seen a ghost." He said, climbing up onto his favourite stool and only too aware that something was very amiss.

"Better now you have arrived Mateo."

What is been going on?" he asked, looking back suspiciously at the threesome collecting their belongings.

"Would you like to join me in a glass of the best brandy?" I said reaching for the Carlos 1. "Then I can tell you what has happened." I said, watching while the unwanted guests left the premises.

"So from what you have just told me Jacqueline, I gather you do not approve of elderly ladies toying with the young blood of Spain," Watching him savouring his drink, I felt I was in no position to judge.

"Which reminds me, we are coming up to the very last event this year of the bullfight. Would you and the children like to come with me to Palma.?"

"Yes very much so. I have never actually been to the bullfight. I have only ever watched it on the television."

"Good, I will take you and the boys out to lunch and then we will drive to Palma."

"What day is the bullfight?

"Friday."

"That means I will need to change my two days off that week to Monday and Friday, I will have to ask the teacher Dona Antonia if the boys can have the afternoon off. Thank you, I look forward to it."

Parking the motorbike against the wall I could see the grey van, belonging to Andres, also parked outside Jose's supermarket. Collecting a wire basket from the stand at the front of the shop and proceeding down the first aisle, Andres approached me.

"Have you got the Credit Letter with you? I asked, my eyes still fixed on the tins of asparagus.

"Yes. Are you going to pay me?"

"Eleven thousand pesetas, that's right isn't it?" I said, putting the shopping basket down to take out my purse.

"Señora, that will still leave two letters outstanding."

"I know, today this is all I can manage." I said, counting out pesetas notes into his grubby hand and acutely aware of the heavy male musk smell of his body.

"This Credit Letter is well overdue," Andres said, rifling through the bundle of crumpled papers inside his jacket pocket. "Which means that the next Credit Letter is due very soon. I will be around to the "Bolero" shortly to collect it." He said, handing me the credit letter before adding the eleven thousand peseta notes to a thick roll of notes held in a rubber band.

"No Andres, I will bring the money to you." I said, turning away to take several tins of tuna fish and jars of olives from the shelves. Standing out of sight, watching the transactions taking place, Jose held several Signed Credit also waiting to be paid.

The following day, with just a handful of local men in the bar for '*tapas*' and drinks, and the children back to school, there was plenty of time to prepare the evening meals.

"Jose, I did not realise I had left the door open." I said, irritated that preparing sherry trifle had been interrupted. "Still, it's nice to see you." I said, looking beyond him at the stranger with him.

"The best cognac for both me and my good friend here Rodriguez.' Jose said, hugging the fat man by his shoulders.

Taking the "Carlos I" from pride of place, on the shelf next to the picture of Manacor hewn in copper, the honey-coloured nectar was served into brandy goblets.

"No make it three glasses, one for you as well."

"No thank you Jose, I've been adding up how much brandy I am offered during the day and it is far too much."

"Rubbish, cognac is great for settling the stomach. Anyway, Rodriguez here," Jose said, addressing the corpulent middle-aged companion. "He has come here today to look at his handy work. He is the boss of the carpentry business, in Felanitx, who supplied and fitted all the woodwork in the "Bolero".

"Really!" I exclaimed, hoping to God that he had not come to collect a considerable amount of money still outstanding. "Rodriguez, what a fine Spanish name." I said, deliberately setting out to flatter the flabby man with the piggy blue eyes.

"In ten days Rodriguez celebrates his fiftieth birthday. And we would like you to prepare a special meal for the occasion."

"What did you have in mind?' I asked Jose, while looking across at Rodriguez with jowls hanging over the collar of his shirt like a rooster's wattle.

"Some of your special vegetable soup followed by fresh lobster." Said Jose.

"And for sweet?"

Speaking for the very first time, Rodriguez answered the question.

"Chocolate éclairs, double cream and topped with nuts and chocolate sauce. It is my favourite."

"Shall we say eight thirty? And two bottles of pink champagne, on ice please, and have it uncorked at least one hour before we arrive." Concluded Rodriguez.

Once the two men left, I returned to the kitchen to finish the trifle. But within a minute, Jose was back.

"I almost forgot." He said, taking papers from his jacket pocket. 'I have been holding onto these Credit Letters, all signed by your husband, in my possession for several days. They are all due for payment." He said, handing them to me.

Quickly attempting to tot up the amounts in front of me, in disbelief, I shook my head. "Jose, these Letters amount to over twenty thousand pesetas. And I just don't have that amount tight now."

"Okay, so how much can you afford to pay?"

"Not more than six thousand pesetas." I said, running my fingers through my hair.

"Okay, at least that something. Leave it with me, I'll contact the companies in Palma and get them to hold off for a week or two."

"But listen Jose, I cannot guarantee to have the rest of the money to give you in two weeks. With winter coming on the takings in the "Bolero" are dropping all the time."

"What you need to do now is to organise special functions for the locals. We'll discuss it when we come for the birthday celebration."

Meanwhile, peering over his thick-rimmed glasses and drumming his chubby fingers, on the dashboard of his luxury car, Rodriguez watched for Jose's return.

"What did you go back for?' He asked.

"The usual business, I didn't want to embarrass her in front of you. 'Jose said, sliding into the leather seat alongside his friend. 'I'm holding several Signed Credit Letters that are due for payment."

"Can't she pay?" asked Rodriguez turning the ignition on the Mercedes.

"Not all at once, no. She's given me six thousand pesetas."

"How much more is left to pay on the Letters?" asked Rodriguez driving slowly over the bridge alongside the ravine.

"There is another fourteen thousand that is due immediately, and then more later this month."

"She is married right? So where is this husband of hers?' Rodriguez asked pulling up in from of the supermarket.

"He has gone back to England for the winter."

"What! and left that charming woman on her own. How irresponsible is that I wonder."

At lunchtime, on the day of the bullfight, after collecting me, we drove on to the school to fetch the boys at school. From there we drove to a local restaurant, close to the school called Es Espinegar, for lunch. There was no problem as to what the children wanted to eat. The choice was always the same Calamari alla Plancha - fried squid with chips. While studying the variety of specials on the menu, Mateo chose wild thrush with fresh herbs, wrapped in cabbage leaves, and basted in white wine. However, for me, having seen these beautiful songbirds laid out in boxes for sale in Felanitx market, I declined joining him. I chose instead the 'speciality of the day" and consisting of stuffed aubergines with fresh tomato sauce and chorizo sausage.

"I'll tell you something Mateo," I said, climbing into the seat of his car next to him, him with the boys in the back, "That meal was just beautiful thank you. But wild thrush wrapped in cabbage leaves will not be added to the menu in the "Bolero".

With the arrival on the scene in the sixties, of Manual Benitez, bullfighting had regained its popularity.

"El Cordobes", as he was known by his adoring fans, revived an interest in the blood sport that rivalled Spain's passion for football. With the explosion of television, this rugged and fiery young Spaniard brought the fights into the home of the Spanish. Displaying suicidal tendencies "this Beatle of the bullfight" turned bullfighting into a cult attracting the highest paid matador of all time.

Manuel Benitez of Cordoba, from where he took his name, was the youngest child of four. Born into a home of abject poverty, his mother died when he was young. Thereafter the task of rearing Manuel in one room, muddy and cold in the winter and intolerably hot in the summer, was left to his thirteen-year-old sister. As a self-confessed, juvenile delinquent Manuel rarely attended school and was regularly beaten by the local police. The only thing this boy achieved, banged up with little food and subjected to brutality, was to sharpen his brain and burn his lean body down to muscle and bone. On one occasion, playing truant from school, Manuel happened to see a film, about bullfighting, that was to transform his life. While the connoisseurs and aficionados of bullfighting poured scorn on Manuel's 'rather sloppy and crude technique with the cape, the rest of Spain adored him. As a Matador, "El Cordobes" possessed a charisma and bravery that was to set him apart from the rest. At the pinnacle of his career, he netted one million pesetas for every fight.

Arriving in Palma, to witness the afternoon fights, there was never any chance that they were going to see the 'Messiah with cape'. Instead standing quietly at the kiosk, on the outside of the circular building, we waited while Mateo queued for the tickets.

"Because we are almost into winter, I have selected seats in the sun rather than in the shade." Mateo said, returning to join us and escorting us to five seats on the second terrace back from the barrier. Sitting on concrete benches, covered with red plastic cushions, opposite the gates where the bull would enter, I had time to look around. With four banks of seats, only half occupied, the scene was far more intimate than I had envisaged. Watching relaxed Spanish families, chatting, drinking, and sharing food, the atmosphere was more like a picnic than an impending fight.

"It's not going to be too brutal is it Mateo?' I asked, glancing sideways at the boys.

"We have seen it loads of times on the television mum. Haven't we? Said Michael digging Terry in the ribs and continuing to blow bubbles with gum in his mouth. Leaning forward to rest his elbows on his knees his hazel eyes fixed on the bull-ring Terry stayed silent. At the same time, like many other youngsters present and seemingly oblivious to their surroundings, young Edward licked the ice cream cone bought by Mateo.

As a recorded fanfare of trumpets sounded, eyes of the audience turned towards the tunnel on the far side of the sanded and raked ring. With an immediate silence, so the attention of the audience was drawn to men, in black woollen hats, peeping out from pillboxes set proud from the wooden barrier.

"Who are they?" I asked.

"They're called '*novillos*'" Mateo replied. "They are aspiring young matadors who assist the Matador, and also practice the art of bull fighting."

When the heavy gates on the other side of the ring opened and nothing appeared, so an even longer silence prevailed. It was only with a good deal of banging and shouting, from the depths of the tunnel, did a bull poke its nose out from the gloom and into the light. With only his dark outline visible through the gates, swinging his head back and forth, the bull tested the air. Following several hard cracks to the rump, the noble creature stepped out tentatively onto the golden sand. With a back rippling with muscle and his dark coat glistening in the late afternoon sun, looking about him, the bull ambled off to the left. Meanwhile leaping out from one pillbox, like a sprung jack-in-a box, a young 'novillo' appeared. Flicking his cape, of yellow silk on one side and magenta on the other, in the direction of the stationary bull, he disappeared back into his protective hideaway.

"So what was that all about?" I queried.

"It's a way of testing the bull. The 'novillo' is assessing the bull's reaction to the cape. Up until now, that bull has never ever seen a man on foot. The first four years of a bull's life is spent grazing on the lush grasslands of Southern Spain where it is only ever encountered men on horseback. These bulls are especially bred for their qualities of aggression and bravery. That 'novillo', is summing up the characteristics of this animal. He needs to establish whether this bull is going to show bravery or cowardice. Do you see that man over there?" Mateo whispered, pointing towards a man dressed in a head-hugging black cap and standing behind the barrier on the far side. "That is the Matador himself. He too is assessing the bull's reactions to these very alien surroundings. Some bulls are so timid and frightened by the noise of the crowd they try to leave the ring by jumping straight out over the barrier."

"So how much does a fighting bull weigh?" I asked, studying the bull's girth.

"At four years old, somewhere in the region of five hundred kilos."

Suddenly, with the appearance of a second 'novillo', leaping out from his pillbox, any attempt on his part to goad the bull into an affray was met with a passive stare. Accordingly spurred on by the rebuff, pushing and kicking the cape before him, this second 'novillo' stamped and strutted in front of the bull. Nervously backing up towards the centre of the ring, the bull stopped still. Then at this poignant moment, dressed in his figure-hugging suit of pink and chocolate velvet and festooned with gold braid, the Matador made his first entrance. Parading around the perimeter of the ring with his woollen cap raised to the applauding crowd, nodding to his two subordinates, the Matador disappeared. Now, looking marginally more distressed, pawing the yellow sand first with one hoof and then the other, the bull stepped forward. With the quarry now standing in a more central position, the two young '*novillos*' appeared once more. With their bodies taught as the string on a crossbow and provocative movements, they flicked their capes across the sand. Now one of the two '*novillos*', cocksure of himself, actually turned his back on the quiet bull. With a signal from behind the barrier, retreating into the pillboxes, the '*novillos*' were replaced by men on horseback.

"Who are these men on horses?" asked young Michael, looking down at the horsemen wearing cream-coloured, wide-brimmed Andalusian hats.

"Picadors, or as some like to call them, the pariahs of the fight."

"Why pariahs?' I asked, admiring the two horsemen trotting passed in their bolero jackets of Prussian blue and brown velvet edged with silver thread.

"You will see soon enough. The task of the '*Picador*' is to weaken the bull by breaking down the powerful muscle tissue situated behind its head. Drawing blood fires the bull into action and injuring him in the neck forces the bull to drop his head. Without doing this, the bull would be far too dangerous for the Matador to take on.'

"That's not fair is it mum?" Exclaimed animal lover Terry.

"From what you are telling me Mateo, it would appear that everything is geared up to be in the Matador's favour."

'Not quite, injuring the animal only takes the edge off its overall strength. It does not prevent the Matador from sometimes being gored."

"Good" Said Terry with a broad grin.

As the proud 'Picador' trotted by, close to us, his chamois leather breeches and medieval-style chain mail armour protecting the lower limbs, could be seen clearly. And held firmly beneath one armpit, the 'Picador' carried a lance armed with a steel tip.

"Good God! I have just noticed that the horse is wearing a blind fold. He cannot see the bull."

"No of course not If the horse could see the bull, the rider would have little chance of getting the horse to move forward." Said Mateo.

Crossing paths in the centre of the ring before moving off to stand at one barrier, while one horseman turned to face the quarry, the other 'Picador' looked on. Totally innocent as to what was happening, instead kicking plumes of sand beneath its girth, the mighty creature tipped his head on one side. Thereby with just one gentle knock from a steel spur, the horseman and his steed moved slowly forward. Standing up in the stirrups, while tilting his head back for a better view, lowering the metal-tipped lance down to the level of the bull's head, the 'Picador' waited.

"The horse sometimes gets hurt. I know because I have seen it on the television."

"Not so much now Michael. Because the horse wears padding all down its flank. But years ago, before the horses wore protection, it was quite common for horses to be killed."

"Really Mateo? Well now I know why it is that Pablo Picasso has such a passion for the bullfight. As well as being a genius in art, he too has a cruel streak." I said.

"Mummy I want a wee." Whispered Edward.

"Not now, you will have to wait." I said,

"It is okay. I will take him." Said Mateo picking Edward up into his arms.

The moment the bull caught sight of horse and rider, turning the horse's flank towards the bulls' flying hoofs, the 'Picador' came forward. Charging in, headlong onto the waiting poised blade, the bull was stunned by the blow. Springing into action, hooking its horns hard up against the padding on the horse, the more the animal fought and struggled with the materiel, so the harder the rider rammed home the lance. Standing high in the stirrups to gain even greater momentum, the blade was turned several times into the bull's neck. While wrenching the blade free, finding its own path down one side of the animal's neck, a rush of dark viscous blood appeared. Considerably weakened and bemused, ambling away to find a spot at a distance from the tormentor, a spume of grey foam appeared at the corner of the bull's gaping mouth. Studying the tottering gait of the vexed animal turning his horse away, the 'Picador' joined his companion waiting at the barrier.

"Oh you are back" I said, as Mateo arrived placing Edward onto my lap. "What about the other 'Picador?'

"It is obvious he is not needed. The first 'Picador' did the job."

Suddenly, appearing from behind the barrier three men arrived dressed in embroidered silk jackets. Carrying wooden batons armed with darts and bound in coloured twine, they strutted across the sand.

"What are these men called?' Asked Michael leaning out watching them pirouetting and leaping into the air.

"They are "Banderilleros." Because the bull can easily outrun a man, they are very brave. If they are to avoid being injured or tossed into the air, their sense of timing needs to be spot on. A grown fighting bull can turn at a ninety-degree angle and toss a man into the air like a rag doll." Concluded Mateo.

"Good I hope he does." retorted middle son Terry, lover of all creatures great and small.

Meanwhile, obviously uninterested in the action, young Edward was busy collecting ice-cream cartons and lolly-sticks from under the seats to make them into imaginary cars.

As one 'banderillero', stamped his soft shoe in the sand, accepting the lure, hooking his upward-sweeping horns first to the left and then to the right the bull exploded into action. Waiting quietly, as the powerful beast pounded forward before diving under the 'banderillero's' raised arm, the skilled man avoided contact. However, for the unfortunate animal sweeping passed, the "banderillero" was able to plunge two coloured darts into the bull's, already, wounded neck. Equally as successful, with the weapon of torture, the same scenario was then played out by another 'banderillero'. However, in the bull's favour was the fact that, managing to deliver a glancing blow, the second young man was spun like a top across the sand. Lying prostrate on the ground, arms protecting his head, any chance of the stressed bull being able to strike a better target, was thwarted by the arrival of a 'novillo'. Creeping onto the sand, jumping, and waving the magenta and yellow silk cape, the bull was distracted long enough for the hit 'banderillero' to get to his feet. Now panting, with the spiteful darts hanging from shallow wounds, the bull dropped his head. In a desperate attempt to rid his body of pain, veering to the left and then to the right, the more the bull moved, so the weight of the barbed darts created convex heaps of flesh upon his bloodied back. Following a signal from a man at the edge of the ring the Banderilleros' marched off out of sight.

As the Matador entered, resplendent in his 'suit of lights', so a great roar went up from the crowd. Holding his black woollen cap high above his head before striding out across the arena, the Matador bowed before the spectator's box.

"Who is that man?" I asked, pointing towards a distinguished looking gentleman, leaning out of a box draped with the Spanish flag.

"He's the arbiter of the fight. Each fight has to be dedicated to him and, in turn, the arbiter judges the Matador's performance".

Striding out around the ring's perimeter, ignoring the bull, again the Matador acknowledged the applause from the crowd. With his shoulder length dark hair caught at the nape of the neck with a black ribbon, visible beneath a magnificently embroidered velvet jacket, the Matador had a white shirt and a black shoe-string tie. With black breeches caught at the knee by ribbons, clad in bright pink stockings and soft black shoes, the Matador carried a red cape over one arm.

"Why is the cape held out at that obtuse angle?" I asked.

"That magenta cape is called a 'muleta'. And that's another word you can add to your Spanish vocabulary." Said Mateo smiling at me. "Because the cape is heavy, the Matador needs to carry a cane beneath to take the weight. Also holding the cape open and wide attracts the attention of the bull."

"I can tell, you are a real connoisseur of the bullfight."

"Is he going to kill the bull" asked Terry wriggling.

"Not yet Terry and stop fidgeting. You need to sit still otherwise you are going to spoil it for the people sitting behind."

"When are we going home. chimed in Edward, abandoning his game of make-believe cars on the ground.

"Oh my goodness me" I said, noticing the fingers of snot dangling from each nostril of the stricken beast standing some ten metres or so from the Matador. With congealed blood glistening on his back and the tongue lolling from one corner of his mouth, the bull dropped his head closer to the sand. Minus preliminary foreplay but merely a few quick 'pas de chat' movements with his feet, strutting with exaggerated movements while sweeping the cape across his chest, the Matador walked forward. Immediately attracted by the movement of both man and cape, the bull also moved. Turning his lithesome body to one side and the cape spread before him, jumping into the air, the Matador accepted the challenge. As the frenzied bull charged directly into the cape so the horns became entangled in the heavy folds.

"Ole" roared the delighted crowd" As the Matador jumped free.

"Ole" was the sound once more, watching the Matador step sideways skilfully freeing the cape.

"While the bull's attention remains focused on the cloak, rather than the man, it gives the Matador the chance to display his skill and artistry with the "muleta".

"How much longer does this torture go on?" I asked, as the Matador went over to the wooden barrier to take a few sips of water.

"Not long now." Mateo said.

"Toro. Hola, toro' called the Matador, whistling and clicking his tongue seductively while stamping towards the animal, in the first throws of death. Laying the cape down onto the sand directly in front of the bull's nose, the befuddled creature bellowed with pain.

As the Matador raised the cape letting it swirl above his head like an eagle, with only inches to spare, the bull thundered passed the Matador's decorated chest. Totally fired up with pain and in a state of turmoil, the animal stopped to grind and pump the sand into plumes beneath its hoofs. Approaching this time with sensual pushing movements from his lower limbs, the Matador held the cape behind his back. Standing erect to expose his entire body to the animal, calling and clicking his tongue, the bull was invited to take the lure. And while the bull charged back and forth in ever decreasing circles, to the front and then to the back, the Matador stood his ground. "Ole!" roared the audience. Thoroughly weakened by the onslaught, its mouth gaping open, as the front legs buckled so the bull's nose hit the ground. With the Matador dropping down temptingly onto one knee, just a few feet from the head, the bull failed to move.

Raising one arm to acknowledge the roars from the crowd, cheekily turning his back on the bull, the Matador walked back towards the barrier. Handed the sword made from tempered steel, so the Matador returned touching the edge. Now side-ways onto the animal, with the sword resting in the crook of one arm, he squinted along the edge of the blade. With the other eye closed, focused on the gaping wound behind the bull's head, amidst a flurry of rapid scissors-movements from his feet, the Matador leapt towards the bull. With one mighty thrust driven hard up to the hilt, severing the spinal cord, the dropped dead.

"Look, do you see how the Matador is cutting off one of the bull's ears? That is indicates it was a good kill."

"We have had enough Mateo, let's go."

"I can tell you were quite affected by the whole experience. You have not said a single word." Mateo said, holding the car door open to let us climb in. Have you heard from Michael lately?" He asked, changing the subject.

"I have had two letters. One when he first arrived and then another letter two weeks ago. He is fine. He has managed to get a job, not in London with his parents but in Sussex."

"Where is Sussex? I am afraid I do not know England at all".

"It is on the coast. Michael is working for a bookmaker in Worthing and he is lodging with my father's sister. She has a lovely house close to the sea."

"It is a good thing he has found a job. Because "Cobassa" is now pressing me about the money still outstanding for the weeks you were back in D43."

"When I write I will mention it to him. That reminds me, I have a birthday celebration coming up shortly and it is to be a special occasion. Jose and this friend called Rodriguez have requested lobster for the main meal."

"So what is the problem?"

"The last time I prepared lobster Thermidor was back in the summer when Michael was there to kill the poor thing. Would you be able to do it for me?"

"Of course. I am going to Palma this weekend to stay with my mother, but I will be back on Tuesday. At the same time, we need to organise a day to visit Palma to apply for your residency. Now you have been here for nine months, without leaving the island. you are entitled to apply for permanent residency." Mateo said, pulling up in front of the "Bolero".

"Thank you. Come on boys we need to take Susy for a walk before it gets dark. Bye," I said, looking back.

CHAPTER 12

Before departing back to England, as an early birthday present, Michael had purchased a baby chicken from Felanitx market for young Michael. Housed in a large wire pen, with a roosting box set on the lowest branch of an olive tree, the well-fed chick was a picture of health. Admired by customers as it roamed freely both inside and outside the "Bolero" it was named 'Gallina Reina'. In the absence of his father, young Michael had adopted the role of head of the household. Brimming with self-confidence, the reliable eight-year-old was proving to be an asset. Cultivating his own piece of garden set against a sunny wall at the side of the bar, the boy grew herbs and vegetables for my kitchen.

Terry on the other hand, was a boy with an attitude. Often difficult to deal with, he could be both morose and uncooperative. Seemingly unable to adjust to the absence of his father, any household chores presented to him were carried out under sufferance. Also not to be outdone by his older brother Terry had acquired a pet in the form of a mantis and because the insect was so bloody ugly, the name of 'ugly' had stuck. At the same time drawn towards the more exotic variety of pets, as well as 'ugly' his mantis, Terry kept creatures such as stick insects, toads, and green frogs, all of which were brought to the kitchen door. Scaling high rocks, balancing on the narrowest of ledges, crawling into caves searching for fossils and quartz crystal, anything that involved danger, fired his imagination. As prime tormentor, Terry preyed on the gentler nature of his younger brother Edward. Aware that his younger brother was frightened by almost anything, Edward was constantly teased. The subject that created the greatest mayhem and distress, was to tell Edward that the giant cacti growing at the side of the road, ate little boys for breakfast'.

With the following Sunday turning out to be busy with lunches, Michael went on his bike to fetch the maid. Not only was the bar full of locals drinking and eating 'tapas' but, unexpectedly, Anna along with the stepson and another woman, came into the restaurant for lunch. And as there was money still outstanding from renting Edgar's villa in August, the entire bill for both drinks and their two-course meal was waivered. That same evening with Ted and two friends drinking and eating sandwiches at the bar two Guardia of Civil, dressed in their dark green winter capes, sat on the outside terrace drinking beer. And it was well beyond midnight before I finally managed to get to bed.

Following information passed on to me by Señor Martinez the schedule for getting the children to school was altered. Upon finding out one bus each morning stopped at the hotel before passing the school on its way to Porto Cristo I acted on the tip. Driving to the hotel, all that was required to persuade the bus driver to make a detour each morning, to collect the children, was a bottle of cheap brandy.

On the Monday, with the premises shut, I listened as the boys scampered about above my head getting ready for school. Lying in the small bed, enjoying the day off, I envisaged the action taking place. With Terry collecting the fresh milk, bread and sweet rolls left by the milkman, Michael prepared coffee in the bar. With the considerable attention given, Michael had become expert at preparing the workmen's favourite morning tipple of 'rasca'-black coffee laced with cognac. However, without my knowledge and excluding young Edward, Michael also made coffee laced with cognac for him and his brother Terry.

Waiting until the boys had left to catch the bus at the beach, I climbed out from the bed. Walking around the back of the building and up into the kitchen, still wearing a nightdress and dressing gown, I was pleased to find sweet rolls and bread laid out for my breakfast. Into November with the weather still pleasantly warm, opening the French doors, I allowed sunlight to flood onto the dining-room floor. Making a coffee before collecting the freshly baked rolls from the kitchen, wandering back into the dining room I sat at a table close to the open doors. With hearing acute as ever and noting the sound of a van approaching on the road below, standing up, I peered around the lace curtain hanging on the doors.

"Oh no," I said to myself, recognising the grey van pulling up on the car park below. Dropping the curtain back into place and trying to gently close the French doors, with so much early winter rain swelling the young wood, I could not manage it. Panicked by the sight of Andres and hoping he had not seen the curtain move, stepping away, I left the doors ajar. Taking a deep breath, I listened to his footfalls crunching on the pebbles on the path.

"God help me." I whispered. placing one hand over my mouth. "When the boys left for school, I did not lock the door behind them".

Gathering the hem of my nightdress and racing from the dining room back into the kitchen, I leaped out through the back door. Fleeing across the rocky terrain and forced to leap right over the wire pen holding 'Gallina Reina', both slippers came off. Now forced to run bare foot, sliding down the building close to the wall stopping to listen before jumping clear of the rockery, I slipped back into the bedroom below. Breathing heavily, leaning hard against the door, I turned the lock. With my mind racing in turmoil, as far as I could remember, the only person who knew where the children and I slept was Mateo.

"What can I do? How can I raise an alarm?" I thought looking at Susy's empty bed and recalling that the dog had been let out when the children left for school. "Out catching bloody rabbits that is for sure."

Hearing the footfalls of Andres, above me, walking from the bar into the dining-room, I knew approximately where he was. What I did not know was that having seen movement from behind the curtain and spotting coffee and abandoned breakfast on the table, the Mallorquin knew I was nearby. Stepping out through the French doors before walking the entire length of the terrace, Andres called out twice. Upon receiving no response, stepping back into the bar closing the door, Andres left. Riveted to the spot, waiting to hear the van door open and close, before climbing onto the bed, I watched him drive away. With legs like jelly and chattering teeth I flopped back on top of the bed. It was only the sound of Susy clawing at the door and the maid calling from the terrace above, some minutes later, that dragged me from the disturbed sleep.

"Mateo, I need to go to Palma today!" I said, arriving at the "Cobassa" offices the next morning.

"Why today?"

"Because I need to chase up the application for a telephone. We have waited for more than six months and a telephone is urgently needed, now, in the "Bolero"."

"In that case we can kill two birds with one stone. Firstly, we will go to the Police Headquarters in Palma to complete the documents, then we can go to the main telephone offices."

Completing all the paperwork necessary to apply for a residency proved not to be a problem. On the other hand, chasing up the telephone application was far more stressful. For over an hour, patiently moving from one glass cubicle to the next doing his utmost to break through the red tape the only thing to be achieved was a promise. from the Principal of the Department, that a telephone would be installed in the "Bolero" within two months.

"What days did you say the "Bolero" is shut?" Mateo asked, driving through Felanitx on the journey back to collect the boys from school.

"Normally Monday and Wednesday."

"Okay on one of those days would you like to go out for lunch and visit the monastery at San Salvadore? There is a good restaurant, at the top".

"Yes, that would be lovely. We visited the monastery once but did not eat there."

"And when did you say you have this birthday party?"

"This Friday coming. I have already ordered a lobster from the fish lady in Porto Colom. Early on Friday morning I will go to collect my usual order of fish, prawns and the lobster."

"Then I will come up at lunchtime to do the 'honours' with the lobster." He said smiling.

"Michael darling, can you do mummy a favour please? Can you go upstairs and look after the bar for me? I can hear customers arriving and I am still showering your brothers" I called, looking around the shower curtain.

Having adapted well to his new role ass barman, familiar with the prices of various drinks, Michael was able to handle money and give the correct change. Standing up on a stool tucked behind the bar, he was now able to reach bottles of alcohol and serve simple drinks. On this Friday evening, arriving later than usual, Ted came in to dine alone. In fact, he was still in the process of finishing his two-course meal, when Jose and Rodriguez arrived for the birthday celebration. Standing, anxiously, at the door leading from the bar into the dining-room, I waited for Ted to ask for his bill. Meanwhile, lingering over his double whiskey and reading a book, Ted's attention was taken by a banging from under his feet.

"What on earth is that noise?" he asked peering over the top of his half-moon spectacles. "That thumping coming from below?".

"Please excuse me, I'll be back shortly."

Racing down through the kitchen and the outside wall to the bedroom below, I found Terry and Edward having a great time jumping on the beds. With order restored and the youngest two back in bed, discarding the apron and replenishing my lipstick, I went back upstairs.

"All sorted out now?" Ted asked, curiously watching as I fussed about emptying his ash tray. "You seem to be somewhat on edge." He said, taking off his spectacles to study the adjacent table set out with fresh flowers. "It must be someone special tonight. Do you know I have the distinct impression that you are trying to get rid of me?"

"No of course not Ted. It is just that Jose and a friend have booked that table for a birthday celebration and I need to go to the kitchen to help the maid with the meal." I said, fidgeting with the box of cutlery on the dresser."

"Do you mean Jose the supermarket owner? Isn't that fraternizing with the locals?"

"Excuse me, fraternising with the locals," I said, "Is an integral part and the bread and butter of the "Bolero" As a matter of fact, I am thinking of staging a supper and dance here for the locals and the residents and of course you will be invited."

After settling his, bill, collecting his overcoat from the hat stand, Ted looked on curiously at the two Mallorquin men seated close to the wood fire.

After despatching young Michael to bed with a generous tip from Rodriguez and Jose, leaving several men including policemen drinking at the bar, the maid and I were left preparing the luxury meal in the kitchen. With the meal finished and the maid paid for her extra time, I joined Rodriguez and Jose to celebrate the birthday. While seated close to the log fire, enjoying drinks, the two men reminisced about the past.

The first thing learnt about, party boy, Rodriguez was, that he was an only child with doting parents. And that as a child, plagued with frequent attacks of asthma and one severe bout of rheumatic fever, Rodriguez managed to dodge conscription into the army.

On the other hand Jose, born in Northern Spain and the eldest son of a family of ten had come from a low and poorly background. Leaning back against the tapestry seats, Rodriguez and I listened while Jose recalled his past. At the age of seventeen, during the Spanish Civil war, he fought with the Republicans against Franco's army.

"The battle was so fierce, not only was I shot in the back twice, but my horse was shot out from beneath me. And because I was fighting against Franco's Nationalist army, I was then a marked man for thirty years. I notice you are sleepy Señora? so it is time we went." Jose said, placing several peseta notes on the coffee table. "Well are you going to tell her or am I?" He said, looking at Rodriguez.

"Those signed Credit Letters that Jose has been holding for you, well I've paid them all in full." Answered Rodriguez, waiting while Jose fanned the Credit Letters across the coffee table.

"But those Signed Letters amount to over two hundred pounds!" I exclaimed.

"Really, if you say so. Sorry we only deal with pesetas. But I have to say." Rodriguez continued, resting a chubby hand on my arm, "It is none of my business., but all these debts should have been put in an envelope and sent to your husband."

"That is easier said than done Rodriguez. It is me dealing with the creditors face to face. As far as my husband is concerned it is a question of out of sight out of mind. And as I cannot promise to pay this money back, I cannot accept this offer from you."

"It's not a loan. There are no strings attached. I have enjoyed a good birthday with great food and in the company of a lovely woman. I have more cash than I know what to do with. I am not married, I have no children, and both my parents are dead. You cannot enjoy money from the grave. You know what they say about no pockets in a shroud?"

"Take these Letters Señora, and do not look a gift horse in the mouth," Jose prompted. "And before we go, both

Rodriguez and I have been thinking about this special Mallorquin evening in the "Bolero" It could be another good way to promote business. We have come up with this idea of a typical Mallorquin meal, with traditional food cooked on the open fire. I could supply all the ingredients needed, from my supermarket at cost price. Rodriguez and I are willing to prepare and cook the food for you. What do you say? We will leave it up to you to decide when."

On the following Sunday, short of a few groceries for lunch, I rode up to Jose's supermarket. Parking the bike at the steps, I spotted the grey van belonging to Andres outside of Pedro's bar. Walking into the supermarket I looked around for Jose.

"Good morning, I am glad I have found you Jose. I have here the full amount owing to Andres on the outstanding Credit Letters. I see he is in Pedro's bar this morning and as I do not want to interrupt his morning break would you pay him and collect the Credit Letters from him?" I asked, counting out the peseta notes into his hand.

"Leave it with me. And have you thought of a date for the Mallorquin supper? Emilio has just departed back to the mainland for the winter months so he will not be able to come."

"Sorry to hear that he is such good company. Any way to answer your question I suggest next Saturday. That will give me time to speak to various customers and to put notices through villa doors. We can catch up on the finer details during the week. Sorry need to go, I have run out of lemons, olives and sugar." I said, collecting a basket.

"Hi there. How's it going?"

"Hello Ted, you are just the person I needed to see. As promised, I am staging the Supper and dance next Saturday. Will you come?"

"No, I cannot make next Saturday because I am leaving for Germany. Having a break in my Berlin flat for a few days."

"Another time maybe Ted and enjoy your holiday. Must fly now I have left son Michael holding the fort in the bar."

"So what nice things have you got on the menu today?" asked Dorothy climbing onto the bar stool next to her friend Petronella Van Gellan.

"One of your favourites Dorothy. Baked hake in white wine with bay leaves. And I am so pleased you two have come for Sunday lunch. I am organising a special local Mallorquin supper next Saturday and I am hoping you two ladies will be able to come." I said, watching Petronella whispering into Dorothy's ear.

"Well that depends. I do not know whether you are aware Jacqueline, but Petronella here lives in the villa directly opposite my brother Ted. And neither of us fancy cosying up by the fire with him for the evening."

"What a coincidence, funny you should say that. Ted cannot come because he is going to be in Berlin for a holiday."

"That is welcome news. Then you can add us to the list."

I did hope that joining them after their lunch, for daiquiri cocktails, Dorothy might disclose something about the ongoing rift with her brother, but it was not to be. Instead sitting with them at the bar, I listened to Petronella talking about her experiences interned in a Japanese Prisoner of war camp, during the Second World war.

In 1942 the Japanese overran the Dutch East Indies. At that time Petronella and her husband, both in their thirties, were teaching on the islands. Subsequently captured by the advancing Japanese army, while Petronella and her two young daughters were put in one camp, her husband and thirteen-year-old son were placed in another camp for men.

Held captive for three years the treatment received was brutal. Plagued by mosquitos, the wet heat and little medicine, malnutrition was the biggest enemy. Handed out one cup of rice each day, it was a question of eating anything else that could be caught. For these women subjected to prolonged starvation, meant that their menstrual cycle stopped. Another issue, prevalent in the camps, was that to obtain fruit and extra rice for the children, it was common for mothers to sleep with their Japanese captors.

"Three years of prolonged deprivation has left Petronella here with poor sight. That is why I have to ferry her around by car.." Said Dorothy, lovingly stroking her friend's hand.

"What a story! So what happened after you were released Petronella? Did your husband and son survive?"

"Yes, once re-united, we returned to live in Holland. But sadly the experiences in the camps and being apart for such a long time, affected us greatly. Now like strangers and no longer compatible we decided to divorce. My husband moved to America with our son and married again."

"And your two daughters?"

"They still live in Amsterdam."

"So how come you finished up living here in Mallorca?" I asked.

"That is a story for another time." Interrupted Dorothy, climbing down from the bar.

"By the way. In order that you can watch this special supper being prepared on the open wood fire, could I ask you to be here sharp at eight next Saturday?

"Of course, we will be here."

On the day of the special supper, the early morning was spent transporting pine wood from the garden, in a wheelbarrow, up behind the premises. Thereafter, taking advantage of the warm autumn sun the children and I took the dog down into the wooded ravine. With the onset of the winter rains, the flowing stream now teemed with fauna and flora. Threading our way through the thick ferns clinging to our legs, an argument broke out between the eldest two boys.

"I want to be on my own." Said Terry, stubbornly marching off upstream towards the cliffs.

"Now do not be away too long. We need to go back early to prepare lunch. Meet you at the beach in half an hour Terry" I called out.

Joining up again later at the beach. Terry said nothing about what he had found in the reeds of a pond. Instead strolling together with Susy, across the sand we met the German mother Mrs Faulhaber.

"How are you? she asked. You must be busy today. As my husband is at sea on the oil tanker in the far East, I will be bringing a neighbour with me tonight. If you like, I could take the children back with me. They can have lunch with Jentz and then I will fetch them back later in the car. It will give you a chance to get things done."

As it turned out they were all back sooner rather than later. I had only just started to prepare the 'tapas' when Mrs Faulhaber arrived in the car park below. Walking out onto the terrace, I could see Mrs Faulhaber was having difficulty trying to restrain Terry, sobbing, and struggling to break free.

"Sorry.' She said, holding onto the fighting boy while hauling him up onto the terrace steps. "I needed to bring the family back. There has been a bit of a disaster involving young Terry and the men working on my new extension."

"Go on, what has happened?' I asked, walking down the steps to grab Terry by the arm.

"Even though it started to rain, waiting while the maid prepared the lunch, I did allow the children to go out into the garden to play. I do not suppose for a minute that you knew Terry had a green poisonous frog in his pocket. Anyway, from what I gather, Terry took the frog from his pocket to show it to the workmen. Naturally alarmed by what they saw, snatching the frog from Terry's hand the workmen flattened it dead with the back of a spade." Mrs Faulhaber said, noticing Terry burst into tears once more. "No matter how much the workmen tried to explain to him that, if threatened, this type of frog exuded poison through its skin, Terry has remained inconsolable. All he has kept saying is that the little frog in his pocket did not hurt him."

"Thank you for bringing them home." I said, guiding the miserable trio back inside.

"I just hate this place." Exploded Terry, his hazel eyes brimming with tears. "I want to go back to England to be with my dad."

"And we don't like you working all the time um." Chimed in Michael supporting his brother. "You are always leaving us on our own."

"And if we went back to England, what would happen to Susy?" I said, taking off Edward's wet socks and shoes.

"We could find somebody to look after her." Terry said, his cheeks still wet from crying.

"And what about the chicken?" I asked, pulling Edward up onto my lap.

"The farm would look after 'Gallina Reina' for me. Could we go back home for Christmas mum?" Asked Michael.

"So you do not really think this place is your home?"

"No we don't." Snapped, dry-eyed Terry.

As usual with young Michael, stationed behind the bar, Mateo was the first to arrive. Helping me to drag tables, between us, from the restaurant into the bar everything needed for the Mallorquin supper was in place. Next to come through the bar doors were the Belgian couple Mr and Mrs Brichot, closely followed by Dorothy and Petronella. Then after applying the finishing touches to the 'tapas', I walked about switching on welcoming lights.

"Buenas noches Señora." Said Jose, coming in followed by Rodriguez close behind. "I will leave these letters from Andres here on the bar. You know what I mean? He said, with a quick wink. "So what have you prepared Jacqueline, for the special meal tonight?"

"A typical Mallorquin meal of slow cooked beef, sealed in goose fat, with herbs and spices."

"Sounds great." Said Rodriguez, walking across the bar to inspect the freshly lit log fire. "If you prepare the food, I'll go and find two large stones." He said, watching Jose tip several packs of, cellophane wrapped, ingredients out onto the hearth.

"What do we need stones for?" I asked, joining the pair at the fireside.

"If you go and fetch two racks from your oven in the kitchen, then I will show you what we do with the stones." Said Jose.

"In the meantime, my son and I will begin serving drinks. Oh good evening, welcome to the "Bolero"" I said, greeting Mrs Faulhaber and her friend now coming through the front door.

"This is my friend Emma. I think it is her first visit to your bar and restaurant. And I have also brought other neighbours with me tonight, for the special meal." she said, guiding two strangers towards the bar.

"Please to meet you both." I said, shaking their hands. "And your names"?

"My name is Lucas, and this is my wife Amelia. We come to spend the winter here in Mallorca. But we live in Germany the rest of the time. We have a house close to the Mona Dam."

"How is it that all German customers speak such good English, while our knowledge of German is absolutely rubbish." I said, greeting them warmly. "Anyway welcome, please take a seat," I said, images of the famous film 'The Dam Busters' going through my head.

At that moment, coming in from the garden, carrying two flattish stones, Rodriguez watched Jose wedge the stones in against the sides of the hot fire. With oven racks duly collected from the kitchen and placed on top of the stones, Jose and Rodriguez began setting out succulent fillets of pork, sliced carves liver marinated in parsley, garlic and oil, and spicy *sobrasada* sausage on plates in front of the fire.

Leaving these obviously skilled cooks to baste the meats with brushes made from the leafy stalks of celery, I went to through to check on the braising meat. Returning wearing oven gloves, the huge terracotta pot filled with braised beef was placed onto one central table. Following another five minutes of basting with lemon juice, parsley and garlic, the glistening cooked meat was laid to rest on plates I front of the fire. While I went amongst the customers serving dry sherry, son Michael carried a tray of 'tapas' around amongst the guests.

"I am most impressed," said Dorothy, accepting the sherry and taking an opened mussel from a plate. "As well as barman Michael is turning out to be an efficient waiter too."

"Please help yourself to the food." I said, setting out the bowls of freshly made salad, cooked rice, together with bottles of local red and white wine.

"What a spread, absolutely delicious." Said Mrs Faulhaber, an hour later, while dabbing her mouth with a serviette. "That trifle of fruit, jelly and sponge soaked in brandy with cream? It is a recipe you must give to me sometime. Can I be greedy and have some more?" she asked.

"I agree, this meal has been worth every penny. Tell me Jacqueline, before you came to Mallorca did you have a restaurant in England?" asked Mr Brichot.

"No not at all. I was a housewife that is all."

"So I assume you have never been to Africa?"

"'No, why do you ask?"

"Well people's background can be interesting. Before coming to live on this island and prior to the Congo gaining its independence from Belgium, I was Commissioner of Police in central Africa for more than ten years."

"That is interesting, because my own father had Dutch ancestors originating from South Africa."

"Didn't your brother Ted serve in the Congo for a while? Petronella said looking towards Dorothy.

"Yes serving in the American army he was in several parts of the world." Said Dorothy. "My half-brother has quite a reputation with women. Anybody who wants to know what he gets up to, the person to ask, is Petronella." Dorothy said, nudging her friend. "Her villa is on the opposite side of the road to where Ted lives. And let me tell you, Petronella's failing eyesight does not prevent her from peeping around the lace curtains, watching the ladies come and go. Ted enjoys the attention it creates because he goes out of his way to brag about how many women he has bedded.

As raucous laughter exploded from the merry customers, so Dorothy's attention was taken by Michael still standing quietly behind the bar.

"I think it is time there was a little whip around for the barman, before he goes to bed. Don't you think?" Dorothy said, handing an empty ashtray around. Grinning broadly while cradling two handfuls of peseta coins, Michael made an exit.

"So continue Mr Brichot, tell us some more about East Africa."

"Before Independence and while the Belgians remained in charge in the Congo, everything was fine. But following Independence and the arrival of terrorist organisations into the Congo, life became so difficult that Madam Brichot and I decided to leave."

"Of course there have been similar problems like that all over Africa, particularly in Namibia." Said Mrs Faulhaber

"Before I put on some music, is there anybody else who would like to tell us a story?

"Well most of us have heard about Petronella's experiences banged up in a Japanese prisoner of war camp." Said Dorothy.

"Yes," I said, glancing at the middle-aged Dutch lady with the clouded blue eyes and plaited greying hair coiled around her ears. I did not say anything, but what I secretly wanted to know, was whether Petronella was amongst the women who gave sexual favours to the Japanese officers.

"I have a story to tell." Volunteered Mrs Faulhaber. "During the Second World War, at the age of twenty, my husband was made captain of a 'u' boat. And on his maiden voyage, sunk by a destroyer in the English Channel he was taken prisoner. Working on a farm in Kent for one year, he was well looked after and learnt to speak good English.

"Brought into the war when he was so young." Said Mateo.

"Yes, that was because by the end of the Second World War Germany had lost so many older men in battles at sea."

"Well you have been quiet tonight Mateo. Have you anything to tell us?" Asked Rodriguez.

"No nothing as interesting as what we have all just heard."

"Mateo is far too modest. He is a black belt in Judo and a skilled diver. He dives to great depths with just holding his breath." I added.

"How do you know that?" Jose asked, his almost black eyes locked onto my face.

"Because we dived together, in Porto Colom, during the summer." I said, smiling at him. "When Michael was still here."

At that point, gazing about the bar, totting up in his head the amount still outstanding for the work carried out in mahogany by his workmen, Rodriguez was undecided as to whether to wait, before presenting the bill of 200,000 pesetas to the proprietor.

"I think it is about time we had more drinks." He said, "Open up three bottles of your pink brut champagne and add it to my bill." Said Rodriguez. "What about you Señora? We know nothing of your past."

"Well I did manage to survive the London Blitz, which killed more than 35,000 people and endured a horrible childhood. Apart from that I married very young, had three sons, and came here to Mallorca to open a bar and restaurant. Anyway, that is enough for now, it is time for some music" I said moving behind the bar selecting the tapes with the best music from the sixties.

Until one o'clock the next morning, drinking champagne and Madeira wine, the customers danced around the bar to the sounds of Roy Orbison, Elvis, and Dusty Springfield. Watching Mr and Mrs Brichot dance to Mick Jagger's rendition of 'It's all over now', was a sight to behold. Quite drunk and held close in Jose's arms, we waltzed together slowly around the bar, to the voice of Sinatra singing 'Moon River'. "I did not know you could dance." I said.
"I can with you." Whispered Jose.

CHAPTER 13

Acutely aware that the next instalment of 900,000 pesetas was almost due, and hoping that on a Sunday, Michael might be with family, I went on the bike to the hotel.

"Can I use the phone please Bernabe? I need to phone the UK. I will pay for the call."

"We have all heard that the supper and dance last night, was a great success. When you decide to put on another one, my fiancée and I would like to come."

"Yes I will," I answered softly, still nursing a sore head.

"Good to speak to you." Answered my mother- in- law. "I am sorry Michael is not here. He has decided to stay in Worthing with your aunt this weekend. Can I give a message? I am sure to hear from him during the week."

"I just need the telephone number of the betting shop where he is working in Worthing." I replied putting down the phone and having already anticipated that the phone call would be a waste of my time.

With the bus driver continuing to collect the boys from the beach, the problem remained about collecting them, from school, in the afternoon. On the Tuesday, the morning started out cool and cloudy. But by the time I left in the afternoon, the rain was sheeting down like stair rods. Pulling up at the school gate, soaked to the skin, I noticed the Dutch father waiting to collect his son, along with other children in the school rota. Keeping his eyes averted while herding the youngsters into his car, before reversing out into the road, he drove away. Meanwhile standing together, in the deep wet grass, and dressed only in their skimpy blue and white cotton gingham smocks my bedraggled trio looked quite forlorn.

"Thank you very much indeed." I yelled at the retreating car. "The Levite that passed by on the other side of the road.' I cursed, hoisting Edward first and then Terry onto the pillion at the back of the bike.

"Wait there Michael. Go and shelter under the covered porch at the entrance of the school. I will be back shortly." I said, kicking the little two-stroke engine into life before weaving from one side of the road to the other, avoiding the potholes filled with muddy water.

At the end of that week, Ted arrived with the man I met at the Mallorquin supper called Lucas, along with another gentleman I had not seen before and introduced to me as Klaus.

"Three glasses of my usual dry sherry." Ted said, guiding his two companions towards the log fire. "We are going to eat our meal here in the bar where it's warmer."

"I am sorry to tell you that I do not have any of your favourite sherry tonight."

"So what have you got instead?" asked Ted.

"Not sherry. Gin and tonic maybe?"

"What do you think? He asked, watching the other men raise their shoulders in muted compliance. "Alright, gin and tonic it will have to be".

Following their hearty meal of sirloin steak with all the trimmings and followed by ice cream and chocolate sauce, Ted asked for three for Irish coffees.

"I remember you telling me Lucas, that you have a house close to the Mona dam?" I said, placing the tray of Irish coffees on the olive wood table near to the fire. "Is that not the place where the bouncing bomb destroyed the dam?"

"Yes that is right. The river Rohr is the place where the bomb broke through the dam. But it was not nearly as romantic as the film made it out to be, nor as devastating to Germany. Within three months both the factories and power stations, situated above that dam, were all operational once more."

"Excuse me, can you come and serve us please." Asked the two policemen, and the only other customers sitting in the bar. "And what are those men drinking?" asked one policeman studying the coffees on the side table.

"Irish coffee." I said, walking over to them.

"What is it made with?"

"Black coffee, and Scotch whiskey topped with double cream."

"That sounds good, we will also have two please." Coming over to the bar, the two policemen watched as I prepared the Irish coffees.

"And we will have the same again. Three more Irish coffees over here." Called Ted.

Knowing, without even looking in the fridge, I did not have enough cream to serve the repeated order, it felt like my heart had sank.

"I am sorry, I do not have the cream to serve more Irish coffee." I said, walking sheepishly across to them.

"You know Jacqueline? You cannot run a business on a shoestring. Since Michael left this place has started to go to the dogs. So, can you give us black coffee and Scotch whiskey? That is of course if you have any whiskey left.." Ted said, nudging Lucas with his elbow.

But the three men were not finished. The moment the two policemen left, so their intimidation continued. Demanding their glasses to be changed, before knocking one full glass of coffee onto the cream tiled floor. Even though I was there in a flash to mop up the coffee, the stain remained.

"It is nearly midnight and I am very tired. Would you please go." I asked, holding back the tears.

CHAPTER 14

The next morning and having not slept a wink, the moment the children left, I drove to Dorothy's villa on the first circle.

"Hello, so what are you doing here so early in the morning?" Dorothy said, opening her front door still wearing her silk dressing gown.

"Can I come in? I need to speak to someone."

"Yes, of course. What is the matter? You are shaking like a leaf and have dark circles under the eyes. Please come in and sit down I have just brewed some fresh coffee.

"Last night I had an extremely stressful time being humiliated and bullied by Ted and two of his friends. It was obvious they were taking advantage of the fact that I am on my own."

"But why would he do that? He is a good customer." Dorothy said, arriving at the table with the china mugs.

"Dorothy I said, ignoring the poignant question "Would you mind telling me what the problem is between you and your brother? Is it because his father is German?"

"Not at all, it is a personal matter. Drink your coffee and I will tell you what you want to know. It involves two stories really. Ted has a flat in Germany and a couple of years ago my son Peter and I were invited to spend Christmas with him and about that time he was seeing a young woman living in Berlin. Anyway, one week before we arrived, this particularly stunning young blond asked Ted what he wanted for a Christmas present. Knowing Ted and what he is like, playfully told her that all he wanted for Christmas was for her to be delivered to him, in a box, naked as the day she was born."

"Oh that is absolutely priceless! So go on Dorothy, what happened?"

"Okay so while my brother was out shopping for presents Peter and I stayed in the flat. Answering a knock on the front door, my fourteen-year-old, was confronted by a life size cardboard box, placed upright in the doorway. Written on a Christmas label, tied with a red ribbon around the box, were the words "Happy Christmas darling. Please open me."

"Oh, I know what is coming." I said, laughing out loud.

"Exactly" Dorothy said, her violet blue eyes rolling. "Untying the ribbon and pulling down the front of the box, standing with a pink ribbon and a large silver ball dangling between her breasts, was the blond Berliner as naked as the day she was born."

"So tell me, how did the girl manage to get from the street into the foyer of the building and then into the box without any clothes?"

"Ted organised it all. The girl arrived in a taxi, along with the folded box. Tipping the doorman he agreed to go along with the plan. Taking the blond first up in the lift he erected the box and put her inside. Waiting for her to take off her clothes inside the box and leaving them at the bottom, the doorman tied the label and knocked on the door. That was how it was done."

"Surely that is not the reason you have nothing to do with Ted?"

"No, a more serious problem occurred between that Christmas and New Year. Switching her allegiance from Ted to my son, the blond gave Peter some lessons in sex education."

"'So your fourteen-year-old lost his virginity to a blond Berliner? What a story!" I said, getting up to leave.

"You know Jacqueline, you are starting to take things far too seriously. The problem is being on your own the stress is getting to you. Take a break from the "Bolero". Shut it for a couple of months and take your family back to the UK for Christmas."

"I am already contemplating that Dorothy. And thank you for cheering me up this morning."

While checking the menu for the Sunday lunches, Michael was left with the task of extricating the flesh of the prawns from the outer shell.

"Without your dad here, you have been such a help to me." I said, ruffling his deep auburn hair. I must get you something really special at Christmas."

'Mum, you're always making promises and then breaking them." He said, tipping the peeled prawns into a colander before taking them to the sink to be washed. "Are we going to go back to England for Christmas?

"I have not made up my mind." I said, deciding not to mention the fact that I had received a letter, from my mother, stating that it was not a good idea. "That's good the prawns are all peeled for the cocktails and I have prepared the roast beef and lemon meringue pie for today.

"Mum, Gallina Reina has not been fed today." Said Edward, walking into the kitchen with the chicken under one arm.

"Michael will you go and feed your chicken. And where's Terry? I asked, herding my youngest son and the chicken back out through the kitchen door. "I've not seen him since breakfast time."

"He's down the ravine with his friend Jentz."

"Will you go and fetch him please. I'm going to have to give you boys, your lunch in the kitchen before serving the customers."

"See what I mean mum? I am the one that does everything, while Terry does nothing. That is not fair!"

"Stop whining Michael and just do as I ask. Go and find Terry, and I'll finish off the prawn sauce." With the sudden rebellion put down, there was just enough time to lay out a pastiche of 'tapas' along the bar.

"You're early today Jose and I see you have Terry with you?".

"Yes, I spotted him in the ravine and brought him back with me."

"Look what I have found mum." Terry said, spreading his hands.

"Are they mushrooms? And can you eat them?" Michael asked leaning over his brother.

"Yes they are mushrooms you can eat, and they called 'cepes.' Said Jose, taking one from Terry's hand. "These are special mushrooms that only grow in the winter. We call them blood mushrooms because if you turn and break them open, the gills and flesh inside are pink."

"Excuse me, are we going to get any service in the restaurant today?" asked Dorothy walking into the bar. "We are all waiting. Mr and Mrs Brichot and their Belgian friends are here along with other customers. And is there lemon meringue pie for sweet today?"

"Yes, it is in the oven cooking I will be there in a moment," I said, still looking at Jose. "Take the mushrooms with you into the kitchen boys, I will be there in a moment. Have you brought that Signed Credit Letter, for "Cobassa", with you?

"No, that Signed Credit Letter is held by "Cobassa" themselves, until such time as it is paid. Why do you ask, can't you pay it?"

"At the moment I cannot pay it, but I do know it is due. I need to go to the bank to find out whether my husband has transferred the money from the UK."

"What if he hasn't?"

"Then I will come back to you Jose."

Zig zagging up the mountain, around the hairpin bends Mateo and I arrived at the Monastery of San Salvador. Leaving behind the statue of Christ towering above us, walking between ramparts, we stopped to study the cross. Standing on the craggy bluff taking in the crisp air. Mateo and I looked out across the panoramic view of the island.

"For any non-ecclesiastical person, wishing to get away from the bustle of everyday life, you can book a simple room here." Mateo said, turning to look behind at the stone monastery. "The Dominican priests, living here, are totally self-sufficient. They grow all their own vegetables and even produce a brand of wine and liqueur."

"It looks as though they keep their own live-stock as well." I said, leaning out over the wall. I can see penned goats, pigs and chickens."

"Yes, they are good farmers. They understand all nature and produce a good quality honey." Said Mateo, pointing to the apiaries dotted amongst the fig trees. "After providing for themselves the honey produced is sold, along with other commodities, in their little shop next to the monastery. I will take you there for lunch."

"Do the Dominican priests ever leave this place" I asked, still leaning over the parapet at the great drop below.

"Once or twice each week, a priest goes down with a van to Felanitx, to stock up with the essentials they cannot produce for themselves. Apart from that it is a life of total abstinence. They are celibate you know, self-sufficient and dedicated to the life of Christ."

"That sounds quite appealing. Sometimes I wish I could be like that."

"What do you mean? Like a nun in a convent?"

"It is tempting because it is a life free from worry and stress. Which reminds me, I am thinking about returning to England for Christmas. Would that affect the application for my residency on the island?"

"No, but is that what you are planning to do?"

"The problem is making sure both the property and the pets are looked after. The farm at the school will look after the chicken but Susy is a problem."

"How long are you thinking of going for?"

"Just a few weeks to catch up with my family."

"I could not possibly look after the dog in my office, but my mother might take care of her in Palma on a temporary basis. Anyway, let us go inside and have lunch." He said, leading me by the hand.

In stark contrast to the austere appearance outside, the monastery inside was filled with warmth and light. Watching jolly-faced Dominican priests, moving amongst visitors speaking English, I was taken aback.

"So they speak English?" I whispered studying their surplices of black serge tied around the waist with rope belts.

"Yes of course." Said Mateo, furrowing his brow." These Dominicans are learned men. Being celibate and choosing the ecclesiastical way of life does not constitute ignorance."

After enjoying the lunch of serrano ham, goat's cheese with artichokes and followed by Spanish tortilla with salad, we sat back drinking mugs of creamy of coffee.

"If you do decide to return from England alone with the boys, I will be waiting here for you. Just do not be away too long." He said, paying for a tray of fresh eggs and two jars of honey from the shop.

Driving to Felanitx and using the phone in the bank, I managed to contact Michael working in the betting shop. Having only just been paid his first month's salary, board and lodging to my aunt and hiring a car, the conversation was short and sweet.

"Sorry, you will just have to go and explain the situation to "Cobassa" and delay payment for another three months."

"And what about us coming to England for Christmas? The boys miss you."

"If you are going to insist with that idea, I will have to borrow the money from my father to pay for your air fares. And that is an expense I could do without. Besides, just where are you planning on staying? Your parents have already stated that they are not keen on the idea of you returning. They think you should stay where you are. Anyway, you still have a couple of weeks to decide what you want to do."

"Thank you, very much Michael." I said banging the phone down.

"Good morning Mateo, I have come to tell you that I have decided to go ack to England for Christmas. So could you ask your mother to look after the dog? Also I have brought the money to pay the second amount for the construction of the "Bolero". I understand you are holding the Signed Credit Letter of 900,000 pesetas? At the same time I want to pay the money that was still outstanding on D43."

"I am quite surprised. I had a feeling that Michael might not be able to pay the full amount. Anyway it is good news. It relieves the pressure on you." He said, opening a drawer under his desk and putting the envelope inside. "I will count it later and then bring the Signed Letter to you."

One week before Christmas, a notice was placed on the door of the "Bolero" informing the customers we were shut for holidays. However although I had managed to settle some of the outstanding bills, I was not able to settle the large amount still outstanding with Rodriguez.

"Tell you what, he said, leaning over the bar. "I will make a deal. If you bring back one of those tape-recording music centres from England, like you have here, I will cancel the bill."

"Done." I said, shaking his hand.

Two days later, with the "Bolero" locked up, the pets taken care of and the two-stroke bike in the storeroom, Mateo took up to Palma airport.

"Have a good rest. Enjoy your stay with the family and come back to me." He said, kissing me on the cheek.

"Look after the property and I promise I will write to you."

Walking into the arrivals lounge at 4 o'clock in the morning, the boys were the first to spot their father looking sleek, groomed, and wearing a Crombie overcoat. After eventually finding the luggage, for the entire hour's journey from Heathrow to London, an awkward silence prevailed.

"So where are we staying?' I asked, looking across at Euston station.

"Look it is five in the morning and I am not in the mood for talking right now. I have been working in Worthing today before driving here to collect you."

"Well what do you expect if you book a cheap night flight."

"As far as I know, the arrangement for today is that we leave the boys with your parents. A temporary bed has been made up for them in the front room.'

"'And us?"

'Well it is Christmas Eve" Michael said, irritably. "And my parents are busy in the flower shop today. Anyway while you are here, we can use that top bedroom in the flower shop. My younger brother Terry is away most of the time living with his cousin in Dagenham."

Arriving at my parent's house at 6 am and placing the drowsy boys between pristine sheets on mattresses on the floor, Michael and I drove on to Dalston. Remembering to side-step the creaky stairs before creeping past his parent's bedroom, we climbed the next flight to the room at the top. Within ten minutes, with his sexual drive sated, Michael was sound asleep. Left lying there, my eyes open, my mind was in a turmoil. Going down to the kitchen later, to join the family for breakfast, John and Ivy were already out working at the front of the flower shop.

"So what are we doing today?' I asked, pushing the unwanted toast around on the plate.

"Well it is Christmas, I thought we'd collect the boys and go and buy them a few presents."

"Then I will need some money to tide me over during the Christmas period." I added.

Christmas day spent with my parents turned out to be a disaster. Il-tempered at the best of times, and now having to cater for guests, my mother was at her worst. Smouldering with anger, as he hacked away at the turkey, a hostile environment prevailed. And the moment the Christmas pudding was out of the way, so my father launched into the attack.

"And you," he said, his piercing blue eyes flashing, "abandoning your post at the "Bolero". Did you ever stop to think how difficult you have made things for your husband here?" he asked, watching his son-in-law smirk. "And leaving the pet dog with some stranger?"

"I think it is time to go Michael." I said, collecting the Christmas presents.

Arriving much sooner than expected, the rest of the day was spent with Michael's own welcoming family. Later that night, with the boys sleeping on cushions on the floor in the top parlour, Michael and I went up to up to the top room. Lying on a lumpy double bed that felt like coiled snakes, staring up at the cracked ceiling, I yearned for connection. Instead silently fingering me, beneath my nightdress, Michael rolled onto me.

The following morning, with the flower shop closed for Boxing Day and the rest of the family still asleep, I watched Michael splashing aftershave onto his chin.

"When will you be back?'

"There are a lot of race meetings today. And for most of the days leading up to the New Year as well."

"'So what am I supposed to do with the children and very little money, until you return?"

"Look I need to save as much money as possible to take back to Mallorca to pay the outstanding bills. I am paying to rent a car as well as giving money to your aunt for my keep and lodging." He said studying his image in the mirror over the kitchen sink.

"I notice you have deliberately avoided asking me how I managed to pay the bill of 900.000 pesetas on the signed Credit Letter to "Cobassa?"

"That is just short of seven hundred pounds."

"Yes."

"You need to stop beating yourself up about this. Look I am not. The fact that it was paid is all I need to know." Studying him standing, looking relaxed, his legs slightly apart and with his weight put onto one hip, made me think of Michelangelo's statue of David.

"So you do not want me to tell you how it was paid."

"No, just leave it." He said, popping the comb into his suit pocket, and putting on his overcoat. "Sorry, I have got to go. Here, take ten pounds that should see you through until I get back for the New Year."

In the intervening period between Christmas and the New Year, writing to Mateo, I gave him my address. Two weeks into January I received a letter back, telling me that due to exceptionally wet weather, rain had seeped in under the doors and window frames of the property. Taking it upon himself, Mateo had summoned Rodriguez to fit wooden shutters to all the windows and doors in the "Bolero".

Writing to Mateo telling him of my decision, not to return to Mallorca until the spring, did not go down too well. At the same time needing to earn money, temporarily, placing the eldest boys in a local school, I took a temporary job in the City. But of course leaving Edward with my mother- in- law, I knew was an extra burden she could have done without.

The fact of the matter was, there existed a close rapport between us, that made me closer to her than to my own mother. Feeling guilty about her workload in the flower shop, feeding my family, coming in from school, as well as preparing a meal on my return from work, I minimised the workload. Each evening cleaning the dishes, catching up with personal chores washing clothes and ironing, I prepared meals for the next day. Saturday was then spent cleaning the old Edwardian home from top to toe. Only on Sundays, when Michael returned from Worthing, did we take the children out around London.

At the same time, now aged 19 the youngest son Terry continued to give anguish to the family. Having left school at 15 without qualifications, against his mother's wishes but encouraged by his father, Terry had taken up a career in boxing. Now training full time in a Boxing academy in East London and living with a cousin in Dagenham, Terry rarely visited the flower shop.

It just so happened, still in London for March, we were there when my dear grandfather Pop suddenly died. Ten years previously, after the death of my grandmother, Pop had moved into the top flat in my parent's Victorian house. And with the entire family present, we were able to attend his funeral conducted in the Abney Park Cemetery Stoke Newington.

"Your father has been telling me about a friend who has an old Sunbeam Talbot car for sale. I am thinking of buying it to take back to Mallorca. It is a good price." Michael said, as we walked together out of the cemetery.

"I hope it is road worthy" came my reply.

On the 24th of April, my mother's birthday, with the vintage Sunbeam Talbot car weighed down with luggage we set out, once more, on the journey back to Mallorca. Driving off the ferry in Bilbao at eight in the morning and arriving in Pamplona by lunchtime, everything was going according to plan. Sticking to the rules laid down by my husband, about avoiding stopping, and refreshments taken on the hoof, the only concession made was to allow the boys to tumble of the car to pee. On this second occasion, arriving armed with tickets to catch the Barcelona ferry to Palma, we sat watching the car being hoisted, in a wire mesh from the quayside, up and over the side of the ship.

"Oh for God's sake!" Michael said, standing up as the car was dropped from a height onto the open deck. "Did you hear that?" he said, wincing as the deckhand, inside the car, crunched his way through the gears. Later, boarding the old ship, huddled together in one tiny cabin the crossing from

Barcelona to Mallorca was extremely uncomfortable. However despite a sleepless night, the moment the car bumped down the gangway and onto the quayside, we were off to the shops in Palma.

"You cannot park here. "I said, sticking my head out of the side window looking at the kerb "You are on a double yellow line."

"Jacqueline will you please be quiet. I have no intention of stopping here. I am merely turning the car around that's all." He said, now embarking on an illegal' u' turn in the middle of the road.

"Do you ever do anything that it actually within the law?" I asked, as we pulled up behind a line of stationary cars at the traffic lights.

"For fucks sake! I do not believe it!." He screeched, attempting to put the car into first gear. "Look at this." he said, the gear stick in his hand, and pointing to the gaping hole in the floor of the car.

"Michael, do you think you could moderate your language in front of the children, "I asked, conscious of the giggling coming from the back of the car. "You are now holding up a whole line of traffic. And what is more, the traffic police have now seen us."

"I knew it." He yelled, above the cacophony of sound coming from the shrieking horns all around. "That idiot who parked the car on the deck," He said, looking in the rear-view mirror at the traffic cops, approaching, waiving their white-gloved hands in the air.

"Sorry officer, I cannot move." He said, brandishing the severed gear stick through the window under one policeman's nose.

Contrary to all expectations the traffic police were both understanding and co-operative. Within minutes, leaving me at the roadside with the boys and Michael at the wheel, the stricken car was pushed into the nearby garage. And while the car was being repaired, the children and I went into Palma market. Returning one hour later, with the gear stick back in its rightful place, we filled the boot of the car with meat and vegetables. Heading out of Palma across the island, through Santanyi, Campos and Felanitx we were back in Cala Murada at midday.

"Look," Michael said, climbing from the car and pointing towards several bare wires hanging from the terrace walls, "those lovely lights have all gone. They have been pinched."

"It is not all bad news at least we now have varnished shutters on the door and windows." I said, following him up the path. "Apart from the cactus and the castor oil plants that appear to have gone wild, nothing else seems to have changed."

"So who fitted those new shutters?"

"Rodriguez the carpenter from Felanitx who did all the wood-work in the bar."

"Is that the guy we have brought this music system back for?" Michael asked, opening the door of the "Bolero" "Plenty of brown envelopes on the mat I see.". He said, picking them up.

"Everything appears to be as I left it, just dust that is all." I said, ducking under the bar flap. "I'll go and connect the butane gas and rustle up some tea while you open the mail."

"Where have the boys gone?"

'They are out the back playing. Probably Terry is looking for the mantis he left in a box."

"Well I am going to the "Cobassa" offices to collect the spare keys and to pay the latest Signed Credit Letter due. Also, I need to ask Mateo if we can rent D43 for the next six months."

The following afternoon kneeling in the garden splitting young spring shoots, recognising the sound of Mateo's car, I stood up to greet him.

"Can we go inside? I don't have very much time. Is Michael here?"

"No he has gone to the bank in Felanitx."

"When he returns, will you inform him that D43 is available again this year. But we will require six month's rent in advance. When the money has been paid, then I will hand over the keys."

"What about our dog Susy?" I asked, bemused by the cold and aloof attitude.

"I was wondering when you were going to ask. The dog is still with my mother who continues to look after her. When would you like the dog returned?"

"Quite frankly we have enough on our plate right now. Do you think your mother would like to keep her?"

"I will ask. Oh and one other thing I need to tell you before I go. I am now engaged and due to marry in June. My fiancée is a German girl I have known for some time. Her father owns that white villa over there on the far side of the ravine. Look do you see the one with the blue shutters and two white square turrets." Mateo said, going over to the bar door to point. "Her father was here in February having a swimming pool built in the garden. And it was then I started taking out his daughter. And that villa is going to be our wedding present."

Keeping the "Bolero" closed for the first two days, did not prevent the news from spreading that we were back. Predictably and unannounced, on the third morning, the Guardia of Civil arrived to check that all the relative papers were in order. Then at lunchtime that day, I set out the 'tapas' along the bar.

"Buenos dias, Señora." Said Rodriguez. "A little bird told me you were back. Nice to see you. Did you remember to bring me back a tape recorder from England?"

"Yes, it is the villa. I will ask my husband to bring it to the bar."

"So where is this husband of yours?" He asked, gazing around the bar "I am eager to meet him."

"At Jose's supermarket buying gas."

At that moment, huffing and puffing, balancing a bottle of butane gas on one shoulder, Michael came into the bar.

"I cannot believe, how out of condition I am. Too much of the good life in the UK."

"Glad to meet you. My name is Rodriguez." he said, extending on hand in greeting. "I am the boss who fitted the shutters and extra door to your premises, while you were in England. I would be obliged if you could let me know when you intend to pay for the work done."

"Just give me a few days please." Michael said, taking the gas into the kitchen and waiting for Rodriguez to leave.

"I don't like him. He is a fat slimy slob. Cannot wait for me to get my feet under the table before asking for money. He said, returning to the bar. "Guess what? I met Bernabe in Pedro's and he told me that Anna and her husband Edgar are getting a divorce."

"That does not surprise me."

"Also, Bernabe was telling me about a retired English couple who have arrived to live permanently in Cala Murada. That is good news. It's about time we had some more British here to support us."

"Anybody at home? asked Emilio strolling into the bar.

"Emilio, glad to see you. Come and have a drink on me." Michael said.

"I heard you were back. A cognac with ice please." He said, climbing onto his favourite stool and lighting a cigarette.

"You are looking very dapper today. Been on the straight and narrow?" Michael asked, admiring Emilio's navy-blue suite and petrol blue silk tie.

"Yes, I have been with my folks on the mainland during the winter. So where is Jacqueline?" Emelio asked, looking over the bar and into the kitchen.

"She has gone in the car to pick up the boys from school. They have a half day today." Said Michael.

"Yes, I have noticed that you have arrived back in a car. What's the make?'

"It's a Sunbeam Talbot."

"You don't see many of those around here. There is a thriving market in Mallorca for all types of foreign cars and that car would certainly fetch a high price."

CHAPTER 15

At lunchtime, amongst the regular workers in the bar, Ted, Mrs Faulhaber along with the German neighbour Lucas with his wife returned. Also accompanying the newly retired English couple, Dorothy and Petronella came in for lunch. Quite unexpectedly, out of the blue the following day, Petronella came back again accompanied by her daughter.

"It is my birthday next week on the 22nd May, and I wondered if you would like to come to my villa to celebrate the event." She asked,

"Yes of course Petronella. Thank you for the invitation, I will bring an iced cake with me."

Setting off the following week, with the iced cake on the seat, turning down into the cul-de-sac I parked in front of Petronella's villa.

'Hi, there, what brings you up here" Said Ted, rising from his sun-lounger and leaving his sunglasses on a chair."

"I'm visiting Petronella, it's her birthday today." I said, lifting the iced cake from the back seat and slipping the catch on the front gate.

"Oh give her my greetings and wish her a happy birthday from me. When I come this week for my usual evening meal, you will have to tell me how you got on". He said, his china blue eyes bright with amusement.

Petronella's home, with its sprawling Moorish façade, was in stark contrast to any other villa in that area. Escorted out onto the crescent-shaped veranda at the rear I was invited, by Petronella, to sit in the shade of the wisteria.

"What a magnificent view you have from here.' I said, inhaling the heady perfume of the lavender-coloured plumes hanging around my head. "And where is your daughter today?" I asked placing the cake on the table.

"She is in Palma with friends. She will be back this evening." She replied, as I lifted the lid on the box.

"Happy birthday Petronella. And greetings also from your neighbour Ted" I said, taking the iced cake out onto the black lacquered Chinese table.

"Thank you." She said, squinting while trying to read the message on the box.

"Oh I forgot about your poor sight. It is simple birthday wishes in pink writing."

"Make yourself comfortable, while I go and fetch some tea."

Returning with a pot of tea, china cups and cookies, placing the tray to one side, Petronella looked for a place to cut the cake.

"What is your birth sign Jacqueline?"' She asked, cutting, and easing a triangular wedge of cake out onto a bone china plate.

"Sorry?" I said, accepting the cake.

"What month and year are you born?" She asked, pouring the tea.

"April the twenty sixth, 1938 why do you ask?"

"Ah Taurus" She smiled, displaying a full set of yellowed teeth. "So what we have here, is an earth sign symbolised by the bull and ruled by the planet Venus."

"It sounds as though you are into astrology. Am I right?"

"Yes, I am. Tell me do you know what time of day you were born?"

"What a question to ask." I said, spluttering over the cake filled with jam and cream. "'I think it was about five in the morning." I continued, sipping tea to clear my throat.

"If I know the time you were born, I can plot the exact position of the Sun the Moon and the planets at the time of your birth. Our sun, which is also a star, is the prime focus and driving force behind all life on this planet. While the Moon governs our inner thoughts and emotions. Would you excuse me a moment I ned to go and fetch the astrological table?" Moments later returning carrying a glass-topped circular table and a book under one arm, Petronella settled down in front of me.

"This book I have here is called the "Ephemeris Sideral Time" she said, thumbing through the pages. "So you say you were born in 1938 at five in the morning. Ah here we are." she said her forefinger stopping on a page illustrated with the astrological symbols representing the Sun, Moon and the other five planets.

"The Sun was in Taurus, the Moon in Pisces and Mercury in Aires."

"Wow I can tell this is serious stuff" I said, leaning forward to study the squiggles and measurements carved into the glass table.

'Yes, you will see that this table is marked out with the twelve houses or signs of the Zodiac with each house marked off in degrees.

"But degrees of what?"

"Time the earth turns on its axis once every twenty-four hours and revolves around the Sun once a year. The entire solar system revolves around the Sun in an anti-clockwise direction. And these markings" she added, running a finger around the edge of the table, are degrees representing the time it takes for the earth to rotate around the Sun."

"Really?

"I can tell you are not entirely convinced." Petronella said smiling.

"That is because I am not sure I understand."

"Let me see if I can make it clearer. Your springtime sign of Taurus signifies you have a strong affiliation with nature. Venus the goddess of love, plays an important role in your life, while Venus symbolises growth and a healthy sexual appetite.

People born under the sign of Taurus, often have an aptitude towards the arts. Have you ever had the desire to write, or perhaps paint? Are you musical in any way?'

"My father's side of the family are artistic, while my mother is very musical."

"Do you believe in reincarnation and the after-life?" She asked, pouring me another cup of tea.

"Actually, Petronella I have never ever really thought about it." I replied, contemplating my exit back to the "Bolero."

"In my previous life I was Spanish, lived in the 18th century but died from the plague at the age of seventeen."

"So is that why you came to live on this Spanish island?"

"Let me finish please. When I lived in Amsterdam, I went on a holiday to Granada. On my return to Holland I visited a medium who described to me the place where I was buried in my previous life."

"Hang on a moment, so this medium had no prior knowledge of your previous visit to Granada?"

"Exactly"

"How strange. So do you think, in your previous life you were buried in Granada?"

"Yes, on your next visit, I will tell you about the church I recognised where I was buried. I should tell you that this famous medium in Amsterdam, told Winston Churchill about his previous life. It seems that when you return to earth for the second time, you are raised higher on the ladder and with greater wisdom."

"Well surely this must be my first time around Petronella." I said, waving her goodbye.

"What took you so long?" Michael asked, leaning over the balustrade. "I was beginning to think I would have to come and prise you out from there." He added, looking quite smug..

"You are looking decidedly pleased with yourself? What has happened and where are the boys?"

"The boys are at the beach. Did you know it is my birthday today too?"

"Oh, and I completely forgot I am so sorry." I said, placing one hand across my mouth.

"You do know it is going to cost you." He said, his eyes dark and intense.

"How?" I asked, a frisson of excitement washing over me.

"Sex in the kitchen."

Hurrying up the steps behind him, we locked all the doors.

"No you on top." Michael said, sprawling out on the kitchen floor.

"Wow, you are so bloody fast" He said, standing up and slamming me hard against the kitchen.

"Yes, yes," I yelled, my head rolling as he kicked my legs apart.

"Away you go baby." He said, thumping to a fast climax."

"Happy birthday darling," I panted, sliding down the wall to squat on the floor.

"Señores?" came the woman's voice at the back door.

"Christ put your knickers on, the maid is here." Michael said, hopping about putting his shorts back on. "You open the door while I go and fetch the boys."

"Do you love me?" he asked, as we stood together behind the bar waiting for the customers.

"Now and forever Michael you are where I belong."

"Señora," Called Espi the maid from the kitchen. "Customers are waiting in the dining room."

On their second visit to Cala Murada, instead of staying in the hotel, Michael's parents rented a villa for two weeks. Sitting with them in a shady part of the garden, enjoying tea and biscuits, Michael's father studied the expensive English newspaper.

"Who is looking after the flower shop while you are away? I asked my mother-in-law.

"Don't mention it. Our son Terry is there looking after the two dogs and the shop. Goodness knows what it will be like when we get home but who cares. It is just so lovely to be here with you all and enjoying the rest." She said, closing her eyes and tilting her face to the sun.

"Did you know the Krays have been given a life sentence?" Said John, looking up from the newspaper.

"Is that so dad. No we did know that."

"Look they are not such bad guys. They only killed their own."

"How can you say that dad. The Krays twins were absolute monsters. There you are, frightened to come out into this garden to put washing on the line because of the tiger spiders and yet you praise the virtues of two East End gangsters! I find that difficult to understand."

Following their two-week relaxing sojourn, eating in the "Bolero", swimming and lounging in the sun, Michael's parents returned to the UK.

Arriving back at the "Bolero", following a hair-dressers appointment, it was almost 6 o'clock. Climbing from the car, studying two strangers leaning over the balustrade, I could see Michael charging up and down the terrace like a headless chicken.

"You have been so long." He thundered, slamming his fists on his hips. "We have been standing here for over an hour."

"What is it?" I said, ignoring the remonstrations and looking instead at the three children sitting on the bottom step.

"The men want to take dad's car." Replied young Michael, with downcast eyes.

"Are you sure?"" I said, rubbing his auburn hair.

"These are Customs men from Palma, and they are here to confiscate the car." Michael said, sprinting down the steps towards me.

"Why?"

"You know what it's like here." He said, looking back, accusingly, at the men. "It appears that fetching a foreign car into this country is illegal. We have broken some bloody law or other and I now must hand over the keys to my car. Can you tell me where the logbook is Jacqueline?'

"The logbook is in the glove compartment where you left it and I have the car keys here in my bag." I said, stepping passed the children. "I hope you gentlemen will excuse me, I said, walking around them and into the bar. "But I need a drink. Would you care to join me?"

"No alcohol for us Señora. Two black coffees would be fine" Replied one gentleman.

"I know for a fact," I said, standing at the machine preparing the espresso coffee. "There are residents here in Cala Murada who own foreign cars. So what is the problem?" I asked handing them tiny cups of coffee.

"They live here but do not work here" Chimed in Michael, opening a bottle of Spanish beer. "It would appear, you cannot have a foreign car here if you own a business. Even if residents do not work, they are still obliged to take a foreign car back out of Spain every six months. All I know is that the car is going to be impounded until a decision is made concerning the infringement of the law."

"You appear to be remarkably well informed about all these matters Michael. I would like to lay a bet that when we brought the car into this country, you knew all about this law. Heh, just as I thought." I said, noting the silence. "So how did these two Customs men know that we had brought a foreign car here? We've only been back for six weeks."

"Somebody informed on us."

"Charming and did these men tell you that?" I asked, watching the pair finishing the coffee.

"Yes and they have the make and registration of the car".

"From whom?"

"Your guess is as good as mine. They are not prepared to say. It could have been anybody, you know we have never ever really been the flavour of the month here."

"Oh come on Michael. Let us not indulge in a round of your self-pity. Here take the car keys"

"Excuse me Señora" said one Customs man, aware of the family friction. "But we need to get on with all the paperwork involved."

"Boys, will you please go into the kitchen and get Espi to give you something to eat." I said noticing them sitting on one bench by the door.

"'No, mum we want to stay here. We don't want the men to take daddy's car" Said Terry.

"While you study those documents Jacqueline, I will go and fetch the logbook from the car."

"We will also require your passport and the passports of the rest of your family Señora." Said the second Customs man in Castiliano Spanish.

"So you were not aware that you were breaking the law?" Said the other Customs man, in English, taking a fountain pen from his briefcase and placing it on the bar.

"No I was not. And if we sign these papers," I replied, as Michael re-entered the bar. "We are effectively admitting guilt. So what happens then?"

"The car will be impounded here on the premises with a lead seal put around the steering column. At another date, Customs Authorities will arrive to tow the car back to Palma. Today both the logbook and the car keys go with us, and in due course you will be notified of the fine imposed for breaking the law." Concluded the first man.

"And if I pay the fine, do I get my car back?" Michael asked.

"We cannot answer that. You need to go and see the British Consulate in Palma who might be able to help."

"Hold on a moment," I said, "Speaking about the British Consulate has made me think of something. I hold a Spanish

Residency. Doesn't that count for something?" I answered waiting while the men talked between themselves in Spanish.

"When did you get your Residency Señora?"

"In November last year. Look I will go back to the villa to fetch it. In the meantime, while you wait, would you please like to take a glass of red wine?". Returning ten minutes later, with passports and the Residency, the two men scrutinised both the photograph and the date on my Residency.

"Your permit is more than seven months old. And unfortunately that is over the permitted time limit to keep a foreign car in the country.' said the first Customs man sympathetically, "If the business had been solely in your husband's name, and the car owned by you, this problem would not have arisen. As it is, we have no alternative but to impound the car."

"You really have no idea the inconvenience this is going to cause to us." I said, walking over to the door looking out at the children now seated on the steps. "Not only where the business is concerned, but also getting the three children to school."

"We cannot guarantee that this will change anything, but it could help to reduce the fine imposed. Later back in the office I am going to add a paragraph setting out the extenuating circumstances surrounding your case." Said the first Customs man gathering the papers together.

"Señor? As well as your wife signing these papers, we require your signature on these documents too." Said the second Customs man handing a pen to Michael.

"So we will definitely get a fine." Michael said, adding his signature to the two sets of documents.

"Without a doubt Señor. Now we have both the logbook and the keys all that is left to do now, is to go down and seal your car."

"Muchas gracias Señores." Michael added sarcastically.

It goes without saying the arrival of Customs Authorities in Cala Murada, had not gone unnoticed. And within half an hour of their departure, Emilio, and Jose arrived in the bar.

"We knew something was up, because the Customs men stopped at my supermarket to ask where the "Bolero" was."

"And you told them?" Michael asked, glaring at Jose.

"No, I noticed the Customs, stop Mateo and his new bride in their car outside the hotel." Said Jose.

"With his new bride? When did he get married?"

"A few weeks ago. The couple have just got back from the honeymoon spent with her family In Germany." Interrupted Emilio.

"So maybe it was him who tipped he Customs off."

"No Mateo would not do that. Look it was only a matter of time before they found you. They had all the relevant details concerning the registration number of your car written down" Said Jose.

"You know Michael, I was concerned about that car the moment I clapped eyes on it. Said Emilio hoisting himself onto his favourite stool. "What about serving us two Fundadore brandies."

"So why on earth didn't you say anything?" Michael said, taking down the bottle from the shelf.

"As it was none of my business, I chose not to interfere. But it is not the first time that this has happened in Cala Murada, is it Jose?" Said Emelio, sipping the brandy.

"No, but the circumstances were different. That Belgian family, from the Congo, drove around in their Mercedes for eighteen months before the Customs finally caught up with them."

"Eighteen months! And did they pay the fine and get their car back?" asked Michael, opening a beer for himself.

'Of course not." Emilio replied. "With the maximum fine imposed, of one hundred thousand pesetas, their car was then passed over for auction. And at auction, the Mercedes fetched another two hundred thousand pesetas."

"And presumably, that cancelled the fine." Michael added, drinking the beer.

"You must be joking. In this country it does not work like that. The fine imposed, together with the price the car fetched at auction, all went straight into the pockets of the Customs Authorities in Palma" Said Jose.

"Don't hold your hopes Michael." said Emilio.

Locating the address of the British Consulate in Palma was quite easy. Meanwhile, crossing the stiflingly hot city, to find the gentleman recommended by the Consulate, was more difficult. Meandering up and down a tree-lined boulevard, I eventually managed to locate the address given to me. Pressing the brass bell fixed to black wrought iron gates, a smartly dressed woman ushered me through into a cool marbled hallway.

"Mr Short, my husband is out right now, but he will be back later. Would you care to wait? Perhaps you would like a coffee?"

"Yes please." Sitting in the hall, with its vaulted ceiling and oak staircase spiralling away to the right, I was happy to wait drinking coffee. Then just after one o'clock and appropriately dressed for July, a debonair looking gentleman wearing a Panama hat and a khaki-coloured bush suit came into the hall. Stopping briefly to converse with his wife, I was escorted into an oak-panelled room and lined with books.

"Well, what have we here." Said Mr Short, lighting up a cigar and at the same time perusing the documents on the red leather desk. "The first point I have to make to you is that you probably will not get your car back. Like you, on average, I see about one case each week and the outcome invariably the same." Said Mr Short, rocking back on his chair to rest both leather sandals on the opened drawer at the bottom of his desk.

LIVING THE RING OF FIRE

"It is really a question of how much you will be fined. The Spanish authorities are inclined to be very heavy handed with foreigners who bring their own make of car into this country. But I am quite intrigued," he went on, turning a page, "To see the remarks made by the Customs officer concerning and I quote "your mitigating circumstances? That is quite unusual", He said, allowing the chair to drop forward onto the front legs. "A plea for clemency? Who can say? Spanish law is notoriously perverse. This plea might help, on the other hand. it could go the other way. Anyway at this stage." He continued, retrieving a leather-bound book from one bookcase behind his desk. "Let me see," he went on thumbing through and locating the appropriate page. "Yes, the fines range from one hundred and fifty thousand pesetas maximum, down to five thousand pesetas minimum. In my experience the average penalty administered to foreigners is round the eight thousand peseta mark."

'My God, that is about four hundred pounds!'

"Can I suggest that you come back to me in two days? I think we ought to both pay a visit to the Customs Authorities at the harbour to see what we can find out I am sure they will be holding the logbook and the keys to your car."

"Thank you for your help Mr Short. You will have to let us know how much we need to pay you."

"One thing at a time Señora. Goodbye."

"So who does the American car belong to?" I enquired, walking up the path, exhausted from the day in Palma.

"Flash car isn't it? We have two new customers. Two Yorkshire guys, who have just finished their meal."

"What the same two from last year?"

"No these are two Yorkshire men, who arrived a month ago, to set up a water-skiing school on Tropicana beach. They have only just found out about us. Before that they have been eating in Pedro's and the German bar The Green Parrot."

"That is really something different a ski school."

"Yes, and they are doing well, teaching mostly young Germans women how to water ski."

"Oh yes, and the rest." I laughed. "Anyway I am glad to see that you and Espi has coped well today without me."

"Yes, she has done the washing, given the boys their tea and bathed them too."

"Good, later I will tell you all about the day in Palma with Mr Short. You know Michael you are going to have to submit a statement, written in Spanish."

At the end of that week, walking into the bar, my head was spinning.

What is the matter? You do not look very well" Michael asked with concern.

"It is okay, leave me I think the postman has just been" I said, ducking out from under the bar flap. "Yes there are three letters. One from the bank for sure to tell us that we are in the red. One from my mother and one addressed to you, which looks like Customs." I said, handing it over to Michael.

"What did I tell you?' he said, slamming the opened, letter face down on the bar. "So much for Mr Short's theory that the statement and appeal written in Spanish would help."

"How much is it for?" I asked, wincing at the pain under my arm.

"The fine is forty thousand pesetas. What absolute buggers! They can come and take my fucking car. But as far as the fine is concerned, they can go to hell. And why are you drinking another brandy at this time of the day?" Michael added, looking directly at me. "That is not like you. I think you should go back to the villa and have a lie down you are looking decidedly peaky" He said, taking me by the arm.

"Ouch! That really hurts." I said, yanking my arm free.

"What does?"

"I have got this big lump in my armpit. And it is so painful."

"Show me." He said, easing the arm out of the sleeve of my white blouse.

"Wow you have an abscess forming. Go back to bed for the rest of the afternoon. I will shut the "Bolero" for an hour and ride to Porto Colom to get Espi back to help tonight. Later I will fetch the boys from school."

"You cannot transport Espi on the back of a two-stroke bike."

"Why not? Spanish women ride, side-saddle, on the back of motor bikes all the time. And if needs be, she can stay overnight in the villa until you feel better."

Feeling somewhat revived after two hours sleep Espi and I were back, side by side. working in the kitchen.

"Those demanding bloody Germans are here again." Michael said, peering through the port hole in the kitchen door. "You know who I am talking about, the furrier from Berlin with his family who always wants to see the meat before it is cooked. Also Ted is here, seated in the dining room with another man I have not seen before."

"Let me look," I said, pushing open the kitchen door. "I remember that man. He came into the bar one night, during the winter months with Ted. His name is Klaus, and he is an unpleasant individual. Will you please take this food out to Monsieur and Madame Brichot and stop complaining about the customers" I said, pushing the tray of food into his hands.

"You can serve them yourself, and those impossible Germans because I have had enough. I am off to serve in the bar."

The next morning with the pain in my armpit more intense, I drove to see Dr Planas in Port Colom. Coming out of the surgery with a prescription for antibiotics and instructions on how to draw and lance an abscess, I went back to Cala Murada. Following two days of antibiotics and administering the hot poultice treatment, the abscess eventually burst. Sleeping soundly for the first time in a week and feeling quite euphoric, sending Espi home to rest and Michael to the beach with the boys, I began writing a letter to my mother.

However, within half an hour, hearing a car screech to a stop below, I walked onto the terrace to see what was happening. Climbing out from a stranger's car, and the family still wearing their swimsuits, Michael carried Terry in his arms. Staggering up the steps and flopping onto a seat, Michael looked down at the ashen face of his son, cradled against his bare chest.

"What has happened? I asked, as the other two boys entered the bar accompanied by a stranger carrying a bundle of clothes.

"Now, before you say anything." Michael said, defensively "It is not my fault. But we think Terry has broken his arm."

"How on earth did he break his arm going for a swim?" I screeched stamping one foot.

"Just calm down and let me explain what happened. Because the boys wanted to go on the swings as well as for a swim, we went to Tropicana beach today. And you know what Terry is like? One minute we were all together and the next minute he has disappeared!"

"That's right mum. We weren't with him." Said Michael, backing up his father's explanation.

"Thank you so much for your help," I said, turning to the stranger standing with the clothes. "We can manage now."

"Please let me help you. I could take the boy to see the doctor in Porto Colom."

"Oh I did not think of that. Of course, we cannot use our own car." I said, looking daggers at my husband. "Thank you." I said to the stranger, as Michael carried Terry down to the car.

"So now they have gone, what exactly happened?" I asked, sitting alongside young Michael and Edward on the bench seat.

"You know what a dare devil Terry is mum? On his own, he tried to do a backward somersault with a twist, high off the swing and landed on his arm. That kind man saw exactly what happened and brought us all back here."

Within the hour, hearing the approaching car, the three of us were off the seat and out the door.

"They are back." I said, hurrying down the path. At the same time anticipating a possible difficult situation between husband and wife, leaving Michael at the roadside cradling Terry, the sensitive stranger drove away.

"Dr Planas says that Terry has two clean breaks in the lower arm above his right wrist. And what is more? Terry allowed the doctor to set the bones, without an anaesthetic. Not a squeak came out of him." Michael said, beaming with pride at his son.

"Can I have a drink mum?' Terry asked, colour starting to flood back into his cheeks.

"Why are you still looking at me as though I have committed a crime? Boys break limbs all the time. It is not the end of the world."

"It will be, when you get the bill." I said, returning from the kitchen with a glass of orange. "I am wondering why Dr Planas has not plastered the arm. Why has he put a back-slab and heavy bandage instead?" I asked, watching Terry gulp down the juice.

"Doctor Planas is coming in three days. Then he will make the decision as to whether the arm needs a full plaster or not."

"Have you saved my dinner mum? I am so hungry." Terry added, his large hazel eyes gazing at me.

"Of course, mum will make calamari and chips." Sitting close, watching Terry tuck into his favourite meal with his left hand, I knew that over the forthcoming holidays, this exuberant youngster was about to have his wings severely clipped.

With the arrival of the doctor on the third day, the decision was made to apply a light plaster to Terry's broken arm. And discarding his jacket and rolling up his sleeves, Dr Planas went into the kitchen to prepare the mix.

"Would you like to join me for a spot of whiskey?" Michael asked, watching the doctor apply the plaster.

"Thank you, It's always Scotch whiskey for me. Now young Terry needs to rest this arm. That plaster has to remain in place for a month." Said the doctor, taking the bowl back into the kitchen before joining Michael in the bar. And so it followed, by the end of the afternoon, with both men reasonably drunk, the fees incurred, up until then, were wavered. Over the forthcoming school holidays in those hot weeks of July, like a beached whale, Terry was forced to sit on the beach while his friends swam in the sea. The only thing lightening those days was the moon landing. On the 16th July, huddled together over the little radio in the bar, we listened to the iconic words coming from Neil Armstrong as stepping down onto the planet he said. "One small step for man. On giant leap for mankind."

CHAPTER 16

With the arrival of Customs on the 20th July, to confiscate the car everybody, including the customers, stood out on the terrace to jeer as the old British car, harnessed unceremoniously by her nose, was towed away. The only highlight in that miserable month was the moon landing.

At the end of August, as the temperature continued to rise. so concern about Terry's general wellbeing increased. Suffering continued nightmares, it was left to brother Michael to return, raising the alarm at the kitchen door.

"Dad you need to come and look at Terry. He is sitting up in bed staring a and screaming again."

Left to the kindness of Mr Brichot to transport Terry and Michael to see Dr Planas, on their return the plaster on Terry's arm had been replaced with a heavy bandage.

"The arm has not mended. Dr Planas seems to think that, when we have been busy Terry has probably been using the arm and even swinging on it. Dr Planas has now given me a referral to go and see an orthopaedic surgeon in Palma tomorrow."

At that point, all the anguish and frustration felt by Terry, boiled to the surface. Covering his face with his hands, he burst into uncontrollable tears. The following morning Mr Brichot took Michael and Terry to Palma to have the bones reset under a general anaesthetic. Later that day, Leaving Terry in the hospital, the two men drove back to Cala Murada.

Once again in Mr Brichot's car, collecting Terry two days later, with the arm heavily plastered from the shoulder to the wrist, all Terry could talk about was the kindness he received from the Carmelite nuns. However having been presented, by the "Brides of Christ", with a bill for one hundred and twenty pounds, Michael was not nearly so impressed. That same night, with Terry sitting bolt upright in his bed screaming, young Michael was back at the "Bolero" raising the alarm.

"I'll go Jacqueline. You man the bar and take the orders while I ask Espi to carry on in the kitchen alone."

Arriving back in the villa, to find Terry still yelling, the reason for the pain was quickly identified. The plastering around Terry's elbow was so heavy and tight it was restricting the blood supply into the upper arm. Immediately setting about a mini operation, cutting the plaster in two places at the elbow joint, Terry flopped back onto the bed.

"You know?" Michael said on his return to the bar, "I literally had to rock that boy to sleep. I can tell this accident has hit him hard. He must be so run down because now he has an abscess forming on the top of his leg. I need to go back to see the doctor and get vitamins and antibiotics for him."

"This is all happening because we are leaving them on their own and free to roam unsupervised."

"So what is the answer?" Michael asked, looking into my face.

"It needs thinking about."

With the arrival in September of the new term, and with Terry's arm finally healed, the children returned to school. However while running down the road to catch the morning bus an accident occurred. Dawdling along behind his brothers, balancing on a narrow wall, and deliberately avoiding contact with the giant cacti that 'ate little boys for breakfast', slipping from the bridge, Edward fell onto rocks below.

"I am so sorry." Said the lady with the French accent, running into the bar with Edward in her arms. "Your other boys asked me to help. They have gone on the school bus while I have run back here with your son.." She said, laying Edward gently down on the bench seat. Following a thorough examination, carried out by the three of us, thankfully, it was discovered that Edward had only cuts and bruises.

For both of us, this was the final straw. There and then the decision was made to pack up the "Bolero" and return home. Leaving Michael in Mallorca, to wind up the business, the children and I flew back to England. With my father-in-law there to meet us at the airport we were taken back on a temporary basis, to stay in the flower shop. At the same time with a telephone never having been installed in the "Bolero", the Cala Murada hotel was used to convey messages.

"Bernabe will you please let Michael know that I have managed to secure a tenancy on a house in Tottenham. He knows that area because that is where we lived when we got married.

Into October and with the arrival of the autumn rains, the four men are now seated undercover. The speciality of the day in Pedro's bar is, locally gathered snails cooked in garlic and served in parsley sauce.

"So where is Emilio?" asks Andres, producing the regular black cheroot.

"Living it up, burning the candle at both ends with his long-term partner, in Ibiza." Says Jose.

"Pedro? we want four beers while you prepare the meal. And when did Michael leave for England? And aren't you in charge of the place until they get a buyer? He asks, looking back to address Bernabe.

"Yes, he went three weeks ago, and I have already heard that there is somebody interested in buying the "Bolero" A woman from Brighton, along with her young partner, are coming to stay in the hotel see the bar and restaurant.

"So how much are they selling it for?" Asks Rodriguez.

"Twelve thousand pounds. For you Rodriguez, that is approximately one million, six hundred thousand pesetas."

"That sounds a good price." Jose says with a shrug, "But of course they still have mounting debts and signed Credit Letters waiting to be paid. Once they are settled, there will not be much left."

"They had a bloody good deal out of me." Says Rodriguez. "For the price of a British made radio and tape recorder, I cancelled the money outstanding on the work carried out in the bar. What the hell! As I said at the time, the "Bolero" had atmosphere and was a good place to eat. I doubt it will be the same in the future."

"Did you know, just before they closed, they were raided by the Guardia? The police absolutely trashed the place looking for drugs." Says Bernabe.

"So I heard. The Green Parrot might have been behind that. You know how that German owner has always tried to bring down any other competition in the area." Adds Jose, leaning back while allowing Pedro to place the beers on the table.

"Maybe, it was 'El Loro Verde' The Green Parrot who tipped off the Police about their English car." Says Rodriguez.

"Perhaps who can tell. Speaking about El Loro Verde, you must have heard about the death of the German Klaus? It was my sister, his maid, who found him dead in the garden." Says Andres.

"Really? How did he die?" asks Jose.

"I have been told it was a stroke. Have you met those two Yorkshiremen, flashing around in an American Buick? Well they have been running a ski school on Tropicana beach. My workmen have been telling me all about them."

"Yes, we have seen them Andres, why?" Asks Bernabe.

"Well they have been spending a great deal of time eating in The Green Parrot and associating with the German girls. I hear that those two guys have been sniffing about, asking questions and purporting to be Mossad police."

"Oh, so then suddenly Klaus stops going to El Loro Verde and a week later is found dead!" Says Rodriguez.

"Correct."

"And here comes our speciality of the day." Announces Jose, leaning back as the steaming bowls of snails are placed on the plastic table in front of them. "Do not forget the long toothpicks to pick out these beauties from the shells." He calls to Pedro.

"You know Jose, we should have added 'Caracoles en salsa de ajo y perejil' to the menu of that Mallorquin night in the "Bolero." Says Rodriguez his small eyes twinkling.

"That night certainly put a large hole in my pocket." Concludes Jose, with a warm smile.

PART II

CHAPTER 17

Returning to work in a betting shop in Soho for one year, Michael was subsequently offered a post, in the North of England, from his previous employer. Having never been further than Watford I agreed to make the move from London to Yorkshire. Not only did the bookmaker Corals put up the deposit on a four bedroomed house in one of the swankiest parts of North Leeds, but they paid the moving expenses along with an advance of money for the furniture.

"Be ready when I get home tonight darling, I am taking you out for the evening." Michael said, flying out of the door late for work as usual. Meeting the postmen and collecting the two letters, placing the latest bank statement into the inside pocket of his suit, the second letter with the Spanish postmark, was put on the car seat beside him.

"Did you manage to get a babysitter for the boys?" He asked, arriving home at 6 o'clock that afternoon.

"Yes that new neighbour I have made friends with, two doors down, she will come in. And where are we going?"

"You look lovely tonight." He said, touching the ruby velvet dress. "We are going to a snazzy place in Alwoodley. I have got a letter from Mallorca I will read it to you later."

"So here we are." Michael said, placing the dry sherries down on the table. "Lots of news from Bernabe some good and some bad. Mrs Harvey is pleased with the way things have gone for the opening year in the "Bolero". She has no regrets about having sold her hotel in Brighton to buy our bar and restaurant. Mr Brichot sends his good wishes and says that if we decide to come back to Cala Murada at any time, he will fix us up with a good villa. "Also," Michael continued scanning through the second page. "Mrs Faulhaber says her son Jentz is taking care of Terry's mantis 'Ugly' and Michael's chicken Gallina Reina is doing well on the farm, laying large brown eggs."

"You will have to tell both the boys in the morning. They will be pleased to hear that."

"Now where was I? Oh yes, Mateo and is wife now have a new baby."

"So where is the bad news?"

"Okay, Emilio has died from a massive heart attack."

"How awful, he was so young." I said, looking down into the glass of sherry.

"Yes, only 43."

"Anything else?"

"Your friend Anna is serving an eight-year sentence, in a Barcelona jail, for trafficking heroin."

"Come on now Jacqueline." Michael added, noticing me bite my lower lip. "No tears I know how fond of her you were, but really it was only a question of time. From the very beginning, it was obvious that Anna was a disaster just waiting to happen. Look It is all behind us now, we sold the "Bolero" for a good price and even after settling the bills we still came out on top with three thousand pounds. Which reminds me, I have had a call from my eldest brother John."

"What does he want?"

"At the moment he has financial problems and because he is behind with his mortgage he could lose his house."

"You are joking! John and Ruth have four young children."

"Exactly, that is why I have agreed to lend him one thousand pounds."

"So now we are down to two thousand pounds?"

"That is not a problem, because now I have a job that is well paid."

Living in Leeds, we experienced a good quality of life. Now as Manager for the whole of the Yorkshire area, Michael flourished in his job. While I made new friends and acquired new interests in art, Michael took up golf. At the same time, apparently settled and contented, the boys attended good local schools. Along with street parties and regular invites to the neighbours, for dinner, we were enjoying ourselves. To celebrate Christmas the following year we drove, all the way in the Rover car, to Austria. After one glorious week of sledging, eating mounds of rich food, and drinking copious amounts of Austrian beer, I came back to Yorkshire pregnant.

Subsequently, in September 1972, I gave birth to a gorgeous, plump, contented baby boy named George. Now with frequent visits from my parents the favourite pastime of my father was to take baby George to Roundhay park in his bassinet pram and accompanied by the Alsatian dog. As big as a young lion, this Alsatian named Elsa, was a dog who knew her strength. And the event that created the most amusement with my father was, given half a chance, Elsa would toss any, submissive, passing dog into the air like a yellow duster.

However, over the following years, becoming somewhat withdrawn and secretive, there was a gradual deterioration in Michael's attitude, not only towards his job, but also towards me. Lying alongside of him, spent after a particularly rough but satisfying session of sex, I felt it was the perfect time to challenge him.

"I sense there is something really wrong Michael. For instance, why are you keeping all the bank statements away from me? If you are in trouble I am sure I could be of help."

"You stay out of it. Your job is to be in the home and to look after the children."

However, leaving young George with a minder to ride my bike, twice each week, to work in one of Michael's betting shops in Cross Gates, did not prevent the arrival of debt collectors at the front door. Coupled with Michael's refusal to reprimand his sons for bad behaviour, the eldest two boys were in trouble at school. Having myself emerged from a strict upbringing the thing I found hardest to accept, was the lack of respect shown me by the eldest two boys. Attending the evening meetings, to sort out the problems with the various teachers, what made things even worse was the fact that I was pregnant again.

"It seems to me Michael, that you have only to touch your braces. Did anybody ever tell you how babies are made?" My father chuckled, upon hearing the news via the phone.

Following the birth of the fifth son Matthew, in March 1978, Michael received the sack from his job. While never ever disclosing the reason for his dismissal all I knew was, handed a golden handshake from Corals, he was shown the front door.

"You do not have to worry. It is not the end of the world. I have plans to open my own betting shop and can promise you, within one year you will be wearing a mink coat."

The place chosen, by Michael, to buy his own betting shop was a unit in Holt Park North Leeds. For the next month, going to the unit to strip out the fittings and the old walls, I remember him coming home, each day, with the blue cotton overalls coated in dust.

"Now I have been open for a few months, I am going to adopt a new system with your housekeeping."

"Why? What do you mean? I asked.

"Instead of giving you housekeeping each week, I will go to the market in Bradford to buy all the meat and groceries we need."

"And what exactly do I do for money?"

"You will get any change left over."

I can hardly believe now, that then aged forty, I was naïve and stupid enough to accept such an outrageous arrangement.

However, three months later, at Christmastime, with nine-month-old Matthew on my lap and the others seated around the kitchen table, a further announcement was made.

"I have some bad news to tell. I will not be able to give you any money for Christmas this year."

"Why not?"

"Simply because the betting shop has not been making a profit and I am now quite behind with the mortgage. Something more serious is the fact that I have not paid rent on the shop and I am in trouble with the Racing Authorities for violating rules with regard to the betting levy. The only way I can think of to avoid bankruptcy, is to use this house as collateral against all the debts."

"How can you think to do such a thing? Why on earth did you not tell me you were in trouble? And what exactly is going to happen to us?" I said, looking around at the boys. "I have given you five sons and the best twenty years of my life and this is how you repay me?"

"I know it must be a bit of a shock. But you will need to survive with just a few pounds until the New Year."

"Do not say another word Michael, just go away and let me think. Come on boys let us take Elsa to the park." Aware that Michael's father had died from a heart attack the previous October, and that his mother was left alone to run the flower shop, walking around Roundhay park lake, I could see a way out.

"So what exactly are you saying?" Michael asked.

"I am saying, with your younger brother off somewhere else, the only other son who knows all about the flower shop is you."

"Of course, that could be the answer. So why did I not think of that myself?" He said, jumping at the chance to shed all responsibilities "Once I start running the flower shop, I will be able to send you housekeeping and maybe even extra to sort out the problems with the betting shop.

Having swallowed the bait, the next afternoon, packing his bags into a taxi before waiving to the neighbours, Michael went off to catch the London train. And the first port of call for me, following his departure, was to visit Tom the second in command running the betting shop.

"You know," Tom said, "Michael has been a really good friend. Both my wife and I have so enjoyed the social evenings in your home. Having said that the trouble with Michael is, he has absolutely no business acumen whatsoever." Tom went on, leaning across the shop counter to present me with several brown envelopes. "These are all rent demands for the shop, that Michael has continued to leave unopened."

"Right Tom, let us see if between us, we can sort out this mess in the betting shop. In the meantime, I need to go to bank to find out how much we are in arrears with the mortgage."

Visiting the Bank Manager, with young Matthew in his pushchair, I was presented with all the spent cheques, previously signed by Michael. There in front of me, in black and white, was the reason for our continued problems. Twenty, forty and sixty pounds each month, one third of Michael's salary, had been used to pay gambling debts with various bookmakers. It was certainly the first time I ever heard of a bookmaker going broke himself. Over the following weeks, as the promised money from London began to dry up, so I realised that my husband would always pose a threat to both me and the children.

Naturally, as anticipated, the moment I made the decision to divorce Michael, so he arrived the next weekend, driving the shop van, to challenge my decision.

"I am not going to allow you to divorce me." He said, looking bothered and walking in circles around the hall. "And what is more? I have decided to take Elsa back to London with me."

"Are you mad? You cannot take an Alsatian back into the middle of London." I said" immediately going into the kitchen to grab Elsa by the collar.

"Where are you going?"

"Away from you." I said, hauling the dog up the stairs and onto the top landing."

"I will just go and fetch her." He called out.

"No you won't." I replied, dragging the heavy dog along the passage, before pushing her in the spare room.

"If you took Elsa," I said from the top of the stairs. "The only thing you will be punishing are the children and the dog and not me." I said, grappling with him as he held my arm. "Stop this, you are behaving like some spoilt child who has had his sweeties taken away." I said toppling backwards down the bottom stairs.

"Are you alright? He said, helping me up. "Okay you win. I cannot stop you from signing the divorce papers. But whatever happens in the future Jacqueline I know, eventually, we will finish up together. You can keep Elsa, but I am going to take Terry back to London with me instead."

"Good, as far as I am concerned that is much better deal." I said, relieved that with the eldest at school and Matthew asleep, they were not there to witness us squabbling over the dog and Terry.

Aged seventeen, having always resented any form of discipline imposed by either his school or me, Terry was completely beyond my control. The following morning with Terry having always favoured his father, sitting in the van tight-lipped and looking straight ahead, I was not given a second glance. However, six hours after their departure back to Hackney, I received a phone call from my mother.

"We have just had your poor husband here close to tears. He has told us all about the scuffle over the dog and having to bring Terry back here to London. Also Michael tells us that because of your unreasonable attitude, he has left you with little money. Anyway, having discussed all this with your father, we want to make it quite clear that if you are intending to go ahead with this crazy idea of divorcing him, you will not receive a penny from us. If you are short of money, our advice is that you go to the Social Security office in Leeds for help."

I have no idea whether the eldest teenage boys ever discussed amongst themselves, the sudden breakup of the family. Sadly, what I do know is, I never spoke to them about my decision to divorce their father. With Tom beginning to turn around the fortunes of the betting shop, I took on a part-time job as an auxiliary nurse in a local hospital. At that time I had no idea that my sister-in-law Ruth had already divorced Michael's eldest brother John.

Having left school with a reasonably good track record, our eldest son Michael began working for an engineering company. Then aged eighteen, having bought a motorbike only to discover that his father had a poor credit rating, another source had to be found to back him. Like a fool, it was left to me to ask a friend to countersign the documents on the higher purchase agreement. However within six months, defaulting on all the payments, the creditors were knocking on my neighbour's front door. At the conclusion of what turned out to be an extremely distressing and embarrassing incident, packing his bags, Michael too went off to join his father in London.

At the first hearing of the divorce proceedings, Michael did not show up. Neither did he appear, for the Divorce Absolute. It was only at the following hearing, arranged by the Registrar, to thrash out the terms of maintenance and costs, that Michael arrived accompanied by his London solicitor.

Coincidentally, it just so happened, that the Leeds Register appointed to deal with the question of maintenance, was the organist from my local Methodist church. Not that it had any bearing on the outcome because although I recognised him, he did not know me.

Watching my husband cunningly screw his hands together, like the character of Uriah Heap in David Copperfield, Michael presented his reasons for arriving at the Court hearing without either the accounts or statements from the flower shop.

"So you now have a part-time nursing job? Is that correct? The Registrar asked, addressing me.

"Yes I do." I replied clearly.

"Having listened to everything you have to say, I now conclude that you are a capable and forthright woman. However, having heard the circumstances surrounding your husband having to go to help his mother run the flower shop, I am going to award the minimum of maintenance to you and the three children."

"What about the property?" I asked, still standing to listen. "I need to sell the house to pay off the debts and to buy a smaller home."

"Yes I understand that. You can sell the house and pay off any debts. But if after buying another property, sometime in the future, you then decide to sell that second house, your ex-husband will be entitled to receive 50% of the value." Absolutely devastated at the severity of the ruling made against us, I returned to Roundhay.

"Hello, we are in a call box on the motorway." Michael said cheerily. "Any my solicitor and I have not stopped laughing. We cannot believe what we have just got away with. Anyway, I just wanted to say that I will abide by the ruling made and send regular maintenance to you and the three boys."

With the financial problems concerning the betting shop sorted out by Tom, selling the four bed-roomed home we then moved, lock stock and barrel with Matthew and the pet canary in his pram, to a modest home nearby.

Following the granting of the Divorce Absolute, I felt desolate. With the start of the menopause, I wondered if I had gone mad? What was I thinking, divorcing the man I was still in love with? With the increasing indifference from my parents, it was now a question of me phoning them first. However, the unkindest cut of all came from Michael's mother. With her turning her back on me, while going through the motions of running a home, but as the same time failing the youngest boys, I was alone. During that dreadful time, I never thought to ask for help.

Meanwhile, Edward aged eighteen, having taken his 'A' levels and achieved grade 8 on the French horn and grade 7 on the piano before deciding to take up a course in acting at Park Lane College Leeds, moved into a flat with students in Headingly. With three sons now gone from the home, left with George and Matthew, life appeared to settle down. The highlight of each passing month, for all three of us, was the regular visit of Michael to spend the weekend. Like the famous pair Richard and Elizabeth, soon it became apparent that although impossible to live with, Michael was equally impossible to be without. Very soon we were back sharing the same bedroom.

Never defaulting with the maintenance, not only did I cook all his meals, but we visited the family haunts. On Sundays, packing up a picnic before climbing into the van with Elsa the dog, we visited Brimham rocks, Harwood House and other favourites on the river Wharf.

With Michael living in London, after passing my UK driving test, I acquired a second-hand Volkswagen car. At the same time, being alone, gave me the opportunity to care for the garden and pursue my passion for art. Joining an art club, I began lessons in painting and drawing. Gradually as my interest in art expanding, so my desire to study art history itself increased. Taking advantage of the odd occasions that Michael had the children with him in London, or on a short holiday, I was off visiting Florence to study Renaissance Art. Meanwhile, the darling of the family, quiet, steady, and level-headed eight-year-old George, continued to do well at school.

"Hello mum." Said eldest son Michael. "We have some news to tell you. Terry is going to get married next week."

"Next week, why have you not told me before?"

"Actually mum, Terry did not want you to know. You know what he is like. Dad and I have eventually managed to persuade him that you should know. He is marrying a Japanese girl on Monday."

"Next Monday but that is in five days from now. I will have to see if I can get the time off from the hospital to bring the boys with me to London. When and where is the wedding taking place?"

"Two o'clock at the Registry Office in Hackney Town Hall."

"Will anybody be at King's Cross to meet us from the train?"

"I cannot guarantee it."

Arriving at King's Cross the following Monday, decked out in our Sunday best, finding nobody there to collect us, did not surprise me. Racing out of the station to hail a taxi we arrived at Hackney Town Hall, just as the ceremony was about to begin. Dressed in a gown of champagne coloured silk, scooped at the hem with silk rosebuds, I watched as this beautiful Japanese girl turned to walk into the Registrar's office on Terry's arm.

Having always supported his father in objecting to the divorce, and now regarded by Terry as a woman of disrepute, the atmosphere at the reception in the Chinese restaurant, was tense Later in the pub sharing drinks, while the boys were welcomed with open arms, I was somewhat ostracised.

"The only reason I am sitting here" Said Michael's mother, taking up the empty chair next to me. "Is because it is my grandson's wedding" At that time the family in London were still unaware that Michael and I were back together again as an item.

During the 1980's drugs and particularly cannabis was rife in all the schools. The first time it was brought to my notice was when I received a call from the school telling me George, along with others, had been caught smoking cannabis in the playground. On his return home from school, I set about him with the kitchen broom. I cannot be sure that this form of punishment worked, all I do know is it helped fuel Terry's destruction of my character.

Shortly after their wedding, Terry and his new bride went to visit Japan. And as Terry's wife came from a high class and wealthy Japanese family, a Japanese wedding had to take place. In typical Japanese style, with Terry dressed as a Samurai warrior, complete with sword, his wife arrived on her father's arm wearing an embroidered kimono and her face concealed in a white hood. Sadly, none of our family was there to witness this magnificent Japanese ceremony in Tokyo. However, on their return to the UK we were able to drool over the photographs.

The next year, Michael and I took Edward and his friend Kay, along with the youngest two boys on holiday to Sperlonga in Italy. And the following year, leaving George and Matthew in the care of a good neighbour, Michael and I went alone on a romantic holiday to Sorrento and Capri.

While in 1986 Edward managed to secure a place, in Swiss Cottage London, at the Central Drama School the disaster at Chernobyl occurred. With radioactive dust drifting towards Yorkshire, there was panic about buying local vegetables.

Now aged fourteen, where sense of humour was concerned, smart young George certainly took after his father. Into High school and while attending the weekly teenage disco, I was summoned by his year tutor. As the High School was literally next door to where we lived, I did not have far to walk.

"Will you please come and get George he is drunk. And do you know what this cheeky young rascal has said to us?" The teacher added, smiling as I entered his study. "My mother is far worse than me. Like Sue Ellen in Dallas she drinks like a fish."

Now aged 27, having had several lady friends, and changing jobs from long distance lorry driver to London bus driver and then selling gas, son Michael was back in Leeds. Having recently had eleven-year-old Elsa put to sleep, I agreed to take care of one of Michael's Staffordshire bull terriers called Cassie. As a way of alleviating my constant worry about my son's lifestyle, leaving George and Matthew with a neighbour I went off to London.

Met at Victoria coach station, I could hardly believe my eyes. Not sure whether it was meant to shock or maybe charm me, but Michael's had had his dark hair permed into the Afro Caribbean style. Taken by taxi down Park Lane to the Hilton Hotel, to be dined in the roof top restaurant, I laughed all the way. Spending that night together in a West End hotel, more than a month went by, before Michael came to see us in Leeds.

"Sorry I have not been here for quite a while. But I have had a bit of a problem in the flower shop. A fire to be precise." He said, handing me a bunch of white lilies.

"A fire? Was your mother there?"

"No, fortunately she was staying with her sister-in-law Phyllis for the weekend."

"Is the shop burnt?"

"Yes there is so much damage to the ground floor, I have had to send mum back to stay in Ilford."

"When did this happen, and how did it start?"

"Sunday lunchtime two weeks ago. I went out the back of the shop to change a tyre on the van and forgot I had left the chipper on in the kitchen."

"So had you been drinking?"

"No of course not."

"Come on Michael I do not believe you."

"There is no point arguing about that now. The fact is, when I went over the road to report the fire at Dalston Police Station, the bloody cops made me wait in a queue. We did manage to salvage some of the furniture, but with so much damage we can only carry on working in the shop in a limited way."

If that news was not bad enough, having decided to sell their Victorian house in Stoke Newington, my parents were planning to move. The reason given for wanting to move from London to Somerset was that my mother wanted to rekindle memories of her youthful years spent with the family in Frome.

CHAPTER 18

With another year going by, seventeen-year-old George began his 'A' level courses. Not only was George settled in his High School, with a part-time evening job in Tesco's, but he was deeply in love with a young woman called Sarah.

For young Matthew, born into the eye of a storm, it was a poor start. Often fretful, frequently sleep walking, and out raking the streets when I was at work, caused great concern. Even paying for a private tutor to come, each Saturday, to give Matthew extra tuition at home did not improve either his behaviour or his performance at school. Having said that, beneath this fractious exterior, there lay a gentle and caring boy. The event Matthew loved to do, was to come and meet me at the hospital where I worked. Eager to come up into the 'Care of the Elderly ward' he would sit, chatting and holding the hands of the elderly, until the end of my shift.

On another occasion, choosing to take Matthew, in the car across from Yorkshire to Frome to visit my parents, proved not to be a good idea. Throughout that weekend spent with them in the bungalow my father was in a bad mood. Struck down with increasingly poor sight and suffering an underlying health problem, he was not prepared to discuss, Matthew and I were under the cosh. Suddenly, out of the blue, my father announced that I was a bad mother. Although that was probably true, with his track record, was he the right person to caste the first stone?

Following the demise and gradual disintegration of the previously flourishing flower shop, Michael's mother was placed into sheltered housing. Meanwhile having lived in Yorkshire for twenty years and aware of own father's health problems, I considered returning to London. At the same time, acutely aware of how competitive London was where employment was concerned, I took a course at Park Lane College in computing technology.

As I suspected, any suggestion of moving to London, was not well received by George. Happy at school, involved with his 'A' level exams and still deeply in love with his childhood sweetheart, George had other ideas. In fact the whole idea that I was prepared to go, and leave him to cope alone, was taken very badly. On the other hand, knowing how stable and mature George was, leaving him under the guidance of Sarah's own very responsible father, I knew he would survive. Putting the house in the hands of an agent, to rent for six months before leaving George with a close school friend, Matthew, along with Cassie the dog and I set off for London.

"So where are we going" I asked Edward, hurrying along behind him. "I can hardly believe this is happening. Some twenty years ago I was taken to see a house, only once in Roundhay, which we subsequently bought and now here I am doing the same thing!" I said, arriving at the front of a smart, three-story block of flats in Finchley.

"It is the ground floor flat we are here to see. I am not sure you will like it mum. I have been looking all around in North Finchley and this is the best I could find. Let us see what you think?" He said, unlocking the front door to the ground floor flat. "I do not have much time. I have to be back for my class at Central Drama School this afternoon."

"How far is Swiss Cottage from here?" I asked, following him through the hall into the smart airy lounge.

"Not far, just a few stops on the underground. That is why I picked this area. This two-bedroomed flat is close to the shops and transport."

"It is just what we need, and I love it Edward. Can you contact the Agent about the letting details?"

"It's not cheap, and a lot more than you wanted to pay mum. This area is close to Highgate and Hampstead, so it is expensive."

"Well until the house in Leeds is sold, I will manage somehow. I have left George living with one of his school friends."

At the end of that month, with son Michael driving a van of furniture and with his latest girlfriend at his side, he pulled into the driveway at the front of the flats. Meanwhile having never driven from Leeds to London on a motorway, Matthew, Cassie the dog and I arrived some two hours later. As it turned out, after paying a large deposit and a month's rent up front, I had no alternative but to sell the Volkswagen car. And with my back now firmly up against the wall, after taking several temporary jobs, I managed to secure a permanent post at The Royal Free Hospital in Hampstead. Now settled ack into the London scene and the house in Yorkshire up for sale, contacting sister-in-law Ruth, we arranged to meet in the City.

"So tell me Ruth, how did you feel about John marrying again so soon after your divorce?' I asked, as we sat sharing tea and chocolate cake in a café near to St Paul's Cathedral.

"I had no problems as such with that. What I did find hard to swallow was, that with John suddenly dying from a massive heart attack, his Council pension went to the new wife, while his own children, Lyndsey, Julie, Richard, and John, received absolutely nothing. Anyway, it is all history now." Ruth said, shrugging her shoulders in the familiar Jewish way. "You know I have to admit he was so bloody handsome. And I never ever really stopped loving John. But once the bailiffs arrived to evict us from our home, with four children in tow, that for me was the final straw. Do you know I had to run several miles to get help from my brother Ashley?"

"I am sorry to hear that. Because at that time, Michael and I were still living in Mallorca, I never heard the details of what actually happened."

"Look I always knew that John gambled and that he was an absolute bugger when it came to paying bills. What I did not know was that he had also failed to pay the mortgage." Ruth said, pouring more tea and cutting her cake. "Do you remember, when we were at high school, how my brother would pay me to clean his shoes?"

"Of course I do. You always treated me to marzipan sweets."

"Well it was Ashley who put up all the money to pay the outstanding mortgage. Jews always consider blood thicker than water. Anyway what about you? You must regret the day I ever introduced you to Michael, on that blind date in Soho."

"Not really. If I had my life again, I would probably do the same thing."

"And so what is he doing now?" Ruth added.

"He is a mini cab driver, living in temporary accommodation."

"Oh I see, nothing really changes. Who would imagine that we would both marry in the same year and then, twenty years later, get divorced?"

"Well whatever happens in the future Ruth, we must always keep in touch".

Having been a heavy smoker since the age of 14, dying at the age of 83, all the sons, including Michael, were present at the funeral. However, now without my father, and my mother having taken derivatives of Valium for years for depression, frequent visits to Somerset were required. At the same time, as the news filtered through that the family home in Yorkshire had been sold, so my ex arrived in Finchley to receive his half of the cash.

"I've been in contact with your solicitor in Leeds, to find out whether the forty-six thousand pounds has actually been transferred into your bank account yet." Michael added, settling himself down into an armchair.

"You have got a bloody cheek. I am surprised my solicitor even thought to tell you anything. Yes the money is here in London, but I need to speak to my bank before I transfer the twenty-three thousand pounds into your account."

"Fine, I can wait."

"You are still such a fool" Exclaimed my mother, upon hearing the news on my next visit to Frome. "How many times have I told you. You are far too gullible and trusting. You should not hand over a penny of that money to Michael. Let him take you to court for his share. And in the meantime gain the interest on that money yourself."

"I cannot do that mum, I have promised."

"You know Michael's track record with money. More fool you. Have you thought what you are going to do with your share?" she asked, while attempting to light a cigarette, and completely missing the tip.

"I am going to use most of it to buy the flat we are renting. With my permanent post as Medical Secretary in the Royal Free Hospital I am sure I can get a mortgage."

"Lucky you, I wish I had never come to Somerset. I miss London and I miss going to the West End to spend money. I absolutely hate it here and would be quite happy if I never ever saw another blade of grass again." She went on, attempting to light another cigarette.

"You know mum, it is taking so much Temazepam that makes you depressed." I said, going into the hall to collect the hoover. "You now have three carers coming several times a week to look after you. Not to mention Linda, the cousin who you have always favoured over me, coming from Salisbury twice a month to take you shopping in Bath. What more do you want? The trouble is you are spoilt."

"I want to be back in London where I came from?"

"Let us see what I can do, I will have to consult with your younger brother." I said, busying myself tidying up the lounge.

With twenty-three thousand paid into his bank account, Michael moved from temporary accommodation in Warburton House, into a flat in Hackney Downs. Following contacts made by son Michael, to a Housing Association in the area, a two-bed-roomed flat was acquired in Amhurst Road. Meanwhile still attending Central Drama School and finding his present accommodation too expensive, Edward moved in with his father. For next few months Michael failed to visit. However, left to cope with the realisation that fourteen-year-old Matthew was stealing from my purse and, buying drugs with the proceeds, I had enough to cope with.

"I think I already told you mum," said Edward, speaking over the phone from the Hackney flat. "That dad has bought a second-hand Jaguar car, and that most nights he is out with his younger brother Terry."

"Yes, you did."

"Well this morning, the moment I saw him come out of his bedroom, walking sideways like a crab across the room, I knew he had suffered a stroke. Of course, you know what dad is like, not wanting to accept what was happening, all he wanted to do was to go back to bed."

"You didn't let him?"

"Of course not. Knowing that could have been fatal, I insisted on taking him to the doctors. And he is now back at home again resting in bed."

The very next week I received a telephone call from the Police in Barnet, to tell me they were holding Matthew, along with other teenagers from his school, caught with drugs. Not knowing what else to do, stuck without transport I phoned Michael for help.

"Don't you worry, I will get over this," he said, pulling up an hour later at the back entrance of the flats. "I am on plenty of blood thinners." He said, his speech still very slurred.

"Would you like to come inside?" I asked, studying him as he stayed seated in the Jaguar car.

"No, I am still weak, I cannot walk too far."

"I understand, thank you for coming Michael. Leave it to me I will go into the Police station to deal with Matthew."

"Thank you, just get in."

Obvious he was still quite ill I did not press him. It was down to instinct that told me he had already spent his twenty-three-thousand pounds. Nevertheless, as predicted, following six months of walking, and swimming each day, Michael was back on his feet. Discarding the ailing and rusting Jaguar, and purchasing a second-hand Russian car, he resumed his job working as a mini cab driver.

Around the time of Michael's mother's death in 1994, son Terry and his Japanese wife moved from their rented home in Devon to purchase a one bedroomed basement flat in stylish Islington. Because at the time of the funeral, Terry's wife was heavily pregnant she did not attend the funeral in Manor Park. Following the birth of the first, half Japanese granddaughter, suddenly selling the Islington flat at a huge profit, Terry and his family moved back to live in Japan. As my daughter-in-law's father was wealthy, he volunteered to put up the deposit on a new, earthquake-proof house, on the coast at Chigasaki.

Later came the second wedding of George to his sweetheart Sarah and shortly followed by the wedding of son Michael to a Yorkshire lass. Now with the eldest three apparently settled, a proposition was put to Michael.

"How would you feel about coming back here to live with me in this flat?" I asked. "Not only would it help me to cope with, wayward. Matthew walking around with a spliff behind his ear, but two salaries are better than one. "What do you say?"

With Michael now living with me in Finchley, off to watch talented Edward play the lead role in Macbeth at the Chiswick

Playhouse, followed by the lead role of Hamlet in the Roundhouse Camden, we were indeed back together. However not prepared to share my double bed with Michael, instead giving him the spare bedroom, Matthew slept on the lounge floor. Surprisingly, having left the high school in Barnet with a dismal record, charming Matthew secured a good job.

"If only I had thought to hit Matthew with a broom, like I had with George." I said to myself, watching Matthew strut about, blatantly stoned, in front of his father. "Perhaps things might have been better. You know what Shakespeare said in the play Measure for Measure?' about not having the necessary bits and curbs, the baby beats the nurse?"

It was not long before Michael's car literally died on the road. Now he was left without a source of income and a poor credit rating and it was left to me to find the solution. With my secure job and a clean credit rating, I was able to put a deposit on a good car and act as guarantor on his hire purchase payments. Once more up and running earning good money as a mini cab driver in Holloway and Islington, Michael helped with the household bills while contributing to the repayments on his car. Doing our best to ignore son Matthew, living in the fast lane, life was on an even keel.

Respecting one another's differing interests, while I joined an art club and went line dancing, Michael played snooker and met regularly with his younger brother on Sunday. One night each week, while I attended line dancing on the ground floor of the local club, Michael joined friends to play snooker upstairs.

I have to say that Michael never ever disclosed to his friends that we were divorced. In fact he had continued to refer to me as his wife. And while sitting waiting for the game of snooker to finish, another player came across to make polite conversation.

"And where is it you work?" he asked me.

"She works washing windscreens at the traffic lights." Michael replied. there was never anybody to match Michael's sense of humour.

Arriving in Frome on the Saturday morning, rather than the Friday night, my mother was not well pleased.

"Now that your father has gone, I am virtually a prisoner in this God forsaken bungalow! You have no idea what it is like, only being able to see out of one eye." She said, closing the offending right eye "I have had so many near misses with my cigarettes and lighters, my home help tells me I have scorched the coffee table. I have dropped the lighter, still alight, onto my lap and burnt holes in my best dress. And look," she said, raising her plump thigh, "I have burnt an even bigger hole in the side of the chair."

"Perhaps we should put a fire bucket containing water next to you in case you set light to yourself. Like the jilted bride in Great Expectations?"

"Do not be spiteful Jacqueline. You sound like your father. I have to tell you, daughter dear, that as this is a Bank Holiday weekend and my carers are all away, you and I are going to be alone for three days."

"Good, then we will have to think of ways to occupy ourselves. Did you know it's Derby Day today?" I said, reaching across for the newspaper. "As a point of interest, we could have a bet on the horses." I said, turning to the right page to find the runners and riders for the race. "Pick out a horse mum and I will go and put the bet on with bookmaker down in Frome town. And at the same time, what would you like me to get for your dinner tonight?"

'I want, roast pork with apple sauce and all the trimmings. And while you are in the supermarket, don't forget to buy me two more packs of cigarettes.'

"You smoke far too much."

"At eighty-eight it's the only enjoyment I have left. Please show me the paper and give me the magnifying glass so I can pick out a horse with my one good eye."

In an unusually nostalgic mood, my mother selected horses numbered five and thirteen. It so happened, that collectively, 513 were the numbers on my father's Police uniform. Later that afternoon, returning with the shopping and the betting slips, we sat in front of the television to watch the big race. Despite not picking the Derby winner, but still enjoying every mouthful of the roast pork dinner, my mother sat smoking.

"I can hear the ice cream man in the road. Would you like an ice cream for your sweet mum?"

"Yes, I would like two choc ices."

Leaving her to enjoy the ice cream, I went outside to walk around my late father's beautiful country garden. After stopping to smell the honey-suckle and lift the purple heads of clematis in full bloom I went back inside the bungalow.

"Are you alright mum? I asked, noticing she was somewhat subdued. "It is nearly ten o'clock and I am feeling tired. Do you mind if I go to bed?

"No of course not. I have music on the radio, and a cup of tea, I will be fine, goodnight."

Within one hour, suddenly dragged from my sleep, I was aware of somebody banging on my legs.

'Get up! now" My mother said, standing next to the bed in her nightdress. "I do not feel very well." She said, turning away. Immediately responding to the urgent call while holding one outstretched hand, I followed her down the hall.

"Mum, it's is only eleven o'clock." I said looking up at the cuckoo clock, feeling exasperated that she was having one of her usual bouts of hypochondria. Without speaking but pulling me hard into her bedroom, she stopped in front of her bed. Turning her around and looking into her ashen face, I knew she was dying.

"Are you in any pain?" I asked, gently settling her down and placing her head onto the pillow.

"No," came the soft and breathless reply.

Running out to the phone, within fifteen minutes, an ambulance was outside the bungalow. Following a quick examination, sitting alongside the driver racing through empty country lanes, two crew members inside the ambulance attempted to resuscitate her. Sitting waiting in a small reception room, a doctor came to tell me she had gone.

"She is here in this room here." He said quietly. "Would you like to like to sit with her to say goodbye?"

"Yes." I said, walking through the opened door, to sit at her side. Taking hold of the still warm hand, I turned the wedding ring around between my fingers. It was only during one of the more recent visits, that my mother disclosed, to me, the circumstances surrounding the tragic death of my sister. I always knew that this accident had weighed heavily on her mind. Out of respect for my mother and determined that the story should go with her to the grave, leaning over to kiss her forehead, I whispered, "Rest in Peace."

"Excuse me," called a nurse as I appeared back in the reception area. "Are you Mrs Weet's daughter?"

"Yes, I am."

"And is there not anybody to take you home?"

"No I am alone."

"Then wait a minute and let the hospital call a taxi. Are you sure you are going to be alright?"

"Thank you, I will be fine." I said, looking back once more where my mother was resting."

Back at the bungalow, sitting on the sofa alone dressed in my mother's old cardigan, I waited for the dawn to arrive before contacting the family. A week later, with the Frome Solicitor reading out the Will, I learnt I had not only inherited the bungalow but also a considerable amount of money.

Three months later, in late August and with the bungalow sold, the family arrived in force to clear out the property. While I orchestrated the removal of the furniture and my mother's personal belongings, four sons and Michael took on the task of loading the hired van.

"Okay, that's it." Said thirty-six-year-old Edward, walking to the back of the van before shutting the doors. "Can we have the keys to the bungalow dad, so we can lock up and go?"

Looking decidedly sheepish, Michael stood back to watch his middle son slip the heavy padlock through the hasp on the van doors. "Just a minute Edward, I'm sorry but I have a confession to make."

"Come on dad, none of your jokes today please. I have got a long journey back to Leeds tonight." Snapped eldest son Michael.

'The keys to lock up the bungalow, are in the dressing table, at the front of the van." Michael said.

"On the van! Do you mean the dressing table that we put on first?" Said Edward, his eyes wide in disbelief.

"Yes" came the meek reply.

"Dad, how you have ever managed to reach the age of sixty-two and still remain in one piece is a bloody miracle. You know what grandad Weet always said about you? Dell Boy from Only fools and Horses." Edward said, walking to the back of the van. "That's it everybody start unloading the van."

"So where have you been?" Michael asked, standing at the back door of our Finchley flat with his hands on his hips. "While waiting for you to arrive, we have had fish and chips, and unloaded half of your mother's furniture into the garage. I have to say you do look exhausted." he said walking towards me.

"I forgot it was the Notting hill Carnival today. Getting out of Paddington station and finding a bus back to Finchley was a nightmare."

"Come on in, sit down and put your feet up. I have prepared you a special treat of tinned corned beef, with beans and chips. So tell me," Michael said, coming from the kitchen with the plate in his hand. "Now you have inherited this money what do you intend to do with it?"

"Buy a good second-hand car. Pay off all the outstanding mortgage on this flat, and then later this year I will retire from my job in The Royal Free."

"Good that all sounds a good idea."

"Wait," I said, putting down the knife and fork. "There is something else I intend doing. I am going to book a holiday to South Africa."

"Why South Africa?"

"Because that is where the Dutch ancestors, on my father's side, came from two hundred years ago."

PART III

CHAPTER 19

Retiring from my job in the March, I booked a two-week holiday with Saga holidays to fly to Cape Town in South Africa. After spending a few days in the Lord Charles Hotel Somerset West we were then taken. by coach, to Gordon's Bay. The favourite watering hole of Jeffrey Archer. From the outset, I was totally smitten by the beauty and climate of the Southern Cape. In between the well organised trips visiting the Winelands, Camps bay, and the historical sites in Cape Town, I was off alone studying the prices of property in the area.

The convivial atmosphere, amongst the guests staying in Gordon's Bay was such that I made various friends. Sitting with three ladies, about my age, from Keighley and Howarth in Yorkshire there was plenty to talk about. With all three women being married to wealthy farmers, coming to South Africa during Yorkshire winters, was a regular occurrence.

"Hello and good evening everybody. I hope you have enjoyed your evening meal." said the Saga representative. "Tonight, I have organised a visit from a local jeweller to show you some of the beautiful diamonds from South Africa."

"Oh, how lovely" Was the unanimous chorus. "Can we actually buy them?" asked one of the Yorkshire ladies.

"Of course." Said the representative, welcoming the well-dressed, white, diamond dealer into the spacious lounge. With all eyes fixed on the pouch of blue velvet, taken from his briefcase, the roll was opened to reveal several pairs of both diamond and Tanzanite earrings.

"Aren't they just divine." Said the lady from Keighley, holding up a pair of diamond and tanzanite earrings against her ear."

"How much are these?" she asked, gently placing them down on her hand.

"In rand or pounds Madam."

"Pounds."

"Seven hundred."

"My goodness! That is cheap as chips."

"Excuse me Mrs Hall, can I interrupt." Said the receptionist. "Your husband is on the phone calling you from Yorkshire."

"What is the time in Yorkshire?" She asked, turning to look at me.

"About 8 o'clock.. In March we are just one hour ahead of them." Naturally while Mrs Hall went through to take the call, the valuable earrings were put back in the velvet cloth.

"Darling, what a time to call me. I am right now thinking to buy a pair of diamond and tanzanite earrings from a dealer here in the hotel."

"How much?"

"Seven hundred pounds."

"Forget it, keep cards in purse lass." Was the response she received from her tight-fisted husband. Meanwhile, hesitating, studying a pair of drop diamond earrings I decided not to buy them.

Hoping to break the circle of drug taking while still sleeping on the lounge floor, Matthew was dispatched to Australia. Up in the Northern outback, picking bananas amongst the snakes and spiders, and running with dogs to kill pigs, for the next year her was out of our hair. And as the saying goes, as one door shuts so another one opens.

Now aged thirty-seven and still single, middle son Edward suddenly announced he was gay. Meeting up with him for Sunday lunch in a pub in Islington, Michael and I were introduced to the French partner named Bernard. With two of his brothers openly homophobic, nobody could envisage the problems Edward's coming out would ultimately cause.

Following the death of the old dog Cassie, in the second week of September, Michael and I went on a week's holiday back to Cala Murada. Who would have guessed that sitting in the café of the Monastery at San Salvador, that we would suddenly freeze and stop drinking coffee?

"Que esta pasanndo? Que Passa?" The Mallorquins called, rushing towards the small screen of the television situated over the bar. There we all sat, opened mouthed, watching as the second terrorist plane hit the Twin Towers in New York.

Two months later in November, I attended an exhibition in a hotel near to Victoria Station. Having seen an advertisement in the newspaper, I was keen to meet the representatives from Cape Coastal in South Africa. Escorted around the exhibition, by the Principal Pat Lawson, I was handed pamphlets on properties for sale, as well as the maps and photographs of the whole area.

"Come to South Africa. Come and see me in my offices Jacqueline, and I will introduce you Fishhoek."

"So how do you fancy coming to South Africa for a few months?" I asked, clinking our whiskey glasses together to celebrate the New Year.

"Why four months? That is a long time."

"If I decide to buy a holiday home in the Cape, we will need that amount of time to look around."

"Is that what you are going to do with some of your inheritance?"

"Maybe."

"Okay great, when are you thinking of going?"

"I thought the middle of March to the middle of July. It is the most beautiful time in South Africa. Not as hot as the previous three months."

Arriving on the overnight flight from Heathrow, we then took a taxi to the hotel where I had stayed with Saga. This luxury hotel also called The Lord Charles happened to be the bolt hole for, British Airways crews, resting from the long-haul flights.

Following three days spent in abject luxury, and making love in a king-sized bed, we set off by train on the one-hour journey from Cape Town to False Bay. However ignorant of the procedure regarding the various compartments in the train, the fact that we were in carriages used by maids and workers, did not bother us. It was only later we found out that 'whites' preferred to get in the Metro Plus compartments. As the train made its journey around the coast towards Fishhoek, the view was quite spectacular.

"So you made it." Pat Lawson said, greeting us as we walked into the Property Agent Cape Coastal. "I so hoped you would come. How long are you here for?"

"We are planning for months." I replied.

"And you want to rent a property and at the same time have a look around at the area to possibly buy?"

"Yes that is the idea."

"Well I actually own an apartment, here in Fishhoek where you can stay, free of charge, while I look for a house for you to rent."

The place found by Pat Lawson for us to rent, three days later, turned out to be situated in the next resort of Glencairn. Perched halfway up the hillside, above the road and overlooking the beach stood this quaint cottage constructed in wood. Chintzy, somewhat old fashioned and comfortable, it was the perfect place to stay. Strolling through the well-equipped kitchen into the lounge and up a little flight of steps, it did not take us long to choose which, of the three bedrooms, we wanted to share. On our very first night going out into the dark, investigating the back garden, we saw the first wild porcupine.

The next morning, sitting together in the double bed drinking tea, watching the sunrise, we saw the early morning train, coming around the bend towards Glencairn. After spending the entire morning walking along the pristine beach, after studying the timetable at Glencairn station, we boarded the train back to Fishhoek.

"So what do you think of the cottage?" Pat asked, "And are you happy with the price the owner is asking? She is a good friend who lives on the mountain, on the other side of the Nature Reserve."

"So that expanse of water with reeds and footpaths, opposite the cottage, is a Nature Reserve" Said Michael.

"Yes, Glencairn Nature Reserve is very well known."

"It is all perfect. Where do I sign? I would like to pay, in full, right now." I said.

"And could you please tell us where we go to hire a car and buy a map."

"Of course Michael. Anything you need to know, Cape Coastal is here for you."

The very next morning, following a hearty breakfast and a long walk on the beach, armed with a map and Michael driving the hired car, we set off up the road towards the town of Simonstown.

"Hang on." Michael said, slowing the car as we approached the local Naval Museum. "Look, I can hardly believe it." He said, pointing across the road towards a small grocer's shop on the right. "That Indian shop was here when I came to Cape Town in the Navy."

"Good God! How long ago was that?"

"I was nineteen." He said, pulling off the road and stopping in the car, next to the Anglican Church. "At that time in the fifties, the port of Simonstown was still governed by the British and the cruiser I was on, actually docked here. You know what sailors are like?" Michael said, smiling at me. "At weekends, boarding the little train, we all went off to Cape Town. Drinking and living it up for the entire weekend, we staggered back here at dawn on Monday morning. So that

I could sober up before going back on board, I always went over the road to that Indian grocer to buy a pint of milk."

"So nothing has altered much Michael." I said laughing.

"Come on, let us drive up into Simonstown and park the car. I can remember now, the view from the top across the harbour is great." He added, driving passed the Naval barracks before turning left, close to the Simonstown hotel.

"Do you see that other hotel on the other side of the road called 'The Lord Nelson?" Michael added, excitedly. "That pub is actually named after Lord Nelson."

"What the Lord Nelson?"

"Yes of course. As a young midshipman the sailing ship he was on, docked here to take on fresh supplies of fruit and wood to mend broken masts. And because young Nelson was always so sick at sea, he would stay here to rest and recuperate."

"Really? I had no idea you are so well-informed Michael."

"About the naval history, I am. Come on, let us go back and have some lunch in that pub, next door to where we are staying."

"You mean The Southern Right?"

"Yes, I think that is the name of a whale. Let us go and introduce ourselves."

Over the next few weeks, finding the shopping Malls, the library, petrol stations as well as the local supermarket called Pick and Pay, took some considerable time. We had only been in the lovely cottage for two months when, out on his morning walk, Michael spotted a house up for sale.

"You need to come and have a look at this property further up Glencairn Road. And the managing agents advertising this property are no other than Cape Coastal."

"What a coincidence, I said, standing looking up at the sign erected on the corner. "And just look at this garden I said, meandering up the side wall studying the aloes and flowering strelitzia. "Come on. let us drive to Fishhoek to speak to Pat."

"That property has only recently come onto the market and there is quite a story attached to it. The young owner wants a quick sale." Said Pat Lawson, from behind her desk.

"Why?" Michael asked.

"Because he has been involved in a shooting incident with Simons Town police, he needs quick cash to appoint a good lawyer. As well as, possibly, pay off the cops."

"That sounds a bit like my home in Hackney." Michael said, with a wry smile "So when can we go and see it?"

The following afternoon, we were taken by Pat Lawson, to view this large corner property built in the early 60's., with round stained-glass windows in the porch.

"Just look at those." I said, walking through the porch with the stained-glass windows and pointing at the dark teak floors.

"Yes, that is a real bonus about this property. All the floors are fitted with African teak floors. Only recently the whole kitchen was modernised." Pat said. "You will note that the combined lounge and dining room, stretch the entire length of the front of the house."

After checking out the bathroom, separate toilet and three spacious bedrooms we followed Pat out into the back garden.

"So what is that little house down there?" I asked, walking down the flagged pathway.

"This property was one of the first to be built here in Glencairn. And that little building used to be where live-in maid stayed. "And as you can see," Pat added, opening the wooden door. "It is now a utility room with a washing machine, a shower and another toilet. This could be handy if you have visitors to stay."

"How much does the owner want for this property?" I asked.

"In English money? forty thousand."

"That is so cheap. And what is the procedure for buying a property here?" I asked.

"In South Africa, once a deposit is paid, it is a binding contract that cannot be reversed. Ten percent down with the balance paid on completion. That normally takes approximately three months to four months."

Within a very few days, with the offer of thirty-eighty thousand pounds accepted by the owner, a deposit was paid on 94 Glen Road.

By June, patiently waiting for things to transpire, winter arrived with a vengeance in South Africa. Along with heaters needed at night in the cottage, to save on the electricity, at lunchtimes we went to sit near the log fire in the "Southern Right" pub.

"Did you see that?" I said, standing up with the glass of Savanah dry in my hand. "I think that was a whale." I said walking across to look through the bay window.

"Yes, that is a Southern Right whale." Said the barman "They come from the Antarctic every year in the winter months to breed. You will see them, all the time now, until November."

"That is incredible." I said, walking out onto the terrace and into the teeth of the icy cold North wind to watch the majestic mammal, showing off, spy hopping and breaching out of the sea to attract a female. Little did we know that, at lunchtime the following Sunday, we were about to witness the most spectacular show of all. Standing on the steps in front of the cottage we watched as, cars, coaches, and hordes of visitors, arrived on the road below, to film, two pairs of whales actually mating close to the beach.

"I can hardly believe it. They are in shallow water." I exclaimed, yelling excitedly.

Do you know why that is?" Asked the owner emerging from the pub to watch. "Whales are mammals they breed like us. Because the female is underneath him, she needs to come up to take a breath. That is why we can see them so well in shallow water."

"Has David Attenborough filmed this spectacle for one of his series, I wonder?" Michael asked. "I did know what Sir David said about the promiscuous Southern Right whale and all I can say it that it must have made the female's eyes water!"

Reluctantly, going back into the cottage to prepare the Sunday lunch, we received a phone call from son Michael. While I basted the roast beef and turned the crispy potatoes Michael went on to describe the events going on just off Glencairn beach.

"Dad, you need to go back down there with a van, serving hot tea and sandwiches, you could make a lot of money."

In the July, on the recommendation of Pat Lawson, we took a trip to the Hex River valley. Driving on passed Worcester and through the German built Huguenot Tunnel, bursting out from the 4 km tunnel, we arrived in the Du Toitskloof valley below snow-covered mountains. Driving on towards the destination, in the De Doorns, neither of us had ever witnessed before such spectacular scenery. Turning down several unmade roads between cropped vines, we arrived at the De Vlei Country Inn.

"I am sorry," Said the heavily pregnant young woman, coming out of the beautiful old building to greet us. "The owners John and Bernadette are on holiday in Mauritius for the winter."

"So can we stay for two nights?" I asked, noticing the exaggerated limp as she escorted us onto the veranda.

"Yes, of course. There are several rondavels for you to choose from."

"What is a rondavel?" Michael asked.

"Come with me, I will show you" she said, taking several sets of keys from an old desk in the hall. "My name is Florence by the way."

"We cannot believe how cold it is here Florence" I said, shivering while noticing her scanty thin dress beneath her cotton apron.

"Yes, we have snow on the mountains for at least three months in the winter." She said glancing back at the gigantic mountain range behind. "As well as welcoming visitors this is an estate producing wine. And the winter frosts help to set the vines. If you decide to stay, I could prepare you a meal. But as I am simple Khosa woman. the food will be simple and African style."

"How absolutely charming. We would love to stay. And are you here alone Florence?" Michael asked.

"Yes, I have escaped, with my small boy, away from a violent husband. John and Bernadette took me in and allowed me to stay here to look after the house in the winter. During the summer months I will work in the vineyards."

For the next two days, frozen for most of the time, but snuggled up beneath duck duvets, gazing up at a circular roof made from reeds, held together with poles, Michael and I were as happy as sandboys.

On the last morning, following a substantial cooked breakfast, we waited in the flagged hallway, to pay the bill.

"So when is your baby due?" I asked, handing Florence a large tip.

"Two months mama and thank you for the extra rand."

"Take care Florence, we will definitely be back."

With Michael taking his usual constitutional walk through the Glencairn Nature Reserve, I was left measuring up the windows of the new holiday home.

"The place you need to go for all furnishings, including furniture is Wynberg." Said the previous owner coming through the, open, porch door.

"Where is that? I asked, stepping down from the ladder.

"Back up the line towards Cape Town. Because it is a predominantly black suburb, everything is much cheaper there than here, in this predominantly white area."

"Well thank you for the tip."

"It is a pleasure mam. I wish you both joy in 94 Glen Road."

One of the very first things I noticed in South Africa, particularly about Afrikaans men, was the respect and politeness shown towards women. With one suitcase filled with quality cotton material, trimmed with African motives, we flew back to the UK. And while Michael went back to work as a minicab driver, I packed boxes of belongings, to be sent via sea freight, back to South Africa. With money transferred from my bank in London, to the bank in Fishhoek, we waited for a completion date on the property to take place.

About that time with Edward's partner Bernard now living with him in Michael's Hackney flat we frequently met. On the occasions Michael went to Hackney to see his brother, I joined Edward and Bernard for Sunday lunch in Highgate and Hampstead. Sitting together I became acquainted with Edward's French partner called Bernard. Meanwhile, with son Matthew deciding to extend his stay in Australia, life went on an ordered fashion.

"I have just had a phone call from Ruth." I said, shutting down the sewing machine after completing another set of curtains. "Before we go back next week, we have to go to Ilford to see her. She has just had a cancerous breast removed."

Flying back into Cape Town for Christmas, finding somewhere cheap to stay in Fishhoek, hiring a car we rushed around, like lunatics, visiting shops in Wynberg buying everything needed to furnish the new home. In fact, we had only been settled into the holiday home, before the first encounter with baboons occurred. With Michael laying stretched out at the top of the garden, dozing in the sun, I stood in the kitchen cooking lamb chops for lunch. Suddenly acutely aware that something had walked behind me I looked around to see a baboon jump up onto the breakfast bar.

"Michael," I said, raising my voice, "Please will you come in."

Knowing from experience that I was not one to freak out, recognising my alarm call, Michael came running.

"What?"

"Look," I said, pointing at the baboon digging into the fruit bowl. "That is it. I am off, goodbye." I said, pulling the lamb chops away from the flame before fleeing into the bedroom.

"Get out! Get out," Michael shouted, waving his arms frantically and chasing the baboon out of the back door.

"It is okay Jacqueline, you can come out of the bedroom now" He said, coming to find me. "What are you doing in the wardrobe?" He laughed. "Did you see that little bugger? He went with an apple in one hand and a banana in the other."

Over the Christmas period the first neighbours, called Neville and Cynthia Romain, came by to introduce themselves. With Cynthia about my age and her husband Neville, some twenty-five years older, they were both extremely enlightened and well-educated couple. While Cynthia, of Jewish origin, was born in Southgate North London, Neville was an American whose Jewish family fled the San Francisco earthquake at the beginning of the century.

"Can I come in?" asked, Cynthia standing just inside the stained-glass window in the porch with a cake in cake in her hand.

"Of course, I said, "I was just finishing putting up the curtains in the small bedroom."

"It is all looking very smart. You certainly made a good choice to buy a property, on this side of the valley."

"Why?"

"You have to remember that we are in the Southern Hemisphere and that means we have a north facing sun. All the properties on the mountain, on the other side of Glencairn valley, are in the shade for most of the winter months and that makes them cold. I have made this cake for you. So are you going to invite me for tea?" Enquired, forthright Cynthia.

"Yes of course."

"I knew the previous owner of this house very well. Ian was a charming guy, and I took his lovely collie dog, called Shadow, to the beach every day. Two years ago, we had the most enormous fire come sweeping down over the mountain at the back here from Simonstown."

"Oh yes, Pat Lawson told us about it." I said, setting the tray with china cups on the table.

"Here in Glencairn, with the flames close to the back garden, the fireman gave us only ten minutes to get out. So off I went with darling Neville, with passports, money, photographs, jewellery and the cat under one arm."

"Where was the owner of this house?"

"Ian was in Cape Town working, while Shadow was here in this house alone. Hearing in Cape Town what was happening, riding back on his motorbike, watching the flames rising from Glencairn he was stopped by a roadblock at the top of the road. But that did not stop Ian. Crashing through the Police cordon he raced back here to save his young dog. With the puppy Shadow, tucked inside his leather jacket, driving back he crashed through the barriers for a second time. You know Jacqueline," she said pensively, "The problem here is, with young men able to get locally grown cannabis, at will, they get into these rumbles with the police. So where is that handsome husband of yours?" Cynthia asked changing the subject. "Neville and I were wondering if you and Michael would like to come to have lunch with us on New Year's Day. As a good Jewish woman, I am a good cook."

"Michael is in Fishhoek right now buying fishing tackle. We would both like to accept your invitation, but we have surprise visitors arriving tomorrow. Our son Edward and his partner, on holiday in America, have decided to make a detour and to stop off and see us before travelling on to Australia."

"So bring them too. We would love to meet them."

Despite flying directly from the States to Cape Town, feeling exhausted, did not prevent us from taking Edward and Bernard straight down to Elsje's river for a picnic. Enjoying the toasted sandwiches filled with dried Biltong, raising our glasses filled with gin and tonic, we wished the couple a good holiday. Arriving on time at the home of Neville and Cynthia, for the New Year, following a delicious meal served with the best South African wines, our guests Edward, Bernard, along with Michael and me, sat back to listen to the enthralling conversations that were to follow.

"Previously, both Neville and I worked in Rhodesia, as journalists. Following Independence, it was re-named Zimbabwe. Following a series of revealing articles, written by us, concerning the misdemeanours of President Mugabe we were put at the top of his hit list. And that is why we had to flee the country and come to live here in South Africa. My darling Neville here," she said, stroking his hand tenderly, is famous. Not only has he written books, produced films in Australia and the States, but fluent in several languages he worked for the CIA."

"We did notice the American flag, hanging above the front door, as we came in." Said Edward.

"Yes, I am indeed still an American. And even though Cynthia and I have lived in nearly every other part of the world I can tell you," Neville added, looking out across the valley to the mountains beyond. "There is nowhere else to compare to South Africa. My Jewish parents," he went on, pouring us all another shot of malt whiskey, "Came here with seven children at the turn of the century. And my father was one of the first Americans to build himself a fine house close to Camps Bay. After developing more sites along that coast, it did not take him long to became wealthy."

"How interesting." Said Edward. "My mother was telling me about the devastating fires you had here in Glencairn and how you had you had ten minutes to escape?"

"Yes, that is right." Said Neville.

"And did you hear about us having a baboon come in through the back door last week?" Michael asked, savouring the first malt whiskey.

"Take my word Michael, you can expect more than a baboon through the back door." Said Cynthia. "Both the Puff adder and the Cobra snake live in the caves behind us. And when they are driven out from their natural habitat, by fire, they come down from the mountains and into the gardens."

"It was Cynthia who spotted a cobra in our lounge." Said Neville.

"So what did you do Cynthia?" Bernard asked,

"I phoned the local snake man, but by the time he arrived fifteen minutes later, the cobra was nowhere to be seen."

"Oh my God." I exclaimed.

"Unlike the Puff adder, Cobras are shy and will try to hide if they can. And that is what this snake had done. Going around the lounge, quietly lifting up all the furniture the cobra was found curled up asleep underneath the sofa."

"Did the snake man kill it?"

"No of course not Michael. Snakes are a protected species here in the Cape. You are not allowed to kill them,"

"So what did he do with it?" Asked Edward.

"Grabbing it firmly behind the head and placing it in a cotton bag, he took it to False Bay hospital.to have the fangs milked."

"Milked?" Asked Bernard.

"Yes, the serum is collected to help victims of snake bites."

"Well I must thank you both for inviting us. What an absolutely captivating afternoon we have had." Said Edward, shaking Neville by the hand "This will certainly be something to go into the diary of events on the trip."

"Do not forget to contact that security company I told you about Michael." Cynthia added, waving us off down the front steps.

Late the following day we drove to Constantia to share a meal at a late 18th century wine estate, built in the Dutch Style called Buitenverwachting. Stepping from the car in the late evening sunshine we stopped to admire the mile upon mile of vines, laden with under-ripe grapes and surrounded by a mist of blue agapanthus, Working as Maître d'hôtel in Greenwich and being a connoisseur in fine dining, was the reason why this venue was chosen by Bernard. The event that stands out about this wonderful evening was the dessert I ordered. A minute grand piano made of dark chocolate with a raised lid in stranded sugar, with tiny white chocolate keys and served with clotted cream.

With time to spare the following day, before the flight to Australia, we took Edward and Bernard out to Cape Point. Paying the high price to take the cable car to the top, we leant over the wall to look at the 260-metre drop to the emerald sea below.

"This is the farthest point of South Africa" Said, Michael. "What you see in front of you is the Southern Atlantic. There is nothing else, now, between us and Antarctica. Just think of it," He said, inhaling a breath into his lungs. "The air quality here is so clean and pure we are the first to breath it."

"That is very cleaver thinking dad." Said Edward, looking around at his father.

"I think it was Sir Francis Drake who said to Queen Elizabeth the I, and here I quote, 'Mam, I have just visited the fairest cape in all the world.'

CHAPTER 20

On Cynthia's recommendation two security guards from ADT came to give us an estimate to have an alarm system put into the house. Walking behind the two men, built like barn doors, places to put the keypads were discussed. Sitting altogether around the kitchen table, while I read the contract and attempted to absorb the codes to get in and out of the property the security men spoke to Michael.

"So how are you spending your time here Sir? Are you a surfer, a swimmer, or perhaps you just sunbathe?"

"I do go to the beach each day to swim and now I have joined Fishhoek Bowls Club I go there twice a week. Great company with many ex-pats now living in Cape Town. Also, I have started fishing in Strandfontein."

"Excuse me Sir?" Said one guard looking quite startled. "Do you go fishing alone at Strandfontein?"

"Yes, why not?

"You can only fish from that beach in a group When we fish there we go four or five men strong. The reason being, the criminal elements from the township of Khayelitsha, lay in the sand dunes, taking pot shots at the whites on the beach."

"Oh! The mind boggles." I said, laughing. "That sounds like a scene from 'Only Fools and Horses'."

"Sorry mam?"

"Forget it. It is a private joke about a programme on UK television."

"So would you like to take time to consider this alarm system?"

"No it all seems good. Please show us where we need to sign." I said.

"A good choice mam, I can guarantee, that within a few minutes of the alarm being activated, you will receive an armed response."

Completely abandoning the idea of fishing at Strandfontein, while Michael played bowls in Fishhoek, I took up several activities of my own. Enrolling with The University of Third Age at Muizenberg, I attended the monthly meetings. Attending church on Sundays in Kalk Bay with line dancing another day, I joined an art group in Fishhoek. Not content with these various activities, what I loved the most was going to the local township. Two mornings each week I attended a school in Masiphumelele to help with the younger children. Sitting with them on their little stools, going over the basics of counting and saying a few words in English. The highlight of these mornings, spent with these delightful black children, was playing games. Putting on the disc of Paul Simon's 'Graceland', dancing around playing the game musical chairs, we sang the refrain 'Diamonds on the soles of her shoes.'

Although Glencairn beach was both wide and beautiful, it was also barren. And for that reason most leisure time was spent enjoying the facilities in Fishhoek. It was while sitting at the outside beach café, overhearing the nearby conversation, we became familiar with the problem of the Great White Shark.

"So that is the shark spotter's cabin we can see." I said, pointing to the top of the mountain on the right of Fishhoek beach.

"Yes," said the man on next table drinking his Rooibos tea. "Two guards take it in turns to sit there from early in the morning until six at night. We keep asking for shark nets to be installed along the beach but so far nothing has happened."

"Do you get any attacks?" Michael asked.

"It is rare, but yes sometimes. If the sea is calm, with the aid of strong binoculars, the shark spotter can look down to the seabed. But problems occur when the sea is rough."

"So swimmers are completely reliant on the spotter's good eyesight." I said.

"Not quite, he also has a loud whistle which alerts a siren situated here, just outside the fish restaurant."

"And that works no attacks?"

"Not recently mam. Problems occur when swimmers choose to ignore the warnings."

Following the revelations concerning White Sharks, we went down onto the beach to stretch out in the sun. Suddenly alerted by the sound of movement we both sat up.

"Quick, the trekkers have a catch." Said one young Cape Coloured guy running by.

Standing up to join the growing throng, we too set off down the beach studying the two lines of men running apart while opening wide a bell-shaped net.

"Look at the weight of that net. They have a huge catch." Michael said, watching the silvered fish thrashing wildly on the wet sand.

"Of what?" I said, taking off my sandals to wade out into the water.

"Yellowtail and snoek, mam." Said one man taking a plastic bag from his shorts.

The fight put up between the two-foot long jumping Yellow tail and the Trekkers was awesome! And as the wrestling match took place so customers, with plastic bags, arrived to buy the catch. Meanwhile restaurant owners, alerted by Trekkers with phones, were encouraged to come to Fishhoek beach. Withing minutes, vans and cars were rolling down the slopes and onto the beach. Carrying boxes filled with ice, the now gasping fish were placed into boxes before being loaded into the backs of vans.

"Well you could not get fresher fish than that" Said Michael. "Next time we come to Fishhoek we need to bring the camera and some bags in the boot of the car.

Only once, during that four-month stay, was any attempt made to fool the burglar alarm system. Sitting in the car waiting for Michael to activate the keypad, I realised we had forgotten a shopping bag.

"Where are you going?" Michael said, watching me run behind him.

"It will be okay I have a plan."

Upon arriving fifteen minutes later, carrying the bag of lager Michael was confronted by two guards coming around from the back of the house with guns cocked at the ready.

"Hold it guys. You can put the shooters away. We are the owners."

Only once the security guards had gone, feeling contrite, did I confess my sins. Knowing that one small kitchen window was slightly open, squeezing one arm through, I managed to grab the bag from the sink.

Before leaving Glencairn that year, intending to enhance the gardens, we decided to return to De Doorns.

"Wait Michael," I said, as we drove from the Huguenot tunnel, around sharp bends alongside the Hex river. "Did you see the name of that wine estate? It was De Wet."

"So?"

"That is the Afrikaans equivalent of my surname Weet."

"How on earth do you know that?" Michael asked, pulling off the road and into a ditch.

"Because after my first trip to South Africa, I did research regarding my ancestors."

"So your ancestors could have originated from this part of South Africa?"

"Maybe."

On this, our second visit to De Vlei, we were met by the hosts Bernadette and Juan. Almost immediately placed into the back of his four-wheel drive, we were given a guided tour around the estate, the air now heavy with the smell of ripe grapes.

"So what are those little boxes on the end of the vines for, Juan?

"They house fireworks on timers, that go off at intervals. The loud bang keeps the baboons and birds away from the ripened fruit."

"You have certainly captured the art of producing good wine." I said.

"Not always, it has taken years of experience. When the Dutch first came to colonize the Cape, the wine they produced was undrinkable. It was only after the French, my country men," Juan said, looking back "Brought vines from France that good wine was produced on the Cape.

"So how is Florence?" I asked.

"She us well. She now has a baby girl. You will see her tonight when she serves the evening meals. With many guests here, during the summer months, Bernadette and I do the cooking."

Sleeping in the same rondavel as our previous visit, joining the guests at breakfast I was pleased to see Florence looking so well. Relaxing around the outdoor pool for the morning, armed with a map and instructions from Juan and Bernadette, we set off to find the garden centre. Driving up and down tiny roads and around vineyards, for an hour, we attempted to locate the place marked on the map.

"Excuse me," Michael said, winding down the car window. "Could you tell us where this place is." He asked, pointing to the cross made by Juan.

"Oh you mean the knackery" Replied the Khosa woman in a marked Afrikaans voice.

"Knackery?" Repeated Michael "What is a Knackery?"

"Kwackery," she said, showing the gap in her front teeth. "is the Afrikaans word for a garden centre."

"Thank you." I said, taking note of her missing front teeth.

"Do you know I think that must be a tribal thing."

"What is?" Michael asked, parking the in the garden centre.

"Khosa women with their front teeth missing. Florence has missing front teeth too. On my next visit to Masiphumelele I will find out."

Arriving back in Glencairn, the next day, the car laden with plants, we set about the task of finding a gardener. It was left to the neighbours, next door, to give us the name of a gardener. During the last week of our five-month stay, the Malawian gardener planted the frangipani, pin cushion protea and young acacia trees in the garden.

Over the space of two visits to South Africa, being introduced to porcupines, whales, baboons, snakes and sharks we had, in effect, encountered Glencairn's equivalent of the Big Five. Leaving Rand and keys with the neighbour. along with extra money to pay the gardener we returned to England. Returning from the constant hit to our senses in South Africa, did not appear to affect the vastly different lifestyle of London. With Matthew planning to move from Australia to visit his brother Terry in Japan, for seven months we remained in the UK That Christmas we spent in Yorkshire first with George and Sarah and the new baby in their home in Roundhay and followed by the New Year spent with Michael and his partner in Harrogate.

Departing South Africa the previous year I had relinquished the hired car, so arriving back in Cape Town a taxi was waiting to take us back to Glencairn. During the fifty-minute journey from the airport around False Bay we were asked questions, by the driver, about life in the UK.

"So how are things here?" asked Michael, looking out at the open sea.

"Lately it has been difficult. We had a fatal shark attack here in Fishhoek a month ago."

"What happened?" I asked.

"Do you know about the women's group that meet every morning, to swim from the rocks on Jagger's walk?" the driver said, looking back at me.

"You mean that walk under the cliffs out to the headland between Fishhoek and Simonstown." Said Michael.

"Yes, well an English lady, who retired to live here twenty years ago was killed while swimming at seven in the morning."

"Hang on a moment." I said. "So what happened to the shark spotter and the alarm system on the beach.

"She was a long way out in deep water and swimming back stroke with a rubber hat tight over her ears she did not hear a thing."

"Did the shark spotter sea the shark?" Michael asked.

"Yes, waving his arms in the air and blowing his whistle he ran down the mountain. But it was too late. Leaving just the red swimming hat on the surface, the seventy-year-old was taken down in two gulps."

"Oh my God! It is like something from the film Jaws." I said.

"Welcome back to South Africa." Added Michael.

Before the arrival of Edward and Bernard, for their second visit, I purchased a second-hand car. Naturally meeting them at the airport, the topic of conversation was the shark attack.

"The strange thing is," I said, turning to address them, "I hear that although that lady knew of the dangers, she had believed she would meet her maker in the sea."

Staying with us in Glencairn, for the first two nights of their holiday, once again, we were invited to share lunch with the Romains. Following one of Cynthia's specialities of pot toasted chicken with chilli, pineapple, and macadamia nuts, we sat to listen and learn more about Neville's extraordinary life.

"When we lived in New York, Neville was a body-guard to Edward the VIII and his wife Wallace Simpson."

"And I can tell you, she was not a nice person" Said sweet old Neville.

"Well we always knew that, because of Edward's abdication, the Queen mother did not like her" I said.

"That is right. On one occasion, escorting the couple through the revolving doors of the Waldorf Hotel, Wallace dropped one of her white gloves."

"And guess what?" said Cynthia. "When Neville bent down to retrieve the glove, he was stopped from doing so by Wallace telling her husband, formally the King, to do it himself."

"Thank you both for your hospitality." Said Edward, as we prepared to leave. "We need to keep returning to South Africa for further instalments."

For the rest of their two-week holiday, the gay couple were booked into a luxury hotel in Simonstown. Meeting up the next day, we took them to the famous fish restaurant, in Simonstown, called Salty Sea Dog.

"The two most popular fish on the menu here is hake, which is a deep-sea fish similar to our cod, or king clip a fish with firm flesh like our Halibut."

"I notice that the kingklip is almost double the price of the hake." Said Bernard.

"Yes that is because over-fished Kingklip is now a protected species."

While Edward and Bernard went for the Kingklip. Michael and I stuck to our favourite Hake and chips. Later, stuffed from the huge meal, we set off up the road passed the South African war ships.

"Stop the car dad." Edward said, pointing to a troop of baboons loping along at the edge of the road. "Look at that lead male, walking with the females and babies close behind. I need to take some photographs." He said, winding down the car window.

"No please shut the window." Bernard demanded. "Did you see the size of the teeth on that dominant male?" He said, rolling his eyes.

"Those eye teeth are almost the same length as a lion" Said Michael, waiting while Edward took shots of the troop. Then driving beyond the entrance to Cape Point and down the other side of the mountains, we stopped to take photographs of surfers on Scarborough beach. Then driving on through, aptly named, Misty Cliffs, Michael parked the car near to Noordhoek beach.

"I do believe this expanse of sand was used to produce some of the shots in the film "Ryan's Daughter. I said.

"And" added Michael, "because the sea has many rocks just below the surface, this area is littered with shipwrecks." Driving up and around the treacherous mountain pass at Chapman's Peak, Edward and Bernard witnessed one of the most spectacular scenic views in all the world."

Handing the car keys over to Edward, while we took a rest from the guided tours, the couple went off on their own. Thereafter for the following days they visited Cape Town, took the cable car to the top of Table Mountain, visited Camps Bay, and went in a truck up around Kirstenbosch gardens to see the famous flowering King and Queen protea.

"So what is next on the agenda?" Asked Edward handing back the keys to his father.

The following day. walking together down the jetty at Hout Bay, we stopped to buy tickets for the boat trip out to Seal Island.

"Good morning everybody and welcome aboard." Said the skipper as we motored out beyond the peninsula and towards the series of rocky islands "You will notice immediately that these islands are over-crowded with seals. And because they are so over-crowded young pups, hanging on by the skin of their teeth, fall back into the sea. You can imagine folks," said the skipper, waiting for the inevitable response, "This is a bonanza for the waiting sharks."

"Oh, that is just awful." Said one horrified tourist hiding her eyes.

"Not so mam." Said the skipper. "Nature has a way of taking care of itself. We have far too many seals eating the shoals of fish. And for that reason we, as fisherman, are happy to let the white shark control the seal population."

Driving first to the brandy cellars in Stellenbosch and on through wine estates of Franschhoek the two-week holiday came to a climax at the De Vlei Country Inn. And on their first morning, lounging round the pool, Edward taught Bernard how to swim. For all of us, the highlight of those two days at De Vlei was helping with the grape harvest. Moving alongside the workers, crouching beneath the box-shaped vines, we gathered the black grapes. Then, cradling the dessert grapes in our hands, they were laid into to padded boxes.

"Where are they going to?" Asked Bernard"

"By tomorrow morning, these grapes will be on a plane to Japan. We workers, earn a fraction of what these grapes will be sold for Tokyo."

The last evening, sitting in front of the Rondeval taking snapshots and drinking their own gin and tonic, raising their cups to the camera, Edward and Bernard said, "And here is to a memorable holiday in South Africa." They said, smiling.

A week after their departure back to the UK, while Michael went to watch test cricket at Newlands, I conducted an illustrated Art Talk, for U3A, in the Muizenberg Pavilion. As it turned out that talk on 'The Life of Michelangelo' turned out to be just one of a succession of talks concerning Master painters, I did in and around the area.

During those four months, something else we did on a regular basis, was to go to buy fish from the Trekkers. Beginning to understand the tides, we knew when the Trekkers would be trawling their nets. Returning to Glencairn with a bag of yellowtail, storing some in the freezer, the rest was grilled on the barbecue. Having recently joined the monthly meeting at Gordon's Camp opposite, Michael had studied the technique of cooking fish and meat over an opened oil drum.

"Before we go back in June," I said, watching him turn the crisped fish on the olive wood fire, "I want to add a water feature to the back garden" Ex-pats at the Gordon's Camp gave me the name of a good builder. I have already drawn up a design and asked him to come."

The following morning, a six-foot tall, striking-looking bearded Afrikaner named Dani, came striding up the garden to greet me.

"Mm," He said, studying my drawings while rubbing his dark beard. "It can be done but it will not be cheap." he said looking back at the black workers. "Building a water feature on two levels will require fetching large rocks from the top of the mountains."

"So how much?"

"At this stage mam, I cannot say. I will work it out and come back with an estimate."

Two days later, with a good price agreed upon, work on the water feature began.

"Jesus, what a weight!" Dani said, exhaling air from his lungs while lowering one enormous rock to the ground. "And to think, prizing this brute out from the mountain I disturbed a puff adder."

"So what happened?" Michael asked, watching two workmen lift another heavy rock from the wheelbarrow.

"What do you think? I Killed the fucker with my leather boot. That is why we always wear these high boots."

"But Dani snakes are a protected species here and you are not supposed to kill them." I said.

"Mam, because cobras are shy reptiles they will leave the scene. But a puff adder will always stand its ground. When you are confronted by a puff adder, it becomes a question of you or it.

"Skinned and cooked on an open fire, they taste just like chicken." Said one of Dani's men."

"Oh my word! What with scorpions in the garden sink, a black widow spider in the post box and venomous snakes that are good to eat, South Africa has it all," I said, walking back down the steps.

At the end of June, with the water feature complete and the cemented pools left to dry and leaving the car battery inside the house and the car locked in the garage, we returned to the UK. On this occasion, planning to stay for seven months, the first port of call was to fly directly to Tokyo to attend Matthew's Japanese wedding. At the same time we were in Tokyo, we went to visit Terry and his Japanese wife, and to gloat over the beauty of our half Japanese and half English granddaughter called Phoebe, Ai in Japanese.

Having lived in a Leasehold property for more than ten years, returning from Japan to find even more bills and extra costs on the property, I thought about selling the property. Conscious that maintaining two homes while flying around the world was depleting my bank balance, the flat in Finchley was put on the market. At this time, with Edward working in a West End theatre and Bernard working as a maître d'hôtel in Greenwich they also wanted to move from Hackney and to buy a house.

Pooling resources and moving back into Michael's flat, had certain financial advantages. However, with Michael living ever closer to his errant younger brother, the move also had its downsides. While with me, Michael continued to tow the line, on the other hand, once out with his brother it was a different matter. Now aged 70, having decided to retire from his job as a mini-cab driver, Michael was playing bowls four afternoons a week in Victoria Park. On Michael's occasional trips with his younger brother to France by ferry, I often queried what they were up to. However, with the stay in Hackney at an end, leaving the, still, unsold flat in the hands of Estate Agents we returned to South Africa.

CHAPTER 21

With no overseas visitors expected, the following two years were spent enjoying South African company and staging dinner parties in the house. With the beautiful water feature now finished, Dani and his wife Rita also became firm friends. Meanwhile, extending our knowledge of South Africa, we visited the hot-water Springs at Montague, joined the tractor ride to the top of the Langberg mountains and flew to Namibia.

While no visitors arrived from the UK, we did receive company in the garden. Even though Glencairn had monitors to look after the baboons, that did not prevent the troops from jumping over the walls. The moment we heard monitors blowing whistles and banging sticks, we knew the baboons were on their way.

"Look at that cheeky devil," Michael said standing at the back door looking up at one dominant male, sitting on our neighbour's roof eating an apple.

"That is not all." I said, running in to join him. "Several females and their babies are playing in the water feature.

"Right, watch this, he said, tucking the head of the garden broom beneath his armpit before lining up the handle at the baboon. Staying exactly where he was, there was no way the canny baboon was going to be fooled into believing that Michael was holding a gun.

"You know what Michael," I said, "The way that male is looking at you, he wants you to go back indoors and have a lie down."

55

In 2008 before returning to England for eight months, Michael our son came for a holiday. And during his two-week stay he and his father went to Newlands to watch the test match between England and South Africa. While back in Hackney, Ruth phoned to tell me the cancer had returned and spread.

Then returning to Glencairn the next year two cousins, the siblings of aunty Eileen, arrived for a holiday. Because, like me, they had endured a childhood bereft of love, there existed a close bond between us. Spending the first days of their holiday, taking Sybil, Terry and Terry's wife on sightseeing trips, the week ended in Kalk Bay. Thoroughly enjoying fish and chips at famous 'Kalky's, the five of us walked down the jetty to watch the trawlers entering the harbour with their afternoon catch.

"Just look out for the seals." I said, pointing towards the coloured woman gutting the fish.

"Oh yes, look that fat seal is coming right up the steps to catch the guts," Said Sybil.

"These workers, cleaning and selling the fish, are called Cape Coloureds. More than two hundred years ago, they sailed here to find work" Said Michael.

"So where did they come from?" Asked Terry.

"Some from India, others from Malaya and even the Philippines. All the different nationalities are famous for their curry."

"Do you think you could live here permanently Michael?" asked Terry's wife Mary.

"No, but Jacqueline could,"

"That is true. I have already told my son Edward that if I die in South Africa he should spread my ashes on the sea here in Kalk Bay."

During the second week of their holiday, with Michael happy playing bowls in Fishhoek, I took the cousins to visit the school in Masiphumelele. Introducing my family to the Principal of the creche and stepping over the rows of sleeping children lying on the floor taking their afternoon nap, we tip-toed outside.

"You will notice that the shacks, are held together with just anything that comes to hand. Planks of wood, sheets of corrugated iron, rolls of plastic sheeting. You name it, they use it." I said.

"But the shacks are so small and packed in together like sardines. How do they manage?" Sybil asked,

"They are extremely adaptable. In point of tact the interiors are comfortable with carpets, fridges and, also with televisions. Unfortunately, it is in the winter when they use paraffin heaters that problems occur. With children packed into the sleeping area at the back, heaters get knocked over."

"I can imagine that must spell disaster." said Terry.

"Exactly because the shacks are so close to one another fire jumps and the fire engines have difficulty getting in. The township it self-sufficient. It has its own butchers, and as you can see, fruit and vegetable stalls spread out along the roadside. They even operate their own funeral directors. It is true to say that for the most part it is the women who worked the hardest."

"I can see that." Terry said, studying a row of men seated outside a shebeen.

"I love the way the women are washing clothes in a metal bucket, with their babies strapped to their backs." Said Mary.

"Do you know those black babies just never cry. Rocked and bounced up and down on their mother's backs and hoisted around for, on demand, breast milk, they are happy babies. Also, the Khosa women are extremely protective of their young. Conscious of the adverse effect drugs being brought by the Nigerians and other tribes into the township is having on the youngsters, it is not unheard of for the women to gang up and physically attack them. It is not unheard of for these illegal immigrants, entering the township, to be killed."

Even though I am aware of the violence, I still love coming to help with the children in Masiphumelele." I said, as we drove out of the township onto the main road.

"I do not think I could handle that." Said Mary.

"Yes there are plenty of women that go to the same church as me who would never dream of coming here. It is true to say that although Nelson Mandela did manage to bring some changes to South Africa, there is still a that needs to be done. Especially the crime against women."

Taking the family on the next trip to Stellenbosch, staying overnight in a hotel built in the Dutch colonial style, the next morning we set off on a tour of the wine estates.

"So why are there roses planted at the beginning of every row of vines?" Sybil asked looking out of the side window.

"Having come from a family of florists, I can answer that question." Said Michael. "The rose trees act as a doctor to the vine. If disease is seen on the roses, then the growers look for bugs and problems on the vines."

"How ingenious is that!" Said Terry.

"Yes it has taken the Afrikaans years to develop that knowledge and to produce good wine.

"So where are we going now?" asked Mary.

"The famous Hot springs at Montague. We can wallow and sweat in the mineral waters all afternoon and then enjoy a good meal. Tomorrow we are off for a fun trip on a tractor to the top of the Langeberg mountains." Boarding the tractor the following day, we went on the 'white knuckle' ride to the top of the mountains.

"We always try to leave the best to last." Michael, said, as we slowly turned into the entrance of the De Vlei Country Inn."

Following a hearty breakfast the next morning, served by Florence, we set off to find the kwackery.

"What are we here for?" Asked Sybil.

"This is the garden centre where Jacqueline likes to buy plants. I can tell you Sybil, it took us some considerable time to work out that kwackery is the Afrikaans word for garden centre."

"So where are you heading for now?" Asked the pleasant young woman packing the plants in a box.

"We are going to Noit." Michael replied.

"To where?" she said, looking quite startled.

"To Noit, for white wine."

"Excuse me sir, but I do not think you are." She said, placing one hand over her mouth. "What you are saying is the slang expression, in Afrikaans, which means 'to fuck'."

For the entire journey back to Cape Town, thinking about the faux pas Michael had made, we fell about laughing.

"I think you should have said Nuit, as in the wine Nuit St Georges." I said, "But because of your flattened cockney voice the vowel came out as Noit 'to fuck' in Afrikaans.

"What a wonderful holiday we have had." Said cousin Terry pushing the trolley of cases into Cape Town airport. "Can we come again next year?" He asked.

With Michael playing bowls in Fishhoek and receiving an invitation to have afternoon tea with Dani's beloved wife Rita, I was taken to Glen Marina in Dani's truck. Having previously heard all about this property built on the top of the mountainside, I was eager to see the 'House that Jack Built.'

"Cutting out two levels from this mountain, it took us seven years to build. And you can see we have not finished it yet." Dani said waiting, while I looked over the precipitous drop on one side of the wobbly steps.

I will leave you two ladies to enjoy your afternoon. Have a good day." Dani said, smiling and slapping his wife's plump bottom.

"Welcome to Glen Marina, I am so glad you could make it. Said rosy-cheeked Rita. "Please come in, I have just taken cakes from the oven.

"So how big is this house?" I said, looking at the kitchen and large living area.

"Up that flight of stairs there are three bedrooms Now into our early forties and with the family working and living abroad Dani and I now have the place to ourselves."

"You must have married young?" I said, watching Rita come to the table with a tray of warm scones.

"Yes, I was eighteen and Dani nineteen. And still we are in love. You know to start each day,." Rita said buttering the warm scones, "Dani brings me tea and sitting together in bed, we discuss the day ahead. After kneeling to say prayers, Dani makes loves to me before going to work."

"Really? What every morning?"

"No not every morning, about three or four times a week."

"Well saying your prayers first before sex and then going to work, sounds a good idea to me." I said, knowing that during the day Dani hit at least one bottle of whiskey.

On Michael's return that day, I could not wait to tell him all about the house built on the mountainside and the lively afternoon spent with Rita.

On one morning driving into Masiphumelele, before leaving the car parked in front of the school, I went around to open the boot. While retrieving books and drawings prepared for the lesson I heard what I thought were gunshots. Not sure exactly where the shots had come from I carried on walking into the school. It was only while in the kitchen serving the breakfast of 'pap' to the children and hearing an ambulance stop in the next road, that we three women discovered what had happened. And that two masked men, from the township of Khayelitsha, had arrived to hold up the local doctor. Producing guns, the men demanded that all drugs and money in the surgery be handed over. However, with no ready cash on the premises, the only thing the doctor could give were drugs in the cabinet. Not satisfied and with the holdup plan thwarted, the doctor was shot through the hip anyway.

Returned to Hackney for the following seven months and with the flat in Finchley sold, life went back to normal. With Michael going his own way, I joined local bridge classes and visited all the art galleries in London.

However, events in South Africa were not quite so mundane. From various sources, including a newspaper report. we learnt that there had been two fatal shark attacks in False Bay. The first death occurring in Noordhoek, when a nineteen-year-old surfer was taken directly off his surfboard. And the second fatal attack when, a holidaymaker from Johannesburg, was killed while swimming in the kelp on Fishhoek beach.

"So no shark nets yet" said Michael reading the latest article in his newspaper out loud. "That will damage the tourist industry."

Back in Glencairn by the middle of January, we drove to Cape Town airport to await the arrival of the cousins for their second holiday. Because some thirty-five years previously, Terry, Mary and Sybil had all come to visit us when we had the bar and restaurant in Mallorca, I considered them special guests. Watching them appear, into arrivals at 9 o'clock in the morning, I ran forward to greet them.

"So lovely to see you all again" I said, hugging all three of them.

"It does not seem that we have ever been away." Said Mary.

"So come on Michael, what have you got lined up for us this time?" asked Terry, getting into the front passenger seat beside him.

"Fishhoek beach"

"What for? The swimsuits are still in the cases."

"It is a surprise. About this time, the new team of guys will be there to put out the shark nets. It is good news, Fishhoek has finally got nets on one side of the beach.

"What? You did not say anything to us last year when we swam there nearly every day without nets." Said Mary.

"No because then we always relied upon the shark spotter and the sirens. And if you remember Mary, on the occasions the alarm went off, the exit from the sea up the beach, was like the Anzio landings."

"That is true." Sybil laughed.

Parking the car alongside the café before taking off our shoes, the five of us walked down the beach. At this point and now familiar with the routine, nine slim black men wearing wet suits and their curled dreadlocks tied up onto their heads, posed for the cameras.

"You will notice," Said Michael. "So that the nets do not interfere with the Trekkers fishing, or possibly whales in the bay, they have netted off one third only of the beach."

"They are quite incredible. On my morning walks I have watched them. The way they swim out, diving down to secure those heavy nets close to the bottom, they look like seals themselves."

During the previous nine years, neither Michael nor I could remember just how many times we had visited Table Mountain, Kirstenbosch gardens, Hout Bay or studied the penguins on Boulder's beach. However, with an invitation from Dani and Rita for supper, enduring being bored, we took the cousins to see the penguins. Then on the return journey, back through Simonstown before making the sharp turn to the left into Glen Marine, we drove up the mountain road to Dani and Rita's house.

"The only thing that is not allowed in our house," said Dani, greeting us with open arms on the top step, "is smoking. Apart from that it is a question of anything goes." he added, striding across the living room to stand behind the little bar. "And what would you folks like to drink?"

"Shall we have our usual gin and tonics?" I asked, Sybil and Mary.

"Why not, yes please." Replied Mary.

"And for you guys what can I get you? Beer, lager or something stronger?" Said Dani retrieving a variety of glasses from the shelf behind the bar. "And for you my darling, do you want your usual Campari, orange and ice? He said, looking across Rita.

"Yes please" she said, joining the group and placing a tray of sliced Biltong onto the bar.

"My God! Are those real shark's teeth?" Terry asked, looking up at the two sets of shark jaws hanging on the wall behind the bar.

"Yes they sure are." Dani replied, placing slices of lemon into the three gin and tonics. "My eldest son and I, between us, own a small boat. And together we fish from Miller's point."

"What do you fish for?" asked Michael, accepting a glass of beer.

"We dive with bags attached to our chest, to poach abalone."

"You poach the shell-fish abalone?" Asked Sybil.

"Yes, because abalone fetches such a high price here on the Cape, they are worth the risk involved. Diving down to gather them from the rocks, the sharks are often at our backs."

"Good God! So have you ever been attacked?" said Terry, his eyes filled with terror.

"No, we always carry one harpoon gun between us. And these little beauties on the wall are to prove it."

Following a sumptuous meal of roasted meats and vegetables, cooked on the indoor barbecue, our glasses were continually topped up with a variety of alcoholic drinks. Still seated around the table, watching big man Dani cradling two tiny chihuahuas to his chest, one of which sang on demand, it was truly a night to remember. I cannot now recall exactly what we drank, but what I do remember is that by midnight we were all absolutely smashed. With the host out cold on the sofa and Rita only just able to stand, we saw ourselves out of the front door and into the darkness.

"That is a lot of good," I said, tottering sideways to take hold of the flimsy handrail. "Leaving us out here with only two small lights here at the top. I cannot see a bloody thing."

"I agree, that is one hell of a drop over the side." Said Terry.

"Okay so what you three girls must do, is sit down on your backsides and slide down from one step to the next." Said, Michael.

"You have got to be joking." I said, while considering the suggestion.

"Right, let us go girls." I said.

With skirts up around our thighs and giggling the whole time, we slid down the stony stairs. For sure, by the time we reached the bottom, I was not the only one with wet pants. How a very drunk Michael managed to drive down from the mountain, in the dark and along to Glencairn, without encountering a police roadblock, was a miracle.

With the cousins back in Brighton and following another eight months in London, we returned to South Africa. And this time, on Dani's recommendation and to celebrate the New Year we drove to a place near Ceres called Klondike. Surrounded by mountains, this baking hot bowl was famous for producing sweet black cherries. Spending one whole day up ladders eating and picking cherries, loaded up with half a dozen boxes, we drove on to spend a night in a mountain retreat close to Paarl. The following morning, finishing his cooked breakfast consisting of two fried eggs and several cups of black coffee, Michael suddenly became ill. Ashen faced, staggering out onto the terrace, he was violently sick into the hibiscus plants. In fact Michael was so poorly, I had to drive the car back to Glencairn.

Later going around, distributing boxes of cherries to the neighbours, I stopped off at Cynthia's house.

"It sounds to me like he suffered a heart attack or maybe a small stroke." Said Cynthia, accepting the box of cherries. "He needs to see a doctor."

"He has no medical cover in South Africa, and so he will not do that Cynthia."

"But he could get free treatment back in the UK."

"Yes he knows that, on the NHS."

Calling again, the following week, to give Cynthia an update on Michael's progress, she had a story to tell concerning the houseboy called Derek. Employed by our Indian neighbours as an odd job man, forty-year-old Derek, lived and slept in the garage at the front of the neighbour's house. Everybody in the neighbourhood knew that on Saturday, once paid, Derek would set off across the valley to buy alcohol from the liquor store next to the petrol station.

Apparently on the Saturday before we arrived back from Paarl, walking into the storeroom at the back of the petrol garage, one female attendant spotted a cobra asleep in the corner. Rushing out to raise the alarm, two male attendants armed with metal rods, approached the back room. At that crucial moment, emerging from the liquor store already worse for wear and noting what was happening, Derek chased after them. Stopping them from killing the aroused cobra and picking it up by the tail, Derek was bitten on his wrist. However, thinking that alcohol might help dilute the venom, drunk Derek set off running back into the liquor store.

With alarms bells sounding all around the garage one astute customer standing at the pumps, managing to grab hold of Derek and push him into the back of his car, drove him around to the hospital in False Bay. However, upon discovering the hospital did not hold the necessary antidote, Derek was driven at speed to the Victoria Hospital in Wynberg. Gravely ill for several days, barely conscious and with his poorly arm the size of an elephant's trunk, Derek made a full recovery.

Around this time, with Michael hinting he might not return to Africa, my eyesight began playing tricks. The problem I had, was driving from sunlight into dark shadow. Particularly beneath trees, I could not decipher objects on the left-hand side. Although I had always had regular checks at the opticians, for reading glasses and sunglasses, suspecting this might be different, I made an appointment to see an ophthalmologist specialist.

After studying both eyes, using high tech equipment, the specialist confirmed I had a common condition associated with the elderly called 'Wet Age-related Macular degeneration. After further detailed examination of the troublesome left eye, the specialist confirmed it was, in his opinion, 'beyond redemption.' On the other hand while the right eye also had a leaking and damaged retina, the specialist considered that with a series of needle injections, the problem could be contained but not cured. Unlike Michael, with money in my South African bank account I agreed to pay for private treatment.

As a special treat for my birthday that April, I booked a four-day holiday to Victoria Falls. Of course to enter Zimbabwe, not only did we need mosquito medication but as British citizens, we needed a special Visa to enter the country. Being singled out at immigration and having our documents and passports scrutinized by the police, we then handed over another extra levy to enter the country. At that time, with President Mugabe out of favour with the British but a close ally of President Zuma of South Africa, we Brits were getting a rough ride.

Staying at the Victoria Falls Safari Lodge on the Zambezi river was, undoubtedly, one of the best holidays we ever had together. Taking the Sundowner cruise along the river to watch the elephants come through the trees to drink, followed by a candle-lit dinner was a special birthday treat.

What a morning it turned out to be, walking along the pathway next to the Falls and getting soaked to the skin. Arriving back at the hotel, looking exactly like drowned rats, the rest of the afternoon was spent drying out our passports and American dollars on top of the bed.

At five o'clock the next morning, joining a group at a special retreat in the bush, we walked alongside young lions for more than an hour. Later driven to a conservation area caring for abandoned elephants, we were invited to take a ride. Watching these huge creatures arriving with their keeper, to stand on the hillock well above us, we were invited to choose which one we would like to ride.

"Okay, I'll go on the big one." Michael said, as the big male came around the deep pit waiting to be mounted.

"Good, I would much prefer to ride the littler one." I replied.

"Oh, I have to tell you" the keeper said, leaning over to me. "She is special to us. We rescued her from a big fire where her mother was burnt."

"Brilliant! That is all I needed to know. Riding an African elephant that has had a traumatic childhood. I bet I am going to finish up in Botswana."

Fortunately, I did not finish up elsewhere. In fact the whole holiday was the most wonderful experience. Underneath the white mosquito nets, close to the Zambezi river was the very last time Michael and I aver made love to each other.

CHAPTER 22

Returning later that year back to the UK, close to Christmas, we received an invitation from Matthew now in the Philippines to attend the christening of the first half Philippine grandson. With Michael not choosing to stay at home, I agreed to fly on my own to Manila. To celebrate this special occasion in the Catholic calendar, prior to the tip, I made a series of hand puppets.

Apart from struggling through, near, typhoon conditions and breathing in some of the most polluted air on the planet, it turned out to be a most exhilarating experience. Staying in a house, without running hot water, a shower that had just packed up, and a toilet only operational with a bucket of water, was quite mind blowing. With my Philippine daughter-in-law having to ask two younger sisters to wash be down, in the afternoon, with a bowl of warm water balanced on the toilet seat was indeed different. Sleeping on the actual floor of a small room with most of the glass missing from the window, says it all!

Having said that, the actual day the christening took place was a day to remember. Following the beautiful ceremony in the Catholic church, a reception took place in the local square. Following a gargantuan meal of roasted pig, platefuls of mango fruit and cake, all set out on a raised plinth. Then assisted by Matthew we presented a Punch and Judy show for all the children living in the complex.

As a special gift made for those not present, Joy had asked a local potter to throw special Christening mugs. On one side of each mug was the photograph of baby boy Matteo, while on the other side was a reading from the New Testament. The fact that Matthew's brothers, back in the UK, did not bother to acknowledge the gifts, left me feeling both sad and ashamed.

"So I can see from the sign outside, that you have sold your house?" said the retired doctor, climbing out from his car.

"Yes. It is so kind of you to offer to take me to the U3A venue in Cape Town today. With the troublesome eyes I seem to have lost the confidence to drive on the motorways through to Tygerberg."

"No problem at all. I live just down the road." He said, placing my digital projector in the back of his car. "So where are you thinking of moving to?" he asked, holding the door open for me to get inside.

"I am looking for an apartment in Fishhoek with better security."

"With the amount of crime going on here at the moment, that sounds like a sensible idea. I was most impressed with your art lecture last month in St James Kalk Bay."

"You mean the Life of Picasso? That is a favourite talk of mine."

"And your talk today 'Godfathers of the Renaissance'? that is something very different."

"Yes, I am always stretching my repertoire."

Driving on through Wynberg the doctor turned left towards the motorway.

"Do you mind if I turn the radio on?" he asked, turning hard left again off the main road and down onto the semi-circular bend leading onto the M4.

"Pollsmoor prison!" I said, looking out to the left, "That is where Mandela served some of his 27 years."

"Yes, that is right. Said the doctor, pressing one button on the dashboard.

"Good morning everybody." Said the announcer on radio station. "On February the 14th, this is the ten o'clock news. Overnight there has been a shooting at the home of Oscar Pistorius and his girlfriend Riva Steenkamp has been found dead. Nothing more is known about the circumstances, but the police and reporters are there at the house now."

"Wow!" Said the doctor, his eyes wide. "That is going to be one hell of a story. There have been rumours that Oscar Pistorius and his entire family are into guns and big game hunting."

"Isn't that the guy called the blade runner? He was in the London 2012 Olympic games last year? Michael and I live in a flat not far from the Olympic Park in Stratford where the games took place. It was all over the papers, that being beaten in a race, Pistorius went about trashing the changing rooms."

"Probably. Pistorius is well known for his violent outbursts and temper. He has been in more than one scrape with the South African police. The doctor said, negotiating the tangle of motorway connections around Newlands Cricket ground "In fact, there was an incident in Johannesburg recently, when a loaded gun went off inside a restaurant packed with Sunday diners. Apparently, while Oscar was passing a pistol beneath the table to his friend sitting opposite, the gun went off. The bullet went into the floor under the table but grazed his friend's toe at the same time. Because of his reputation and despite Pistorius being challenged by the restaurant owner, the story went to ground."

"Really."

"And what is more, there have been rumours in our newspapers that Riva has a secret admirer in the form of a famous rugby player from Pretoria. That makes it most interesting, A tragedy occurring on the Valentine's Day? It could be significant." The doctor said, thoughtfully.

With the news of the death of Riva Steenkamp circulating throughout the world, everybody was glued to their radios and television screens, wanted to know the sequence of events. According to a statement made by the doctor living in the same luxury complex, both he and his wife had been woken by lights and a furious argument in the house opposite. Hearing a woman scream they then heard several gun shots.

Sitting on the bed for several minutes, trying to absorb what they had heard, getting dressed the doctor walked across to the Pistorius house. Taken straight through into the hallway by a housemaid, Pistorius was at that moment, coming down the stairs covered in blood, with limp Riva in his arms. Crying while laying her down onto the floor in front of the doctor saying over and over 'please let her live.' Pistorius then disappeared back upstairs.

"Why do you think Pistorius left dead Riva with you, to go back upstairs"? Asked the detective, questioning the doctor.

"My immediate reaction was because the gun was still upstairs, Oscar had gone up there to kill himself"

"Or maybe he went back upstairs to wipe clean Riva's mobile phone." Said the detective with a wry smile.

By the middle of March I had moved, from Glencairn into a two bedroomed apartment, in a secure complex in Fishhoek. With the fire station located on the opposite side of the road of the upstairs flat and with the library and Municipal offices nearby, I felt safer in this four-apartment block called Rebmore.

So now what about Linda, the cousin so favoured by my mother, arriving for her fourth visit to stay with me. Without a doubt my late mother would have approved of her favourite niece, indirectly, benefiting from my inheritance. Leaving behind her, the cold English winters, Linda enjoyed coming to the South African sun. Graced with similar characteristics to our joint grandmother from Tottenham, and as an only child Linda and I got on well. While I went off meeting friends and to keep fit classes, well-built homely Linda was quite content to either read in the bottom garden or sunbathe on Fishhoek beach. Five years my junior and with good eyesight, taking the wheel of my car, we drove along the coast to Knysna on the Garden Route and to visit the cheetah park at Wilderness. For both of us, the highlight of Linda's stay that year was a visit the Mount Nelson hotel in Cape Town for afternoon tea.

Two months after her departure back to Bournemouth, arriving in Cape Town airport for my return journey back to London, I encountered a problem. Standing at the desk, waiting while the air ticket and passport was studied by the Immigration officer, I was asked to step out from the queue. Called across by another official, I was then escorted down a passageway to a small office.

"Would you stand there please madam. I need to take your photograph and to scan your passport again."

"Why? What is going on?"

"Under new regulations, that came into force a week ago, you have overstayed your time in South Africa. Three months is now the limit for foreign visitors. If you want to leave the country tonight, you will need to sign these two sets of papers."

"Sign papers for what?"

"Admitting you have violated the new regulations and accepting the fine that will be imposed."

"So how much is the fine?"

"I cannot say. You will need to go to the South African Commission in Whitehall London. Only after paying the fine there, will you be allowed back into this country."

Anxious not to miss the flight, hardly looking at what I was signing, I went out from the office to join the throng of English businessmen already on their phones calling the UK for legal help.

Arriving back in Hackney that summer, I noticed that Michael had developed a dry cough. Questioning him about the cough, it was dismissed as a summer cold. About a week later, with Michael away for the day fishing at Deal with his brother, I set about the task of cleaning the flat. And while putting away clean underwear into Michael's dresser drawer, I made a startling discovery. Sitting down to eat my meal alone, I waited for his return.

"Have you had a good day?" He asked. "Terry and I have caught mackerel. He has taken some home for his sons and I will put the rest in the freezer."

"Just leave them a moment and come with me into your bedroom." I said, pulling open the bottom drawer of his dresser. "Can you tell me why it is that you have a cosh and cannisters of CS gas in this drawer?" I asked, pointed to them.

"Because living here in Hackney, you never know when we might need them."

"But they are illegal weapons Michael." I said, angrily.

"Why don't you leave me to worry about that,"

As these new cracks appeared in the relationship, so I filled the time with new activities. Joining a group at the Hackney Sports Centre, I went line-dancing, rode bicycles along the towpath from Springfield park to the Olympic park at Stratford. Looking up at Ferry house as I rode by, I thought about Ruth and this place where she lived as a girl.

"So what did the doctor have to say this time, about that cough?" I asked Michael arriving back from playing cricket on Hackney Downs.

"Nothing much. He listened to my heart and chest, took my blood pressure, consulted the drugs I am taking and upped the statins that is all. He could not find anything else wrong. Have you heard how Ruth is?"

"I will let you know later. She has not got long to live and because she is now so ill, she has been placed in the Intensive Care Unit. I am meeting up with her eldest son John outside Bart's hospital this afternoon."

On the day of Ruth's funeral ten days later, planning to go with his brother Terry and cousins to the pub, before arriving at the cemetery, an argument ensued. Categorically refusing to go to the funeral alone, Michael agreed to accompany me. Sitting together in the crematorium, alongside Ruth's four children and the Jewish relatives and with my head bowed, I whispered farewell to my school friend and former sister-in-law.

The following year 2014, travelling by tube to Charing Cross, I walked to the South African Commissioner's office in Whitehall. After settling the fine of three hundred pounds and knowing a further Visa would be needed to re-enter South Africa, the rest of the day was spent moving from one kiosk to another.

"Under the new restrictions, three months is the maximum amount of time you can stay in South Africa." Said the official, studying pages on my passport.

"But I have a house there."

"If you intend to live there permanently, you will need the guarantee and support of a South African resident."

"What exactly does that mean?" I asked,

"A South African citizen willing to sponsor you and to support your application."

"I see. And in the meantime I can only go back for a maximum of three months?"

"Correct."

Making a concerted effort to join the rowdy birthday celebrations in the Army and Navy pub, I took Michael's brother to one side. Not that mattered much, what with the volume of the music and Michael's increased deafness, nothing could be heard anyway.

"Terry please listen to me. I am going back to South Africa for just ten weeks. And while I am away I would like you to keep an eye on your brother."

"Why?"

"I do not think he is very well. I have already spoken to Edward and Bernard, and they will check on him while I am away."

Back again by the middle of March, this time bearing gifts, and the latest magazines from the UK, Linda arrived for yet another holiday. As a divorced woman no matter whether we played crazy golf at Muizenberg, swam from the beach, or sat in church listening to a black gospel choir, Linda and I were good together. Taking me to visit the ophthalmologist in Sun Valley, the idea of having a needle injected into one's eye, made my cousin cringe.

Over this ten-week short stay, having befriended a lady living in the garage in the garden, middle-aged Anne was invited to Sunday lunch. In fact, during Linda's three week stay, Anne joined us on several occasions. On the last evening before Linda's departure back to the UK, Anne and Linda came to hear my talk entitled, 'The life of Van Gogh'. Now very aware that Anne struggled with money, in my absence, she was only too pleased to take on the role of paid caretaker.

Back in London by June, a letter arrived from the Commissioner's office in Whitehall, requesting me to attend a meeting.

"We have now received documentation from a South African resident he said, looking up at me. "You asked your bridge teacher to sponsor you?"

"Yes, I did."

"Well, as Chairman of the U3A in Fishhoek he has written to guarantee you for citizenship in South Africa." He said, thumbing through the passport to find a blank page.

"Here you go," he said, pasting and stamping a special seal into my passport. "You have a permit to stay for up to 48 months."

With no plans to return to South Africa, until the following year, I went to watch Michael play bowls in Victoria Park. Absolutely delighted to see me there on a Saturday, sharing tea with wives and members of the club, Michael introduced me to his friends as his wife. Even though he continued to stride up and down the greens, I was still concerned about the cough. And knowing that some of the family planned a holiday in Cala Murada, I thought about joining them.

"What about us going to Mallorca for a holiday.? I know you must miss the African sun." I said, studying the computer screen. "Look we could go on a last-minute deal in August, for a week to Porto Colom, when George and the family are there."

"But they are staying in a villa in Cala Murada! That is three miles away from Porto Colom."

"So what. We do not want to land on them for their entire holiday. Just take a taxi and visit them for one day."

"It sounds a good idea. Book it up."

Flying from Luton into Palma airport on a hot August afternoon and not arriving at the hotel until midnight, we went straight to bed. The following day, content to just sit and recover from the journey, we waited another day before contacting the family.

"Hello?" answered George, in a clipped tone.

"Hi George, it is your mother speaking."

"I know who it is, what do you want?"

"Surprise, surprise. At this moment, dad and I are sitting on the terrace in a hotel in Porto Colon. Can we come and meet.......?" I managed to say before the phone went dead. Oh!"

"What did he say?" asked Michael, noting my shocked expression.

"He put the phone down on me."

When my mobile phone rang minutes later, I repeated the message, from George, that the family did not want to meet us while they were on holiday.

"You know, Michael said, sitting with his head in his hands, "No matter what has happened in the families, we have always shown respect for our parents. We have never treated them in this way."

With George not stopping to consider the consequences the punitive steps taken towards me, had rubbed off on his father. Within half an hour, in the attempt to alleviate the obvious damage done, Edward was on the phone.

"Because we know how you both must be feeling Bernard and I have decided, tomorrow while George and the family go diving, we will come in the car to take you both out for the day."

As promised, the following morning Edward and Bernard arrived to take us first, to the spectacular stalactite and stalagmite caves at Arta, and then for a late lunch in the Monastery de Lluc. During that awful week on our own, it was the first time I had ever witnessed Michael refuse to swim and avoid the sun.

Into October and with outdoor bowls closed for the winter, Michael became increasingly fretful and withdrawn. Despite receiving assurances from the doctor, his health continued to decline. Looking for an outlet to escape from being with a man not willing to talk and to just read his newspaper all day, I volunteered to work in the soup kitchen at St Paul's Church feeding the homeless. With the original St Paul's Church having been destroyed in the London Blitz this new building with its wide forecourt also accommodated the Saturday Stoke Newington Farmer's market. And as Christmas 2014 approached, so I helped with the Children's play group inside the church.

Spending Christmas day quietly alone, on Boxing day Michael's breathing became so laboured we decided to go on the bus to Homerton Hospital. Following two x-rays of his chest, and another two days later, Michael was diagnosed with the fatal disease of mesothelioma.

Around that Christmas time, embattled in the continued family split, our eldest son Michael was going through one of his regular episodes of not speaking to us. However, upon receiving a phone call telling him about his father's diagnosis, he was down from Leeds the next morning offering his help.

As the news circulated amongst the family, about Michael's terminal illness, so George working for solicitors and holding a degree in law, took up the sword to find out when, where and how his father had come into contact with asbestos: the primary cause of mesothelioma.

Two visits to Bart's Hospital followed by further x-rays confirmed that the lining in Michael's right lung, called the pleura, was filling with fluid. Given the prognosis of just a few months to live, aware that compensation could be involved, legal beaver George was on the ball looking for a London barrister to represent his father.

Having previously arranged an Easter break to visit Bernard's family in France, leaving Michael in the care of a home nurse, along with son Michael with his new partner, Edward and Bernard, along with me, went for three days to the Loire valley.

On the Bank Holiday Monday sitting together on the train in Calais, chatting about our visit to the burial site of Leonardo DaVinci, my phone rang.

"Where are you?" I have kept trying to phone but you have not answered."

"That is because the phone does not work in France. What is the matter Michael? We are on the train on our way home."

"I am here all alone. Michael and his girlfriend Letwin went back to Leeds last night. I have kept pressing this bloody alarm thing around my neck, but nobody has arrived."

"That is probably because it is a Bank Holiday. The district nurses will be in short supply."

"I am in such pain. I have dropped the Paracetamol on the floor."

"Michael, just try and pick up two and take them with some water. I will be home soon."

Leaving Edward and Bernard at St Pancras, I took the bus back to Hackney.

"How has it taken you so long to get here? Michael yelled, as I walked in. "I have been sitting here waiting for hours."

"The train back from Calais was slow and I had to wait for a bus." I answered, distractedly reading the message coming up on the computer screen.

"You are not listening to me. What are you reading?"

"It's a message from Cynthia in Glencairn. Her darling Neville has died."

"How old was he?"

"She says, 96."

"Huh, he should be so lucky. I am only 77!"

"Michael it is no good your being bitter. That is the way it is. You need to accept it."

"But I do not want to accept it. Just look at me. My arms are so thin I am literally wasting away. It is just not fair." He said, pushing the walking frame angrily to one side.

"I know, life is not fair Michael. Would you like me to make soup for your supper?

"Yes please." he added, his equilibrium restored by my undivided attention.

With the announcement in May, of Michael's forthcoming second marriage and with his father too ill to attend, I went on my own to Leeds. The fact that George had refused to be best man at Michael's wedding was hardly surprising. Having Michael come into George's local pub dressed as a cowhand, with a large white Stetson, long cowboy boots and a studded hipster belt, would not have gone down well with his brother George Neither would Michael turning up at his front door, with his first wife on the back of the high-powered motor bike, both encased in leather, with black helmets and dark visors, looking like Darth Vader from Star Wars. It was no secret in the family that both Michael and his first wife smoked cannabis.

As the only person there to represent our family, I witnessed the ceremony of Michael marrying a Zimbabwean nurse called Letwin. Watching him and his radiant new bride posing for photographs on the steps of the Leeds Registry, with friends and members of Letwin's African family present, I was pleased I went. Snubbing anybody in life, had never been my scene.

Arranging that wedding with all the flowers, making the cake, as well as organising and cooking the wedding breakfast, comprising of both English and African foods, took some organising. Raising a glass of champagne to the happy couple, made me think back to George's wedding fifteen years previously. On that joyous occasion, when George married his childhood sweetheart, there was more than one hundred guests present in the exclusive Yorkshire Manor house. I remember how happy Michael was, to be asked to stand in the church pulpit and give a reading from the New Testament expounding the virtue of true love.

With Michael failing to admonish or check his sons, the family remained divided. With five younger males, flexing their muscles and vying for dominance, without a silverback in charge, mayhem had ensued.

For whatever reason, throughout the time I stayed with Michael in his flat, he had not added me to the tenancy. Now watching the sons closing ranks and taking sides around their ailing father, no longer Michael's wife, my position was precarious. With the two-bedroomed ground floor flat solely in Michael's name, upon his death, I would we asked to leave. And as a born survivor I needed a plan.

With the proceedings in full swing to obtain compensation for Michael, following lengthy phone calls and correspondence, and with Michael refusing to appear in court, the barrister came to visit him in the flat. As his ex, only present in the flat to help with the care of my former husband I was happy to sit, as a silent witness, in the corner of the room.

"So Michael when you did your National service, working below the decks of the ship, was there a lot of dust about?" The lady barrister asked.

"Not from the actual shells I loaded into the casings. But I do remember how hot and very dusty it was working down there."

"So let us now go to 1970 to 1980. You worked as Area Manager for the bookmakers Coral's in Leeds? Is that correct?

LIVING THE RING OF FIRE

"Yes, I did."

"And part of your job was to visit other shops in Yorkshire that were either being refurbished or renovated before opening?"

"Yes, when the building work was close to completion."

"Can I ask you what you wore when making these regular inspections?"

"I was always smartly dressed in a navy-blue suit."

"And did you ever notice dust flaying about in the shops, getting onto your suit?"

"Not that I can remember. As I told you, I only visited these shops once the work was near completion."

As the intense and detailed interview continued, so it became apparent that the focus of attention by the lady barrister, was on Michael's ten years employment with the bookmaker Coral's. And at no time did Michael disclose the fact that after leaving Cora's, with a golden handshake, he opened his own betting shop in north Leeds. Not only do I remember, to save money, Michael stripped the walls himself, but also Edward knew his father came home with his dungarees covered in dust. Following a considerable battle in court, by Michael's barrister, Corals legal team eventually accepted liability for the claim of 'possible contamination from asbestos.'

With Michael now insisting that the bathing nurse was 'throwing him around like a sack of potatoes' I took on the task of bathing him myself. And with the NHS installing all the extra equipment in the flat, everything was there to help with Michael's care. Now on regular morphine and constantly falling, twice I had to summon Terry from the pub to help me pick Michael up from the floor. It was only under considerable duress, that Michael, agreed to attend St Joseph's Day Hospital twice a week. Choosing the right moment, while he was away from the flat, I arranged for packing cases to be delivered.

Driving down regularly from Leeds, Michael and Letwin proved to be a great help. On one occasion, driving a van, Michael arrived with an orthopaedic bed to help support and lift his frail father. Meanwhile, ensuring that the visits did not coincide, George also came to visit his father. Also at that time, to help with Michael's loss of appetite, steroids were prescribed by the doctor. However, after taking steroids for just one day, Michael was charging up and down the living room, like a bull elephant in musk.

"Well here I am dying, while you are going to live. he said, stopping on his walking frame and glaring at me. "So what are you going to do once I am gone?"

Of course I did not reply. It was just so sad to witness Michael's complete inability to face reality. Later in the day, speaking via Skype to Matthew in Tokyo about his father's condition, I happened to mention what had been said about wanting to know what I would be doing once he had gone.

"You should have told dad you will send him a post card," Matthew said, true to form and sharp as ever.

"Now you have been awarded this very substantial pay out dad, you will need a solicitor to draw up a Will." George said to his father over the phone.

"But Solicitors are expensive George., Cannot I just write something down on a piece of paper?"

"No, dad it all has to be legal, via a solicitor. You need to decide who you want as Executor, and then I will find a solicitor in Leeds to draw up the Will."

Appointing an appropriate solicitor, but with Michael's increased deafness and failing speech, I was given the task of relaying the conversations on the phone to the solicitor in Leeds. Acting as the go-between, everything Michael said was repeated back to the solicitor, by me. With Edward having already agreed to act as Executor, the first request made by Michael was that he wanted a substantial funeral and with a burial site large enough to take both him and his younger brother Terry. Then with all funeral expenses paid and any outstanding debts settled on thousand pounds was to be given to me, and the rest of his money to be divided equally between his five sons.

Having secretly packed several boxes, in my bedroom, with personal belongings, on Michael's next visit from Yorkshire, I put forward the suggestion that his father be transferred near to his family in Leeds. Once the wheels were in action to find a suitable nursing home nearer his sons. I booked a flight back to South Africa.

Putting to one side the complaints from his father, about paying three thousand pound a month to stay in a nursing home, Michael packed his father up for the journey on the M1to Leeds. Helping to settle him into the most pleasant surroundings and with his family nearby I returned to London. Immediately contacting the overseas freight company, the boxes were collected and taken to Heathrow for transfer, via air freight to South Africa. I went the following two weekends to visit Michael. However, on the second visit, Michael was so ill, he was hardly aware I was there.

"If you are intending to come again next weekend," Said son Michael, "You had better find somewhere else to stay, because we are invited to a party."

"As a matter of fact, I do have somewhere else to stay next weekend Michael." I answered, perfectly aware of the strain this was all having on the family.

CHAPTER 23

Returning to Hackney that day, the very next thing I did, was to write a letter to my husband sending my love and telling him I was returning to South Africa. Then remembering it was George's birthday, I wrote a card to him. Only at the very last moment, writing a note and dropping the keys to the flat inside an envelope, I posted the package to Edward. Boarding the night flight of six thousand miles back to South Africa, by ten the next morning I was back into Cape Town.

"Lovely to see you back" Said David, the regular taxi driver leaving me outside Rebmore flats.

"It is lovely to be back." I said, admiring the explosion of spring flowers in the gardens surrounding the security gates.

Meanwhile, back in England, with the word out that the 'hen had fled the roust', top in the pecking order Michael, was down from Leeds to raid the flat and change the locks. However, quick off the mark Edward, was there ahead of him to retrieve the case of family heirlooms from underneath my bed.

The very first thing I did, upon entering the upstairs flat, was to go and thank Anne for looking after the flat. Following a phone call to make an overdue appointment with the ophthalmologist I went to thank Geoffrey, the bridge teacher, for the glowing report he gave to the Commission in London. It was on the ninth day, while walking on Fishhoek beach in the warm spring sunshine, I received a phone call from Leeds.

"This is George mum, and I am here sitting close to dad. He cannot speak now, but he wants to hear your voice. I am going to put my phone to his ear, on loud-speaker, so he can hear you".

"Go ahead." I said, hearing the laboured breathing. "Hello darling, I am out on my regular walk along the beach and it is a lovely warm spring day. I have been told the Southern Right whales are still here in the bay, but I have not seen any. But today, for the first time this year, the trekkers are back with their fishing nets. Do you remember......?" I said, trying to keep him alert.

"Sorry mum that is enough he cannot listen now."

"Love you now and forever Michael." I shouted.

Following his death, the first person I thought to speak to was Linda.

"I will keep you informed and let you know when the funeral is going to take place."

"Are you going to come back for the funeral?" She asked,

"I am not sure, returning for the funeral I would merely be the piggy in the middle. I will let you know."

"What about your son Matthew in Japan?"

"Although at this time neither he nor Terry know that they have inherited fourteen thousand pounds each from his father, they have too many family commitments to fly back."

Thinking about it and making the decision not to return for the funeral, it was left to Linda to step up to the mark. Standing in representing me and out of respect for Michael, driving from Bournemouth with her son and daughter. Linda was present at Michael's funeral. Being the kind and helpful person that my cousin is, Linda was only too pleased to help George's Yorkshire in-laws, through the labyrinth of unfamiliar backstreets of East London to the cemetery at Manor Park. Armed with the familiar powerful camera, taking pictures of the flowers, including a wreath from me, Linda turned the camera towards those others present. Within 48 hours, via the Internet connection, the images of the mourners were up on my computer screen.

"Well it was all a big strained I can tell you," Linda said on the phone, wanting to make sure I had received the photographs. "to see your eldest standing with cousins from Michael's side of the family on one side of the grave, and George, Edward and the family from Yorkshire drawn up on the opposite side of the grave. It resembled the War of the Roses, The Plantagenets versus the Tudors. And what is more, that younger brother Terry? Well, he arrived directly from hospital, in a wheelchair, looking extremely ill and pushed by one of the sons."

"What was wrong with him?" I asked,

"Alcoholic poisoning, or at least that is what your son Michael told me at the funeral breakfast in The Army and Navy pub. And again, I have to say I felt so sorry for him ostracised by his own family and sitting, instead, with cousins from Ruth's side of the family.

Listening to the encounter of the funeral. I had no regrets about having stayed away from 'The Ring of Fire.' Instead quoting from the funeral booklet sent to me later by Edward, I say "I miss you Michael, but let you go."

THE END

APPENDIX

In 2017, at the same time Oscar Pistorius was serving his extended sentence of six years to fifteen, for killing his girlfriend Reeva, Michael's younger brother Terry was serving a six-year prison sentence for gun crime.

That same year, Linda came again for yet another regular three-week visit to the sun. Then later that year, youngest son Matthew arrived, in August, from Japan with his second Philippine wife and my three half Philippine grandsons to South Africa. For three little boys coming on a 23-hour flight from Tokyo to Cape Town, it was something special. Going around visiting the high spots, having non-poisonous snakes wrapped around their necks, rides on camels, watching penguins, visiting the Lion Sanctuary at Paarl, as well as the Elephant park in Wilderness they were completely overwhelmed by the Cape.

The highlight of their seventeen-day trip, in South Africa's winter, happened on the night before their departure. Leaving me in the flat to cook an evening meal, the family went on their last trip to Fishhoek beach. While Matthew and wife Joy, strolled with the boys along the path above the rocks they noticed a crowd gathering on the rocks. With others ran pointing out to sea. Southern Right whale was spotted launching out from the deep and breaching up into the air before plunging back down below the waves.

"What is going on?" asked Matthew joining the gathering crowds.

"The whale is tangled in plastic fishing line." Replied an onlooker.

"Oh, how sad." said Matthew's wife Joy.

"Quick let us get up onto the bridge over the railway line. We will be able to see much better from there." said Matthew, grabbing hold of eldest son Nicolo by the hand.

With onlookers now on their mobile phones calling for help it was not long before the whole of the viewing area was filled with local press and residents from around the Fishhoek area. With all eyes fixed on the struggling mammal it was twenty minutes or so went by before the rescue team from Simonstown, came roaring around the peninsular into the bay, in their dingy. Already wearing diving gear and with bottles on their backs, plunging into the sea, these skilled team of brave men set off to cut the distressed whale free.

"Oh grandma," Said Mateo, the middle grandson bounding up the stairs and into the lounge, "It was all just so exciting. The men cut the yellow plastic line off the whale and it swam free."

"That is something to tell your friends when you get back to Tokyo." I said dishing up the meal kept warm in the oven.

Once they had left South Africa, with Michael gone with half the family in Japan and the other half in the UK, suddenly I felt alone and vulnerable. With crime on the increase and with muggings, particularly against the elderly living alone, I considered my options. Driving a car with diminished sight, I was not only a liability to other drivers but to my family too. At eighty years of age, if anything untoward was to happen, no way could I expect visitors from six thousand miles away. Making the decision to return to the UK, after selling the car I prepared to leave South Africa. Packing two thirds of all the furniture and belongings into a massive van, everything was then transported by container ship back to England. Just prior to my departure back to England the remaining third of incidental items were distributed between Anne and the township at Masiphumelele.

Arriving back in the UK, the first two weeks were spent in Medway with Edward and Bernard. Then finding a rented house of my own, I moved into the Kent area. And yes, I do miss beautiful South Africa. In fact, the grandchildren, in Tokyo, continue to ask when we are all going back.

It so happens that throughout the time Terry was in prison, Michael kept in touch with his uncle both by letter and on the phone. However, in April 2000 having served half his sentence, released from prison, Terry was confronted with Covid 19 and full lock down.

"Drinking plenty of lager that is the way to stop getting Coronavirus." Terry said over the phone to son Michael.

So here I am, in August 2020 and in the middle of a pandemic, to witness the final scene in this long saga. As matriarch of the family and survivor of 'The Ring of Fire', I am sitting in this Anglican church in Stoke Newington, attending the funeral of my late brother-in-law Terry. Under the new Covid restrictions, only 30 persons can attend one funeral. However, looking around, and counting more than fifty, tells me Terry must have been popular. As well as the friends and neighbours here, Terry was particularly well known in his local pub. However, listening to conversations conducted around me, I can tell the much older men present, are throw backs from Terry's golden years, as well-known boxer at the East Ham boxing club.

So who else, amongst the mourners, is here to represent my family? Looking around the church, a roll call is needed. In the very front pew, sitting alongside his Zimbabwean wife Letwin, I can see Michael my eldest son. Unfortunately, because the family dogs, back in Yorkshire, needed to be cared for, my new Zimbabwean step-granddaughter Nicole, is not here.

So what about second eldest son Terry? The dark ninja with the Machiavellian mentality. The nemesis of my life that I have not seen for more than twenty years? Not present.

Next in line middle son Edward informed of his uncle's death, declined to attend. Likewise, younger brother George, also informed of his uncle's death, declined to attend.

What about son Matthew six thousand miles away in Japan? Now nine years, after the Christening of his son Matteo and still enduring uncharitable indifference from brothers, towards both him and his family, there was no way he was going to be here.

Looking at the youngest son Mark standing in front of the coffin, reading a tribute to his late father, I thought about what had been said the week previously. Upon hearing that Terry was to be cremated. and not buried, the suggestion made by both brothers that the space next to Michael should be reserved for aunty Jacqueline, made me smile.

Perhaps the prediction, made years ago by Michael, that we would eventually finish up together, might come true.

The end

9 781839 755033